D0085191

The Biology of Adolescence

The Biology of Adolescence

Herant A. Katchadourian
STANFORD UNIVERSITY

W. H. FREEMAN AND COMPANY
San Francisco

**Library of Congress
Cataloging in Publication Data**

Katchadourian, Herant A
   The biology of adolescence.

   Bibliography: p.
   Includes index.
   1. Adolescence.   2. Puberty.
3. Youth—Diseases.   I. Title.   [DNLM:
1. Adolescence. WS460 K18b]
RJ140.K37   612.6′61   76–44282
ISBN 0–7167–0376–9
ISBN 0–7167–0375–0 pbk.

Printed in the United States of America

9   8   7   6   5   4   3   2   1

To John Romano
Distinguished University Professor of Psychiatry
The University of Rochester, School of Medicine
Mentor and friend since my professional youth

Preface

The primary emphasis of this book is on the biological changes that take place in the second decade of life, marking the transition of a child into an adult. As a natural consequence of this emphasis, it also deals with the physical ailments and health hazards that can accompany this major developmental stage.

The psychosocial aspects of adolescence have attracted increasing attention in the past several decades. Most texts that deal with this subject pay some attention to the biological changes entailed, but this is almost eclipsed by the greater preoccupation with the nonbiological issues. This book attempts to rectify the imbalance without implying that the biological processes in puberty are all that matter. Ultimately, understanding the developmental events of the second decade, or for that matter any other decade of life, depends on our comprehension of the interactional patterns between biological and psycho-social variables.

Most of the preparation of this book took place when I was in the University Fellows program at Stanford, which was funded by the Ford Foundation. In connection with my larger aim of developing an undergraduate course and teaching materials on the human life cycle, I was further assisted by a grant from the University Fellows. Although I received advice and criticism from many colleagues, students, and friends through the years of this project's development, I benefited particularly in the preparation of this volume from the advice of Julian Davidson, Jared Tinklenberg, and Charlea Massion. Valarie Munden and Carol King were very helpful in the preparation of the manuscript.

October 1976   Herant Katchadourian

Contents

The Biology of Adolescence

Chapter 1

Adolescence and the Life Cycle

"Confound not the distinctions of Thy Life which Nature hath divided, that is, Youth, Adolescence, Manhood, and Old Age; nor in these divided periods, wherein thou art in a manner Four, conceive thyself but One. Let every division be happy in its proper Virtues, nor one Vice run through all. Let each distinction have its salutary transition, and critically deliver thee from the imperfections of the former, so ordering the whole, that Prudence and Virtue may have the largest Section."

Thus wrote the distinguished physician Sir Thomas Browne (1605–1682) in his contemplative observations (Browne 1876). Many others have addressed themselves to this issue throughout the ages, and metaphors abound comparing the progress of life to the unfolding of various natural phenomena. Two apparently contradictory but actually complementary themes pervade these observations: One is that life is a continuous process that, like a river, meanders through time from its source to its destination. The other is that certain major turning points characterize the life cycle, giving it distinctive stages. One can hardly argue against the first premise, but it is easy to disagree over the second, especially in terms of how such stages are to be determined.

This book deals with one aspect of one of these presumed stages of life: the biology of adolescence. But to consider it in isolation is apt to be quite misleading. The changes of puberty do not unfold in a psychosocial vacuum. They are only one aspect of an integrated process of development. Their repercussions affect a person psychologically and socially, and, in turn, physical and human environments influence the biological processes in progress. So, strictly speaking, there is no such thing as "the biology of adolescence" or "the psychology of adolescence"; they are inextricably linked phenomena. Yet, to study these phenomena, it is useful to examine them separately.

To view a given stage of life as if it had an existence of its own can also be misleading. Even if one subscribes to the notion that there are separate life stages, it must be admitted that their interrelationships are what give life cohesion and meaning. Therefore, it could also be said, that there is no such thing as "childhood" or "adolescence" as an isolated entity. The adolescent and adult are anticipated in the child and the child persists to some extent in subsequent stages. Concepts like childhood and adolescence are nevertheless highly useful constructs, and their delineations and subdivisions may serve important didactic and research functions.

ADOLESCENCE AS A STAGE OF LIFE

The term *adolescence* (from the Latin *adolescere,* to grow up) has been in use in the English language since the fifteenth century.[1] But the notion of a transitional stage of life between childhood and adulthood long antedates such usage. Prehistoric man must have been aware of such distinctions, although it is impossible to determine exactly when he began to conceptualize them. Among many nonhuman primate societies, when an animal becomes "pubescent," the fact is clearly recognized, judging from the response of adult animals.

Other common designations for this stage of life are *puberty* and *pubescence* (from the Latin *pubescere,* to be covered with hair). As implied in its etymology, the word puberty refers to the biological changes entailed. It would be preferable to restrict its use to this sense and to use the word adolescence in refer-

---

[1]Monk of Evesham in 1482: " A certen adolescente a yonge man" (*Oxford English Dictionary*).

ring to the psychosocial aspects of development in the second decade. But common usage makes this distinction difficult to maintain in practice.

In the United States, the use of the colloquial term *teenager,* indicating someone between the ages of 13 and 19, has become so widespread that it appears in the statistics of the U.S. Bureau of the Census. For the younger years, "pre-teens" is sometimes used.

Other terms have been used to designate related phases of puberty and adolescence. *Nubility* refers to the later phases of puberty when reproductive maturity and fertility have been attained (Engel 1962). Nubile (Latin, *nubilis*) means "of marriageable age." In the past, *youth* was used to refer to younger people in general. More recently, it has been suggested that youth constitutes the stage of life between adolescence and adulthood (Kenniston 1970).

It is customary to speak of *early* and *late* (and sometimes of *middle*) adolescence (Hamburg 1974). Prepuberty, puberty and preadulthood have also been suggested (Kestenberg 1967*a,* 1967*b,* 1968). Attempts to differentiate the phases of adolescence can be quite useful for research and clinical purposes, especially if an effort is made to correlate biological events with psychosocial ones.

On the other hand, it is not possible to assign specific age ranges to such phases, even if they can be shown to exist. As we will see in subsequent chapters, even the standard biological events of puberty vary in time of onset and duration.

The focus in this text is on the second decade of life because most people go through the transition to adulthood between the ages of 10 and 20. This is when the biological changes take place and to a more variable degree when psychosocial development occurs.

The concept of adolescence, as it is understood today, is mainly a product (some may say artifact) of the twentieth century. But it has a long, if informal, historical background, which is worth a brief digression.

Numerous descriptions of youth can be found in the literature of various historical periods. Although most of this writing is unsystematic and informal, it is nevertheless a source of information about youth and how they were perceived by others in the past. Another rich source is the portraiture of youth (Figures 1.1 and 1.2).

Every culture must somehow incorporate each succeeding generation into its social fabric if the community is to survive as an entity. The ways in which different cultures have accomplished such socialization vary, but one institution that has traditionally performed the task has been the school. The nature of education at a given time is thus a valuable source of information on the status of youth.

In the past century, archeological discoveries have brought to light fascinating details about what is probably the earliest school system to exist. These

FIGURE 1.1
Portraits of young men: (upper left) Filippino Lippi, c. 1457–1504; (upper right)
Giovanni Antonio Boltraffio, 1467–1516; (lower left) Bernardino Pinturicchio, 1454–1513;
(lower right) Sandro Botticelli, 1444–1510. [Photographs courtesy of National Gallery
of Art, Washington, D.C.]

FIGURE 1.2
Portraits of young women by Rembrandt van Rijn, 1606–1669: (left) *Young Girl at an Open Half-Door,* 1645 [photograph courtesy of The Art Institute of Chicago] and (right) *A Woman Holding a Pink* [photograph courtesy of National Gallery of Art, Washington, D.C.].

discoveries consist of Sumerian clay tablets, some of which pertain specifically to Sumerian schools and include the equivalent of our textbooks and student workbooks.[2] The image of Sumerian youth that emerges from these documents is surprisingly contemporary in several ways. The Sumerian schoolboy worked, fretted, and got punished in ways that we can readily comprehend and even emphathize with. Box 1.1 contains vignettes of these interactions.

In the classical period, references to youth were more frequent and specific. Greek philosophers and pedagogues speculated about life stages and formulated opinions about their special features. Their ideas about human nature and development remained influential through the Middle Ages and are still studied today. Especially pertinent in this regard are the writings of Plato and Aristotle. There are 110 characters in Plato's dialogues, 12 to 14 of whom are adolescents (Hall 1904). Plato's writings contain many comments on children

[2]The Sumerian civilization, which flourished in the ancient Near East from the fifth to the second millennium B.C., was the first high civilization known in the history of man. The Sumerians preceded the Semites in the land first known as Sumer and later as Babylon. Their inventions and discoveries include the wagon wheel, the potter's wheel, the plow, the sailboat, architectural innovations, casting in copper and bronze, sculpture in stone, engraving, and so on. Most importantly, the Sumerians invented writing about 7,000 years ago. Known as cuneiform, it was used and borrowed in the ancient world for about 2,000 years. (Kramer 1963).

BOX 1.1

Conversation between a Sumerian youth and his father. [From S. N. Kramer, *The Sumerians*, University of Chicago Press, 1963.]

"Where did you go?"

"I did not go anywhere."

"If you did not go anywhere, why do you idle about? Go to school, stand before your 'school-father' (professor), recite your assignment, open your schoolbag, write your tablet, let your 'big brother' write your new tablet for you. After you have finished your assignment and reported to your monitor, come to me, and do not wander about in the street. Come now, do you know what I said? . . .

"Come now, be a man. Don't stand about in the public square or wander about the boulevard. When walking in the street, don't look all around. Be humble and show fear before your monitor. When you show terror, the monitor will like you.

(About fifteen lines destroyed)

"You who wander about in the public square, would you achieve success? Then seek out the first generations. Go to school, it will be of benefit to you. My son, seek out the first generations, inquire of them.

"Perverse one over whom I stand watch—I would not be a man did I not stand watch over my son—I spoke to my kin, compared its men, but found none like you among them.

"What I am about to relate to you turns the fool into a wise man, holds the snake as if by charms, and will not let you accept false phrases.

"Because my heart had been sated with weariness of you, I kept away from you and heeded not your fears and grumblings—no, I heeded not your fears and grumblings. Because of your clamorings, yes, because of your clamorings, I was angry with you —yes, I was angry with you. Because you do not look to your humanity, my heart was carried off as if by an evil wind. Your grumblings have put an end to me, you have brought me to the point of death.

"I, never in all my life, did I make you carry reeds to the canebrake. The reed rushes which the young and the little carry, you, never in your life did you carry them. I never said to you 'Follow my caravans.' I never sent you to work, to plow my field. I never sent you to work, to dig up my field. I never sent you to work as a laborer. 'Go, work and support me,' I never in my life said to you.

"Others like you support their parents by working. If you spoke to your kin and appreciated them, you would emulate them. They provide 10 *gur* of barley each—even the young ones provided their fathers with 10 *gur* each. They multiplied barley for their father, maintained him in barley, oil, and wool. But you, you're a man when it comes to perverseness, but compared to them you're not a man at all. You certainly don't labor like them—they are the sons of fathers who make their sons labor, but me—I didn't make you work like them."

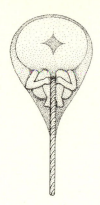

FIGURE 1.3
The homunculus: a sperm containing
a miniature organism. [Redrawn
from L. B. Arey, *Developmental
Anatomy*, Saunders, 1965.]

and youth, as well as advice concerning their upbringing.[3] Plato ascribed the development of rational and critical thought to the time of adolescence and prescribed mathematical and scientific studies for this period.

Aristotle's concept of development was even more systematic. He divided the developmental period into three seven-year stages: infancy (0–7 years); boyhood (8–14); and manhood (15–21). The ability to choose was the critical task to be developed during the adolescent years. Some of Aristotle's observations on youth are contained in a famous statement presented in Box 1.2.

In the Middle Ages, distinctions between life stages were deemphasized. The child was perceived as a miniature adult. Even at the time of conception, a tiny *homunculus* (little man) was believed to exist in the sperm. Because all was preformed, development merely entailed enlargement. Growth was therefore a quantitative rather than qualitative change (Figure 1.3).

In the Renaissance, the scholastic tenets of the Middle Ages were challenged, and new views of human nature and development began to emerge.[4] John Ames Comenius (1592–1670), a Moravian clergyman and educator, advocated relating education to everyday life and teaching in the vernacular rather than Latin. Amazingly ahead of his time, he worked for a universal system of education that would offer equal opportunities to women (Comenius 1923). Comenius also divided the developmental period into four phases of six years each. Adolescence coincided with the third phase (12–18), during which a student learned to "understand and pass judgment on the information collected by the senses." Comenius agreed with Plato that the purpose of schooling during this phase was to train the faculty of reasoning. He thus recommended the consecutive study of grammar, natural philosophy, mathematics, ethics, dialectics, and rhetoric. The fourth phase of development

---

[3]See in particular "Laws," in *The Dialogues of Plato* (Jowett 1953). Plato's educational philosophy is expounded in *The Republic* (Jowett 1921).

[4]For a detailed discussion of these historical developments, see Muuss (1968).

The young are in character prone to desire and ready to carry any desire they may have formed into action. Of bodily desires it is the sexual to which they are most disposed to give way, and in regard to sexual desire they exercise no self-restraint. They are changeful, too, and fickle in their desires, which are as transitory as they are vehement; for their wishes are keen without being permanent, like a sick man's fits of hunger and thirst. They are passionate, irascible, and apt to be carried away by their impulses. They are the slaves, too, of their passion, as their ambition prevents their ever brooking a slight and renders them indignant at the mere idea of enduring an injury. And while they are fond of honor, they are fonder still of victory; for superiority is the object of youthful desire, and victory is a species of superiority. Again, they are fonder both of honor and of victory than of money, the reason why they care so little for money being that they have never yet had experience of want, as the saying of Pittacus about Amphiaraus puts it. They are charitable rather than the reverse, as they have never yet been witnesses of many villainies; and they are trustful, as they have not yet been often deceived. They are sanguine, too, for the young are heated by Nature as drunken men by wine, not to say that they have not yet experienced frequent failures. Their lives are lived principally in hope, as hope is of the future and memory of the past; and while the future of youth is long, its past is short; for on the first day of life it is impossible to remember anything, but all things must be matters of hope. For the same reason they are easily deceived, as being quick to hope. They are inclined to be valorous, for they are full of passion, which excludes fear, and of hope, which inspires confidence. They are bashful, too, having as yet no independent standard of honor and having lived entirely in the school of conventional law. They have high aspirations; for they have never yet been humiliated by the experience of life, but are unacquainted with the limiting force of circumstances; and a great idea of one's own deserts, such as is characteristic of a sanguine disposition, is itself a form of high aspiration. Again, in their actions they prefer honor to expediency, as it is habit rather than calculation which is the rule of their lives, and, while calculation pays regard to expediency, virtue pays regard exclusively to honor. Youth is the age when people are most devoted to their friends or relations or companions, as they are then extremely fond of social intercourse and have not yet learned to judge their friends, or indeed anything else, by the rule of expediency. If the young commit a fault, it is always on the side of excess and exaggeration in defiance of Chilon's maxim ($\mu\eta\delta\grave{\epsilon}\nu$ $\mathring{\alpha}\gamma\alpha\nu$); for they carry everything too far, whether it be their love or hatred or anything else. They regard themselves as omniscient and are positive in their assertions; this is, in fact, the reason of their carrying everything too far. Also their offenses take the line of insolence and not of meanness. They are compassionate from supposing all people to be virtuous, or at least better than they really are; for as they estimate their neighbors by their own guilelessness, they regard the evils which befall them as undeserved. Finally, they are fond of laughter and consequently facetious, facetiousness being disciplined insolence.

(18–24) was to be spent in the university and in travel. The critical task during this phase was the training of the will, including the self-direction of one's own life (Muuss 1968).

The philosophies of John Locke (1632–1704) and Jean Jacques Rousseau (1712–1778) exerted powerful influences in the development of Western liberal thought. Locke emphasized the importance of experience as the fountain of knowledge. Rousseau focused on the innate goodness of the child, the affective aspects of human nature, and individual freedom.

Locke's concept of the mind as a blank sheet (*tabula rasa*) on which to receive the imprints of experience implies an image of the child radically different from the preformationist notion of the child as a miniature adult. Locke believed development to proceed from mental passivity early in life to progressive activity culminating in the emergence of rationality during adolescence.

Rousseau proposed a four-stage developmental sequence: infancy (the first 4 or 5 years); the "savage" stage (5–12 years of age); youth (12–15), and adolescence (15–20). As implied in the second stage, these divisions corresponded to phases in the development of the human race. Rationality developed during youth, and emotional maturation occurred during adolescence, together with the emergence of social responsibility.

The first major contributor to the modern concept of adolescence was Granville Stanley Hall (1844–1924), a leading figure in American psychology and education at the turn of the century. After completing advanced studies in Germany, Hall went to Johns Hopkins in 1882 where he organized a psychological laboratory that rapidly gained prominence. In 1889, he became the first president of Clark University, but he remained active in the field of psychology. He was one of the organizers of the American Psychological Association and the founder of the *American Journal of Psychology* (Hall 1923).

Hall's main contribution to the literature on adolescence was a voluminous work published in 1904 entitled *Adolescence: Its Psychology and Its Relation to Physiology, Anthropology, Sociology, Sex, Crime, Religion and Education.* Apart from its enormous influence on subsequent conceptions of adolescence, his work is especially pertinent to puberty because the model that he advocated was biogenetic in orientation.

Hall was greatly influenced by Charles Robert Darwin (1809–1882) and undertook to elaborate on some of the fundamental tenets of the theory of evolution and to apply them to adolescent development. The German biologist and philosopher Ernst H. Haeckel had proposed the theory of "recapitulation" based on his interpretation of Darwin's work. According to this theory, an organism in the course of its development passes through successive stages that approximately recapitulate the forms of its adult evolutionary ancestors ("ontogeny recapitulates phylogeny"). For example, the embryonal parts of a mammal would pass through adult fishlike amphibian and reptilian phases before attaining the mammalian state (Arey 1965).[5]

Influenced by these views, Hall proposed a parallel theory of psychological recapitulation postulating that during development an individual passes through stages analogous to those that marked the history of the human race. Presumably, adolescence corresponded to the stage of "savagery," the phase through which mankind passed just before entering the stage of civilization.

This view of adolescence was basically biological in orientation: genetic factors controlled physiological events as well as their psychological concomitants, whereas culture and the environment had little effect on them. Other social scientists (including the eminent psychologist E. L. Thorndike) were quick to take issue with Hall's conclusions. Anthropological evidence supported the notion of cultural diversity, which contradicted the genetic predominance underlying the theory of recapitulation. Because of the flaws in Hall's work and the increase in environmentalist thinking in the social sciences, his views were discredited in the 1920s. But at least one of his concepts has persisted, albeit mostly independent of his name and the original reasoning.

This concept is that adolescence constitutes a stormy stage of development. Hall was influenced in this not only by the extrapolation of evolutionary views into the social realm, but by a German literary movement referred to as *Sturm und Drang* (Storm and Stress). This movement flourished in the last quarter of the eighteenth century. Its name is derived from a play of the period.[6] Its themes stressed subjectivity and the unease of man in contemporary society. Its protagonists were often youthful characters in rebellion against the established order, full of idealism, passion, and suffering. The period produced two of the giants of German literature, Schiller and Goethe. The novel *The Sorrows of Young Werther* by Goethe is probably the most famous work of this genre.

Sigmund Freud had no particular interest in adolescence, but Anna Freud and other psychoanalysts of the "ego-psychology" group (in particular, Erik Erikson and Peter Blos) have given much more attention to it. Their views, and those of the majority of other psychoanalysts, have traditionally supported the model of adolescence as a period normally characterized by storm and stress.

The contending view denying this has also persisted since the time of Hall's opponents. Margaret Mead's study of Samoan adolescence in 1928 was a major influence in furthering the view that "coming of age" was not necessarily a turbulent phase of life (Mead 1961). If this happened to be the case in America, the causes had to be sought in cultural and not inherently biological determinants.

---

[5]Even though embryos of different categories of animals do resemble each other in early stages of development, modern biologists do not accept this theory for a variety of reasons.

[6]*Die Wirrwarr: Oder, Sturm und Drang,* written by F. M. von Klinger in 1776. For a study of the literary movement, see Pascal (1953).

   The controversy is by no means settled. Current research on ordinary adolescents has generally failed to substantiate claims of the inevitability and
universality of adolescent stress. Yet some of the recent manifestations of
student activism have fueled the public expectation of "trouble" with youth,
and psychiatrists continue to see a large number of perturbed adolescents in
clinical practice. These two sets of perceptions need not be mutually exclusive.
There may indeed be many adolescents in the throes of intrapsychic or social
conflict, without the element of conflict being a necessary or unavoidable facet
of normal adolescent development. (Offer 1969; Weiner 1970).

THE YOUTH POPULATION

On July 1, 1976, the estimated total population of the United States consisted
of 215,653,000 persons of which 105,181,000 (48.8 percent) were male and
110,472,000 (51.2 percent) female. Those between the ages of 10 and 20
years numbered 45,212,000, constituting 20.9 percent of the total population.
Of the persons in their second decade, 22,989,000 (50.8 percent) were male
and 22,223,000 (49.2 percent) female. Subdivisions of this population are
presented in Table 1.1.

Table 1.1. Projected population of the United
States on July 1, 1976, between the
ages of 10 and 20. (Numbers are in
thousands. Includes Armed Forces
overseas.)

Age (years)	Total	Male	Female
10	3,721	1,899	1,822
11	3,807	1,940	1,868
12	4,004	2,045	1,958
13	4,068	2,072	1,996
14	4,209	2,145	2,065
15	4,282	2,185	2,097
16	4,180	2,129	2,051
17	4,208	2,138	2,070
18	4,249	2,147	2,101
19	4,280	2,160	2,120
20	4,203	2,129	2,074
Totals	45,212	22,989	22,223

Source: U.S. Bureau of the Census 1975, Table 7,
Series 1.

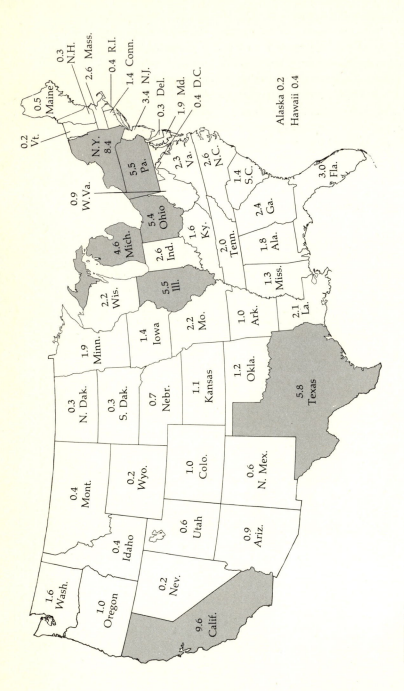

FIGURE 1.4

Percentages by state of the total resident child population in the United States as of July 1, 1968. Of the 70,809,000 under 18 years of age, 44.8 percent were concentrated in seven states. [Redrawn from U.S. Bureau of the Census, ser. P-25, no. 420, April 17, 1969.]

The distribution of children and youth is not uniform across the country. Figure 1.4 shows the percentage distribution of persons 18 years of age and younger. In 1968, that age group numbered 70,809,000 persons of which approximately 45 percent resided in seven states (shaded areas in Figure 1.4).

When we refer to youth, we are indeed talking about very substantial numbers of people. More than 62,000,000 persons are currently engaged full time in the educational institutions of the United States (Woodring 1970). The students constitute 95 percent of this group. If they were to "secede" from the Union, they would constitute a "nation" that would rank as the tenth most populous in the world. The 8,000,000 or so students in the 2,525 colleges and universities alone would outnumber all but four or five of the countries of Western Europe (Katchadourian 1972).

The American population has been growing throughout its history, but the rate of growth has been declining for a long time, except for the "baby boom" that followed the Second World War. The population increased at an average yearly rate of about 3 percent in the first half of the nineteenth century. Then, because of a pronounced decline in fertility rates, this figure fell to an average of 0.7 percent by the 1930s followed by a higher annual growth rate of 1.7 percent (U.S. Bureau of the Census 1975). As a result of the postwar baby boom, there has been a steady increase in both the absolute and relative size of the younger population. In 1940, 45,000,000 persons were under 20 years of age. By 1968, the figure had grown to 77,748,000, and this group had increased from 34.4 percent to 38.9 percent of the general population (Smith and Rice 1972). That postwar generation has now reached adulthood.

Figure 1.5 shows the estimated population of the United States in 1974 and its projected population in the year 2000.[7] Figure 1.6 shows the growth of the 15- to 19-year-old population alone between 1930 and 1970 and its projected increase until the year 2000. In 1974 (Figure 1.5), there were 20,719,000 persons between 10 and 14 years of age. Of those, 10,564,000 (51.0 percent) were male and 10,155,000 (49.0 percent) female. The 15- to 19-year-old group comprised 20,824,000 persons: 10,570,000 (50.8 percent) were male and 10,254,000 (49.2 percent) female. It is expected that, by the year 2000, these figures will have reached 26,240,000 in the 10- to 14-year-old group (13,451,000 males, or 51.3 percent; 12,789,000 females, or 48.7 percent)

[7]Note that in Figure 1.5 (and Figure 1.7) the projected data are for three series. All three are based on the estimated July 1, 1974, population and assume a slight reduction in future mortality and an annual net immigration of 400,000. They differ only in their assumptions about future fertility. The ultimate levels of completed cohort fertility (average number of lifetime births per woman) are: Series I, 2.7; Series II, 2.1, and Series III, 1.7. It is difficult to estimate the annual number of births in future years, and the three series have been developed employing three different assumptions. Series II seems to be a reasonable choice at this time, but one cannot say that it represents the most likely outcome because of many uncertainties. (U.S. Bureau of the Census 1975).

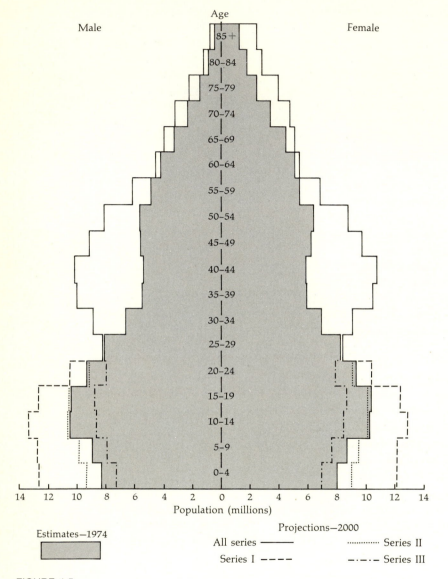

FIGURE 1.5
Estimates and projections of the population of the United States, by age and sex:
1974 and 2000. [Redrawn from U.S. Bureau of the Census, ser. P-25, no. 601,
October 1975, p. 10.]

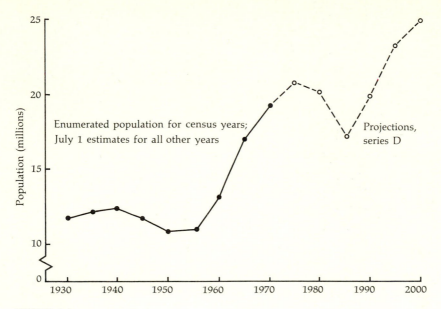

FIGURE 1.6
Teen-age population from 15 to 19 years of age: United States, 1930–2000. [Redrawn from U.S. National Health Center for Statistics, ser. 21, no. 23, 1973.]

and 25,008,000 in the 15- to 19-year-old group (12,765,000 males, or 51.0 percent; 12,242,000 females, or 49.0 percent).

Figure 1.7 shows population trends by age group to the year 2000 for persons 24 years of age and younger. These trends will be determined in varying degree by fertility rates. Note that for the year 2000 the number of 14- to 17-year-olds varies by more than 5 million from the highest (Series I) to the lowest (Series III) birth-rate projection. Considering only those already born, the population of 5- to 13-year-olds is expected to decline during the rest of the 1970s; the population of 14- to 17-year-olds will decline during the 1980s; and the population of 18- to 24-year-olds will increase during the remainder of the 1970s and then decrease in the 1980s and 1990s.

TRANSITION TO ADULTHOOD

One assumption that can be reasonably made about the second decade of life is that it constitutes a transitional period. But is this not true for any other decade as well? The life cycle consists of constant change; thus, are we not always in a transitional state? This is indeed the case. But not all changes

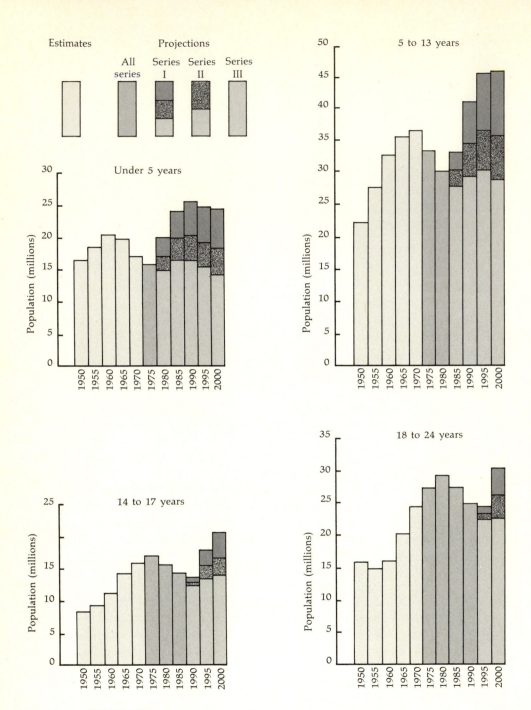

FIGURE 1.7
Estimates and projections of the population of the United States by age: 1950–2000.
[Redrawn from U.S. National Health Center for Statistics, ser. 21, no. 23, 1973.]

are of the same magnitude; nor do they occur at the same rate. A few years make an enormous difference in the life of a child but cause far fewer ripples in the life of an adult. What makes the second decade a particularly important transitional period is the rapidity and magnitude of change and the fact that both biological and psychosocial changes occur simultaneously.

Puberty entails not only growth, which is a property of the entire developmental period, but certain qualitative changes, the most critical being the emergence of reproductive capacity, which more than anything else distinguishes the child from the adult.

The same considerations can be applied to psychosocial development. Cognitive growth during adolescence enhances our thinking by adding extra dimensions without which much of what we consider higher learning would not be possible. Notable progress is made toward emotional maturity, moral development, the ability to participate in interpersonal relationships, and the development of other aspects of the personality. The sense of ego-identity is refined and consolidated. Occupational goals are defined and vocational training gets underway. In short, by the end of the second decade, most people have developed enough competence to get on with the business of becoming full-fledged adults.

What makes the second decade particularly fascinating is the opportunity it offers for observing the interaction of biological and psychological processes. The biological changes of puberty, although variable, are universal and orderly. The changing body elicits psychological reactions (Box 1.3), and a certain amount of self-consciousness seems common (Figures 1.8, 1.9, and 1.10). Beyond that there may be other problems linked to biological changes.

More fundamentally, we need to know much more about the behavioral manifestations of the biological changes and their underlying physiological processes. This may sound like a refrain from the turn of the century, but in fact we are currently in a far better position to investigate these subjects. Rather than relying on such hypothetical constructs as theories of recapitulation, we have accumulated a great deal of knowledge about hormones, for example, and are learning constantly about their behavioral effects.

Biology will progressively tell us a great deal more about puberty. But it will never entirely explain adolescence, because in the last analysis adolescence is created and defined by cultures. Its starting point is the social perception of biological maturation. But societal responses to it vary widely. For example, as adolescent sexuality blossoms, some cultures restrict its expression to narrowly defined limits, whereas others look the other way. All cultures attempt to regulate sexual behavior, but some have more stringent rules than others or apply them more rigorously (Ford and Beach 1951; Marshall and Suggs 1971).

Similar differences exist in the educational opportunities offered, and in the way that occupational roles are defined, that obligations and privileges are

BOX 1.3
The changing body.

I was as light and thin as I have said, because I was undernourished. I ate a hastily poached egg and toast in the morning before going off for my three mile tramp to the schools and I had a meat-tea about five when I got back—and a bread and cheese supper. Most of my time I was so preoccupied with my studies and my intellectual interests that I did not observe what was happening to me, but occasionally and more especially in my third year, I would become acutely aware of my bad condition. I would survey my naked body, so far as my bedroom looking-glass permitted, with extreme distaste, and compare it with the Apollos and Mercuries in the Art Museum. There were hollows under the clavicles, the ribs showed and the muscles of the arms and legs were contemptible. I did not realize that this was merely a matter of insufficient food and exercise. I thought it was an inferior body—perhaps past hope of mending.

To me, in my hidden thoughts, the realization that my own body was thin and ugly was almost insupportable—as I suppose it would be to most young men or women. In the secret places of my heart I wanted a beautiful body and I wanted it because I wanted to make love with it, and all the derision and humour with which I treated my personal appearance in my talking and writing to my friends, my caricatures of my leanness and my unkempt shabbiness, did not affect the profundity of that unconfessed mortification. Each year I was becoming much more positively and urgently sexual and the desire to be physically strong and attractive was intense. I do not know how far my psychology in these matters is exceptional, but I have never been able to consider any sort of love as tolerable except a complete encounter of two mutually desirous bodies—and they have to be reasonably lovely bodies.

H. G. Wells (1866–1946)
Experiment in Autobiography
(reprinted with the permission
of the Estate of H. G. Wells)

I had a pimple on my face that bothered grandma and Aunt Madge a great deal, and even Dona Gabriela's family. Yesterday Clélia decided to take it off in a way she'd learned. She took a redhot coal and threw it in a glass of water; the coal hissed, she opened it up and put it on the pimple, hot. She did it three or four times and the pimple got soft. Then she squeezed it and enough tallow came out to make a candle. When I got home mama called me an idiot because I let anyone do anything they want to me. I said, "I know if I'm an idiot or not. The pimple was growing and it could have got as big as an orange and the Senhora and papa just kept saying over and over that it wasn't anything. I was the one who was getting homelier every day. I'll let anybody do anything they want to if it's for my good." Last night my face was very swollen and Clélia was very worried, but I told her that it wasn't anything and not to worry. Today it's almost gone already.

From the diary of a
Brazilian adolescent,
Helena Morley (March 20, 1894)
The Diary of Helena Morley,
ed. E. Bishop (Farrar, Straus, and
Giroux, 1957)

I was going through a difficult period: I looked awful; my nose was turning red; on my face and the back of my neck there were pimples which I kept picking at nervously. My mother, overworked, took little trouble with my clothes: my ill-fitting dresses accentuated my awkwardness. Embarrassed by my body, I developed phobias: for example, I couldn't bear to drink from a glass I had already drunk from. I had nervous tics: I couldn't stop shrugging my shoulders and twitching my nose. "Don't scratch your pimples; don't twitch your nose," my father kept telling me. Not ill-naturedly, but with complete absence of tact, he would pass remarks about my complexion, my acne, my clumsiness which only made my misery worse and aggravated my bad habits.

Simone de Beauvoir (b. 1908)
Memoirs of a Dutiful Daughter

FIGURE 1.8
Paul Burlin, American, 1886–: *Young Man Alone with His Face,* 1944. [Collection of Whitney Museum of American Art, New York.]

FIGURE 1.9
Pablo Picasso: *Girl Before a Mirror,* 1932. [Collection, The Museum of Modern Art, New York. Gift of Mrs. Simon Guggenheim.]

FIGURE 1.10
Edvard Munch: *Puberty,* 1895. [Nasjonalgalleriet, Oslo, Norway.]

balanced, that political power is shared, and so on. Some cultures pay more attention to youth than others. Some are "tougher" on them, others more lenient. These and other factors determine the extent to which youth will create its "subcultures" and how they will relate to the larger culture containing them.

Complex historical and economic events control these developments. Most social change occurs slowly, but at certain times the process seems to accelerate with bewildering effect. Although it is tempting to assign responsibility to this or that specific event, it is rarely feasible to predict, or even retrospectively to fully understand, the major shifts in the attitudes and behavior of youth. The record of the past half-decade or so is a case in point.

With the benefit of hindsight, attempts have been made to explain the emergence of the modern view of youth. The transformation of the United States from an agricultural to an urban industrial society in the past century and a half is said to have been the critical factor (Demos and Demos 1969). In rural families, youth tend to be miniature models of parents; in urban settings, this tendency is disrupted. Hence, the rift between the generations and the "discontinuity of age groups" (Keniston 1962).

FIGURE 1.11
Albrecht Dürer: *Self Portrait,* at age 13.
[From the Archives of the Austrian National Library, Albertina Collection, Vienna.]

FIGURE 1.12
Alexander Robertson James, 1890–1946: *Black Boy,* 1935. [Metropolitan Museum of Art, Arthur H. Hearn Fund, 1937.]

Young people now spend far more time in school than working. In school, they are segregated with age peers. The prolonged dependence of the young person on the family is mutually burdensome and restrictive. These factors are considered to have been instrumental in transforming the role of young people in society during the last century (President's Science Advisory Committee 1974).

Napoleon was a captain at the age of 16. There is no reason to believe that the biological changes he underwent were basically any different from those of a modern 16-year-old. But the two belong to different social worlds. Whether society will consider a 13-year-old Albrecht Durer (Figure 1.11) "a gifted student" and assign him to extra art classes or treat him on the professional merits of his work is a cultural, not a biological, issue.

In a pluralistic society like that of the United States, it is not easy or even possible to speak coherently of national cultural patterns, or even regional ones. A youth of a particular ethnic group (Figure 1.12) or socioeconomic background may bear no more than superficial similarity to his age peers in other neighborhoods of the same city, even those only a few blocks away. Once again, it is culture, not biology, that better explains such differences.

These few introductory remarks are meant to give some idea of how important a recognition of environmental differences is to our understanding of puberty and adolescence, and to negate any possible implication that understanding biological factors will "explain everything."

Chapter 2

Somatic Changes of Puberty

The biological changes of puberty constitute an exceedingly important aspect of this phase of life. They consist of a great deal that is obvious as well as much that remains obscure. For example, we all know that girls begin to menstruate and boys develop beards, and we have learned a great deal about the hormones that bring about these changes. However, our understanding of the primary mechanisms in the brain that trigger the chain of events that culminate in physical changes is still rudimentary.

The physical changes at puberty are mediated at four levels of control. The highest level of control currently known is in a part of the brain called the hypothalamus. The next is in the pituitary gland, which is under the control of hormones secreted by the hypothalamus. The hormones of the pituitary in turn

regulate the activities of the testes and the ovaries. Finally, the "sex hormones" produced mainly by the testes and ovaries bring about the numerous physical changes of puberty.

If we had a complete understanding of these matters, a logical approach to their description would be in the order outlined above, but, unfortunately, we know most about the final outcome in the form of physical changes and least about the primary brain mechanisms. Therefore, the events are described herein in reverse order, beginning with a discussion of the visible changes of puberty and regressively tracing the events behind the scenes at increasing levels of complexity. This approach will allow us to focus initially on matters that are evident and commonly known, thus making subsequent consideration of that which is less clearly understood more pertinent by placing it against a background of common knowledge and experience.

Puberty is so pervasive that there are hardly any tissues in the body that are not affected by it. The changes that constitute puberty have been classified as follows (Marshall and Tanner 1974, p. 124):[1]

1. acceleration and then deceleration of skeletal growth (the adolescent growth spurt);

2. altered body composition as a result of skeletal and muscular growth, together with changes in the quantity and distribution of fat;

3. development of the circulatory and respiratory systems, leading, particularly in boys, to increased strength and endurance;

4. the development of the gonads, reproductive organs, and secondary sex characters;

5. a combination of factors, not yet fully understood, that modulates the activity of those nervous and endocrine elements that initiate and coordinate all these changes.

These changes produce two major biological outcomes that have profound psychosocial consequences. First, a child attains the physique and physiological capabilities of an adult, including reproductive capacity. Second, most of the major adult physical sex differences become established, greatly enhancing sexual dimorphism.

As universal as these changes are, there are important differences between individuals in the onset, order, and rate of growth at puberty.[2] Yet, if large enough populations are examined, pubertal changes fall into definite and predictable patterns, which are what we will be mostly concerned with here.

---

[1]See also Tanner in Grumbach, Grave, and Mayer (1974, p. 448).

[2]For a discussion of such variability among girls, see Dewhurst (1969) and Marshall and Tanner (1969); and among boys, Marshall and Tanner (1970).

The biological changes of puberty are part of a larger developmental sequence and must be viewed in that context. Thus, although our primary concern here is with puberty, we will briefly examine the general growth patterns between birth and adulthood before turning to the specific changes of puberty.

GROWTH PATTERNS

Growth and aging are lifelong processes that can be examined at the level of cells, tissues, physiological systems, and the organism as a whole. In the first phase of development, in the early embryo, growth is predominant with little differentiation of function. To appreciate the magnitude of growth in early life, consider the rate of gain in weight: an average baby weighs between six and ten pounds at birth; by the end of the fourth or fifth month, the birth weight is doubled; by the end of the first year, it is tripled; and at two years, quadrupled. Adults generally weigh twenty or more times their birth weights. But birth weight is of the order of three billion times the weight of the zygote, or fertilized ovum, with which life starts (Sinclair 1973).

In the second phase of development, which lasts until physical maturity is reached, a balance is achieved between growth and differentiation of function. The third phase spans most of adult life, throughout which most growth is restricted to compensation for losses incurred through wear, tear, and illness. Finally, with further aging even such reparative growth fails to keep pace, and the organism becomes progressively dysfunctional (Sinclair 1973; Harrison et al. 1964).[3]

All parts of the body grow simultaneously, but they do so at different rates. Nevertheless, there are sufficient similarities in growth rates to allow the division of postnatal growth of most tissues of the body into four main types. Figure 2.1 presents patterns of growth in the two decades after birth, expressed as a percentage of final adult size (100 percent).

General growth pertains to that of the body as a whole and to its external dimensions (except for the head and neck). It includes the skeleton and musculature as a whole, the respiratory and digestive organs, the kidneys, the spleen, various parts of the cardiovascular system, and blood volume. Genital growth refers to the reproductive system including testes, ovaries, fallopian tubes, prostate, seminal vesicles, and external genitalia. Neural growth refers to the head, the brain, the spinal cord, and structures associated with them.

---

[3]More extensive accounts of growth patterns can be found in child psychology texts such as Mussen (1970); pediatrics texts such as Barnett and Einhorn (1972); embryology texts such as Arey (1965); and the specialized professional journals.

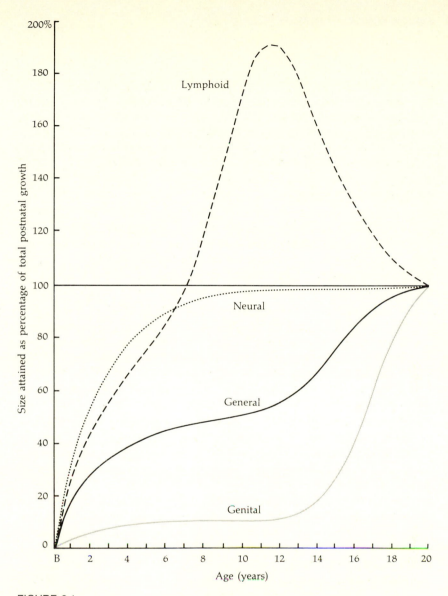

FIGURE 2.1
Growth curves for the four main types of growth in humans. [Redrawn from R. E. Scammon, in *The Measurement of Man,* ed. J. A. Harris, C. M. Jackson, D. G. Patterson, and R. E. Scammon, University of Minnesota Press, 1930.]

Lymphoid growth encompasses the thymus, the lymph nodes, and intestinal lymphoid masses.

The rates of growth during the years of puberty are clearly different for the four types. The general growth curve is steep in childhood, levels off somewhat between the ages of five and ten, and then rises sharply again during puberty until its final leveling off. The genital growth curve follows a similar pattern, but its initial rise is much less marked and the upsurge at puberty more striking. In contrast, the curve for neural development indicates that almost full growth has already been attained by the onset of puberty. In the second decade, structures associated with the neural system have to gain only the final 5 percent of their adult size. The lymphoid growth curve deviates from the general growth curve even more. By age seven, lymphoid tissues have already attained their adult size but continue to grow until about age 12. Then, while the rest of the body keeps growing during the remainder of the second decade, these tissues actually regress.

Development is commonly expressed chronologically. Chronological ages are constant and independent of any other factor. To say that a person is so many years old states a clear and unequivocal fact, but simply knowing the chronological ages of a young person may not tell us very much about his precise stage of development. It was this need for a more revealing measure that led to the development at the turn of the century of the concept of physiological maturity, or *developmental age.*

There are several ways of determining developmental age. The most common is to ascertain skeletal age. The development of bones follows a predictable sequence that is essentially uniform, although its onset and completion varies from one person to another and can be readily checked by the appearance of bones on x rays. By examining a large number of healthy persons during the period of growth, certain developmental standards have been set. These standards indicate, for example, which bones of the hand and wrist should have matured by a given age. A persons' bone age can be determined by consulting atlases containing these standards (Greulich and Pyle 1959). A 13-year-old with a bone age of 13 years would be developing according to the average, or normal, timetable. If his bone age were 14 or more years, he would be considered an early maturer; conversely, if his bone age were less than his chronological age, then he would be a correspondingly late maturer.

The determination of dental age is generally the same as that of skeletal age and is based on the predictable sequence in which deciduous teeth appear, are shed, and are replaced by permanent teeth. The assessment of skeletal age continues to be useful throughout adolescence, but dental age is not after dentition has been completed, usually by age 13.

Another method of determining developmental age consists of establishing morphological age, based on height and similar characteristics. Here again, a person's morphological development is compared with a set of standards derived from the performances of a large number of normal, healthy individuals.

Yet another measure relies on secondary sex characters and is applicable only during puberty. Standards commonly used are breast development for girls (Figure 3.1 on page 55), genital development for boys (Figure 3.7 on page 68), and pubic-hair growth for both boys (Figure 3.6 on page 67) and girls (Figure 3.2 on page 57) (Tanner 1962).[4]

ONSET OF PUBERTY

In the first decade of life, boys and girls grow steadily and quite similarly so that at age ten there are no marked differences in their heights, weights, strength, or the composition of their bodies. They have already attained about four-fifths of their adult height and somewhat more than half of their adult weight. As the second decade of life unfolds, the body seems to get an extra kick that accelerates its growth, brings about sexual maturity, and catapults the adolescent to biological adulthood. Exactly when this process starts and what triggers it are questions to which we as yet do not have precise answers.

We become aware of pubertal changes through their outward manifestations. But at the time they are apparent, other, internal events have long been in progress. By age eight or nine, certain hormones have already increased in amount, although neither the child nor others are aware of it. Even earlier events must have taken place in the brain to trigger the hormonal changes. Under these circumstances, we have no way of knowing precisely when puberty starts.

As judged by its external manifestations, puberty starts in contemporary western youth at about age 10 or 11 among girls and 11 or 12 among boys. But given the wide variability, it is preferable to express the time of onset in terms of a range, from $8\frac{1}{2}$ to 13 for girls (Reynolds and Wines 1948) and from $9\frac{1}{2}$ to 15 for boys (Reynolds and Wines 1951), rather than specific ages. Most children enter puberty within these ages—95 percent of girls show at least one sign of puberty by age $13\frac{1}{2}$ (Di George 1975, p. 1293)—but even at that some perfectly normal exceptions occur earlier or later.

Figure 2.2 includes the average age ranges for the onset and termination of some of the more significant pubertal events. The general sequence is more predictable than the specific dates on which these events are likely to unfold. For example, among pubescent boys, of whatever age, the growth spurt starts simultaneously with enlargement of the penis about one year after the onset of testicular growth. Among girls, there is a close correlation between the growth spurt and breast enlargement. It should be emphasized, however, that even these sequences are not immutably fixed; they can occur in reverse order, especially if the changes are fairly close together. Thus, although breast devel-

---

[4]For further discussion on the assessment of developmental age, see Sinclair (1973), Mussen (1970), and Acheson (1966).

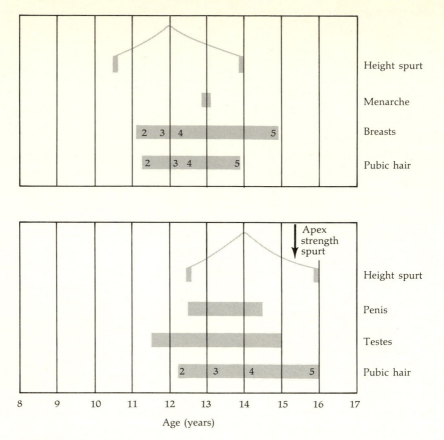

Age (years)

FIGURE 2.2

Sequence of events of puberty. The adolescent growth spurt for girls typically begins at age 10½ and ends at age 14, but it can start as early as age 9½ and end as late as age 15; for boys it can begin as early as age 10½ or as late as age 16 and can end between age 13½ and age 17½. The onset of menstruation can occur at any time between the ages of 10 and 16½; breast development can begin as early as age 8 and be completed by age 13, but it may not begin until age 13 or be completed until age 18; and first pubic hair appears after the beginning of breast development in two-thirds of all girls. Elongation of the penis can begin from age 10½ to age 14½ and can end from age 12½ to age 16½; growth of the testes can begin as early as age 9½ or as late as age 13½ and end at any time between the ages of 13½ and 17. Numbers 2 through 5 refer to the stages of development illustrated in Figures 3.1, 3.2, and 3.3. [Adapted from Growing Up by J. M. Tanner. Copyright © 1973 by Scientific American, Inc. All rights reserved.]

opment usually antedates the growth of pubic hair, in some perfectly normal girls the reverse occurs. It is much less likely, however, that a later event like menstruation would precede either of these earlier developments.

The onset of puberty is consistently earlier in girls than in boys, and the time lag is usually about two years (Kulin 1972, p. 1122). The magnitude of this difference depends on which aspects are being compared: breast budding in girls antedates testicular enlargement by six months; girls grow pubic hair a year and a half earlier than boys; girls reach full height about two years before boys. Summaries, as in Table 3.1 on page 54, are useful in presenting the progress of puberty as long as one does not lose sight of normal variabilities.

CHANGES IN BODY SIZE AND SHAPE

The physical transformation of a child into an adult consists of important changes in height, weight, fat distribution, and body proportion. The figures and the accompanying graphs in Figure 2.3 indicate that more than a uniform and simple increase in size is in progress.

Body Fat

Fatty tissues are found at many sites in the body but what concerns us here is subcutaneous fat, which is deposited under the skin and which significantly contributes to defining body contours.

Subcutaneous fat accumulates quite rapidly during the first 9 months of life, making babies plump. By the age of 1 year, female babies have more fat than males. The gain in fat becomes gradually stabilized and then begins to be lost as children grow up. At about age 7, the process is reversed again: most girls and two out of three boys accumulate subcutaneous fat, which makes prepubescent children chubby and causes some of them to be self-conscious.

With the onset of the growth spurt there is a progressive loss of fat, especially from the limbs. This is most marked at the time of the greatest increase in height. Among boys, it results in a temporary negative fat balance or a net loss, which contributes to the "string bean" look of teen-agers. The loss of fat among girls is not as marked and never produces a negative balance (Falkner 1972, p. 236). As a result, the average teen-age girl enters adulthood with more subcutaneous fat than does the average teen-age boy, especially in the region of the pelvis, the breasts, the upper back, and the backs of the upper arms (Sinclair 1973, p. 43) (Figure 2.4). Consequently, women's bodies are generally more rounded.

This factor also accounts for other differences in physical appearance. Men are generally more muscular than women to begin with, but in addition their muscles are more prominent because of the relative lack of subcutaneous fat. This is why women athletes with highly developed musculatures do not appear as muscular as their male counterparts. The relative paucity of subcutaneous fat also accounts for males having more prominent surface veins such as those of the forearm.

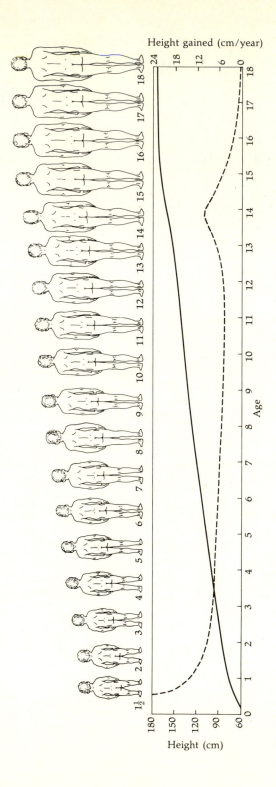

Height gained (cm/year)

Height (cm)

Age

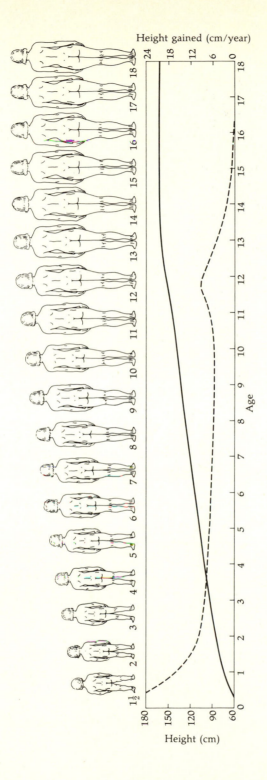

Height gained (cm/year)

Height (cm)

FIGURE 2.3
Rates of growth in development of boys and girls, shown at regular intervals from infancy to maturity. Note the change in the form of the body as well as the increase in height. The height curves (solid lines) represent averages for North America and Western Europe. The curves for velocity of growth (dashed lines) show the increments of height gained from one age to the next. The sharp peaks correspond to the adolescent growth spurt, which occurs two years earlier in girls. [Redrawn from Growing Up by J. M. Tanner. Copyright © 1973 by Scientific American, Inc. All rights reserved.]

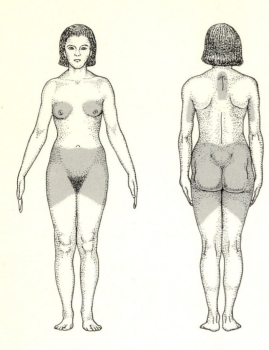

FIGURE 2.4
Sites of fat deposits in the female body at puberty. [Redrawn from D. Sinclair, *Human Growth After Birth,* 2d ed., Oxford University Press, 1973.]

These basic differences between the sexes are subject to much individual variation and are greatly affected by nutritional and other factors. The comparisons therefore hold true only for large numbers of people at similar levels of obesity.

Stature

Growth in stature is one of the more dramatic changes of puberty, making the lanky adolescent a familiar image (Figure 2.5). Progressive growth in height is a continuous process (see Table 2.1 on page 37), and, at age 10, girls have already attained 84 percent and boys 78 percent of their adult height (Bayley 1956, pp. 188–189). What makes the growth spurt in puberty noteworthy is not the overall amount but the rate of growth.

The progressive growth in stature can be illustrated by growth curves (Tanner 1962),[5] as was seen in Figure 2.3. Such curves may show the heights attained with age, as in Figure 2.6, or they may show the velocity of growth, which is

---

[5]The earliest record of this type is less than 200 years old. It was made from 1759 to 1777 by Count de Montbeillard, using his son as the sole subject.

the rate at which height is gained, as in Figure 2.7. The use of the word "velocity" in this respect may seem odd because we associate it with rapid motion,
but it is quite appropriate because growth is a form of motion.

The growth spurt is quite evident in the curves that simply chart progressive
increments in height, but it is much better illustrated by the velocity curves. A
comparison of these curves shows that, although height is increasing throughout childhood, the rate at which this occurs decreases very fast in the first
few years of life and then more slowly until the growth spurt of puberty, when
it is accelerated.

Among girls, the growth spurt typically starts at about age 10½, reaches a
peak at 12, and ends by 14 (Marshall and Tanner 1970). But it may start as
early as 9½ or end as late as 15 (Figure 2.2). Among boys, it usually starts
between 12 and 13 (or as early as 10½ or as late as 16), reaches a peak at 14,
and ends at 16 (or from 13½ to 17½, as shown in Figure 2.2) (Marshall and

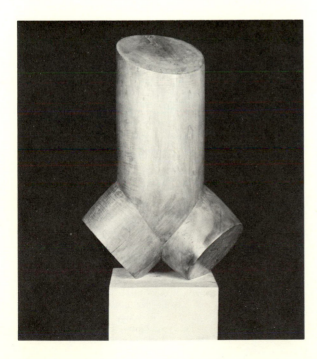

FIGURE 2.5
Constantin Brancusi: *Torso of a Young
Man,* c. 1916. [Philadelphia Museum
of Art. The Louise and Walter Arensberg
collection.]

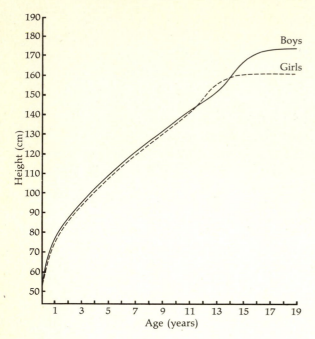

FIGURE 2.6
Typical individual curves showing height attained by boys and girls. [Redrawn from J. M. Tanner, R. H. Whitehouse, and M. Takaishi, *Arch. Dis. Child.* 41(1966):467.]

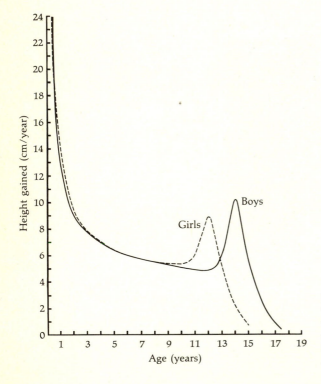

FIGURE 2.7
Typical individual curves showing velocity of growth in height for boys and girls. [Redrawn from J. M. Tanner, R. H. Whitehouse, and M. Takaishi, *Arch. Dis. Child.* 41(1966):466.]

Tanner 1969). Peak velocity of the height spurt is somewhat higher in males than in females (Figure 2.7). In the year in which a boy grows the fastest, he normally adds from about 3 to 5 inches (7–12 cm) to his height; a girl adds slightly less (6–11 cm) (Tanner 1970, p. 94). This means an actual doubling of the velocity of growth, which approximates the rate of growth at age 2.

At the end of the growth spurt, the rate rapidly decelerates. An average girl of 14 and a boy of 16 have already reached 98 percent of their adult height (refer to Table 2.1 on page 37). Further noticeable growth in stature stops at about age 18 in females and age 20 in males.[6]

The cessation of growth in stature is in fact due to sexual maturation. The long bones of the body such as those of the extremities grow at both ends (epiphyses). The sex hormones that increase in puberty hasten closure of these epiphyseal growing plates, eventually bringing to an end further growth in height. The earlier sexual maturation of females is one reason why males are about 10 percent taller as adults. By virtue of maturing later, males have more time to continue growing.

Stature among children is as varied as it is among adults.[7] During puberty, further differences are apparent that are transitory because they result from discrepancies in the rate of growth. As shown in Figure 2.8, curves showing the growth of two boys whose heights are similar at age 11 diverge considerably if one boy grows faster than the other. But by age 17 the slower maturer has caught up.

Another common occurrence is for a girl who is relatively tall before puberty to reach the growth spurt early, which further separates her in stature from her chronological peers. Likewise, a boy who is relatively short to start with will enter puberty late and be seemingly left even further behind. Such discrepancies due to early and late maturation are cancelled out eventually, but while they last they may be cause for concern, as will be discussed later.

Normal patterns of maturation can be classified into the following six groups (Falkner 1972, p. 241):

The first group comprises average children whose growth closely approximates the mean for height and weight at given ages.

The second group consists of early maturing children who are tall in childhood solely because they are more mature than average children; their growth curves lie above the mean curves of average children but not greatly so. They will not be unusually tall adults.

In the third group are early maturing children who are also genetically tall. They are taller than average from early childhood and continue to mature

---

[6]The vertebral column is said to continue growing until age 30 by about $\frac{1}{8}$ inch (Sinclair 1973, p. 25).

[7]As an example of such variation, Tanner points out that if a child of average height on his seventh birthday stopped growing for two years, he would still be within the normal range of height limits for 9-year-olds.

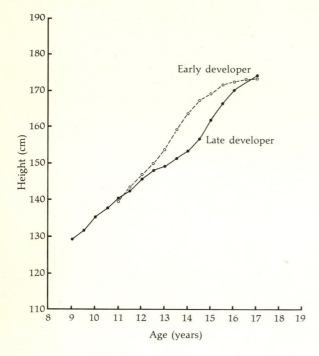

FIGURE 2.8
Height curves during puberty of an early developing boy and a late developing boy. Note that both are the same height at the beginning and end of the growth spurt. [Adapted from J. M. Tanner, *Education and Physical Growth*, University of London Press, 1961.]

rapidly. These children will reach adult status early and will be tall adults. Their growth curves lie well above the mean.

The fourth and fifth groups are the opposites of the second and third groups. They consist of late maturers, with or without genetic shortness, whose growth curves lie below the mean to the same extent that those of children in the second and third groups lie above it.

Many of the children in the sixth group find their way into the "growth clinic." They are children who start puberty much earlier or much later than one would expect. The growth spurt may occur suddenly, before it is expected, or it may be a muted, drawn-out process if it is delayed. Because the "total growth life" of such children is longer or shorter than the average, they may well become much taller or shorter adults than would have been expected.

In addition to lengthening, bones also grow in thickness. During puberty, the outer, or cortical, layer of bones of males grows more than that of females. Dry skeletal weight in both sexes increases throughout puberty but is more marked among males. The overall increase in height itself is the cumulative result of the growth of various body parts. The two constituents in stature are total leg length and trunk length. The legs accelerate in growth first, which contributes to the stereotype of the gangling adolescent. The spurt in trunk length follows almost a year later, but eventual height is due more to an increase in the length of the trunk than in that of the legs.

Leg growth itself is not uniform: the foot accelerates first (but stops growing quite soon) followed by the calf and the thigh. Likewise, the growth spurt of the hand and forearm precedes that of the upper arm. Thus, the more distal parts of the limbs grow faster first, which may unnecessarily worry adolescents who for a while find themselves with disproportionately large hands and feet and do not realize that it is just a matter of time until the rest of the limbs will catch up.

Table 2.1 shows the percentage of mature height attained at different ages. For example, by age 2, boys have attained 49.5 percent and girls 52.8 percent of their adult heights.[8] The reliability of these figures for predicting how tall a

[8]If this sounds implausible, you can check it by measuring the heights of the figures in Figure 2.3.

Table 2.1. Percentages of mature height attained at different ages.

Chronological age (years)	Percentage of average mature height	
	Boys	Girls
Birth	28.6	30.9
1	42.2	44.7
2	49.5	52.8
3	53.8	57.0
4	58.0	61.8
5	61.8	66.2
6	65.2	70.3
7	69.0	74.0
8	72.0	77.5
9	75.0	80.7
10	78.0	84.4
11	81.1	88.4
12	84.2	92.9
13	87.3	96.5
14	91.5	98.3
15	96.1	99.1
16	98.3	99.6
17	99.3	100.0
18	99.8	100.0
19	100.0	100.0

Source: N. Bayley, Growth Curves of Height and Weight by Age for Boys and Girls, Scaled According to Physical Maturity, *J. Pediatr.* 48(1956):187–194.

child will be as an adult depends on the age of the child. At the age of 1 year, they are unreliable, but, at the age of 2 or 3, they can be used to make fairly dependable predictions. Those made at age 8 for girls and age 10 for boys are the most accurate. For example, an 8-year-old girl who is 4 feet tall (which constitutes 72 percent of her adult height) can be expected to grow to be about 5 feet, 7 inches. Similarly, a 10-year-old boy who at 4 feet, 11 inches has attained 84.4 percent of his adult height, will ultimately be about 5 feet, 10 inches.

In puberty, predictions of the amount of growth left, and hence final stature, are better done by reference to skeletal age than chronological age. Ninety percent of the predictions made from such measures are accurate to within $\pm 1\frac{1}{2}$ inches of final height (Tanner 1970, p. 109). Other predictive measures such as parental height are less reliable. It is currently not possible to control growth in stature under ordinary circumstances, but regulation is possible in certain pathological cases in which there is an identifiable cause that can be treated. Nevertheless, the ability to predict adult stature may be useful beyond satisfying the curiosity of those concerned. As Tanner points out, certain careers, like that of a ballet dancer, require that performers be within a limited range in stature. Because training for such careers can begin as early as age nine or ten, foreknowledge of the statistical changes of how tall the child will be as an adult may prevent subsequent disappointment.

Weight

The nonskeletal increments of growth during puberty are greater than those of skeletal growth. By age ten, boys have gained only about 55 percent and girls 59 percent of their adult weight (Heald and Hung 1970, p. 25).

The patterns of weight gain are expressed in weight-attainment curves (Figure 2.9) and velocity curves (Figures 2.10). Weight gain is a composite result of an increase in the size of the skeleton, muscles, and internal organs and in the amount of fat. Weight is a much move variable measure than height because of its greater dependence on such external factors as diet.

Table 2.2 shows height and weight measures for American youth between the ages of 10 and 18. The 50th percentile columns show that 50 percent of the sample population are taller or weigh more than the figures given, and 50 percent are shorter or weigh less. The 5th percentile columns show that only 5 percent are shorter or weigh less than the figures, and the 95th percentile columns show that only 5 percent are taller and weigh more than the figures.

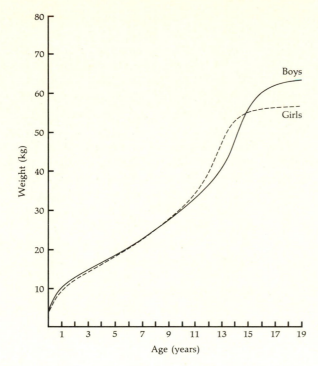

FIGURE 2.9
Typical individual curves showing weight attained by boys and girls. [Redrawn from J. M. Tanner, R. H. Whitehouse, and M. Takaishi, *Arch. Dis. Child.* 41(1966):467.]

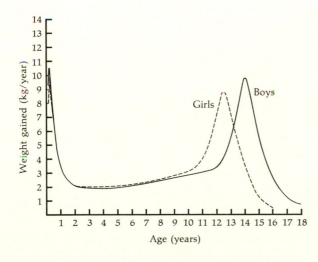

FIGURE 2.10
Typical individual curves showing velocity of weight gain in boys and girls. [Redrawn from J. M. Tanner, R. H. Whitehouse, and M. Takaishi, in *Arch. Dis. Child.* 41(1966):466.]

Table 2.2.   Height and body weight from age 10 to age 18.

Age	Height in inches (by percentile)			Weight in pounds (by percentile)		
	5th	50th	95th	5th	50th	95th
			BOYS			
10	50.6	54.9	59.2	51.4	71.4	91.4
11	51.9	56.4	60.9	53.3	78.9	102.5
12	53.5	58.6	63.7	60.0	86.0	113.5
13	55.2	61.3	67.4	65.3	98.6	131.9
14	57.5	64.1	70.7	75.5	111.8	148.1
15	61.0	66.9	72.8	88.0	124.3	160.6
16	63.8	68.9	74.0	97.8	133.8	169.8
17	65.2	69.8	74.4	106.5	139.8	174.0
18	65.9	70.2	74.5	110.3	144.8	179.3
			GIRLS			
10	49.9	54.5	59.1	48.2	71.0	95.0
11	51.9	57.0	62.1	55.4	82.0	108.6
12	54.1	59.5	64.9	63.9	94.4	124.9
13	57.1	62.2	66.8	72.8	105.5	138.2
14	58.5	63.1	67.7	83.0	113.0	144.0
15	59.5	63.8	68.1	89.5	120.0	150.5
16	59.8	64.1	68.4	95.1	123.0	150.1
17	60.1	64.2	68.3	97.9	125.8	153.7
18	60.1	64.4	68.7	96.0	126.2	156.4

Source: H. L. Barnett and A. H. Einhorn, eds. *Pediatrics*, 15th ed., 1972, p. 1923.
Courtesy of Appleton-Century-Crofts, Publishing Division of Prentice-Hall, Inc.

Musculature and Strength

A substantial contributor to weight gain, as well as changes in general appearance at puberty, is the musculature of the body. Figure 2.11 shows the progressive changes in this regard for the two sexes. Muscular growth usually peaks about three months after growth in stature has peaked.

During puberty, the muscles increase not only in size but also in strength. The increase in strength lags behind the increase in size by many months, but once it has been attained it is appreciably greater than would be expected: the increase in strength is more than can be accounted for by the enlarged muscle mass alone.

Before puberty, there is no substantial difference in muscular strength between boys and girls. But as commonly observed and demonstrated in specific tests (Figure 2.12), a discrepancy emerges during puberty that persists into adulthood (Jones 1949; Espenschade 1940; MacCurdy 1953). The

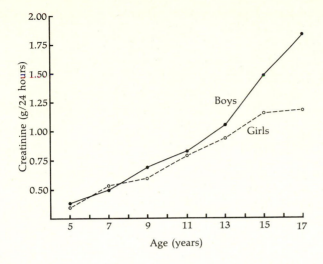

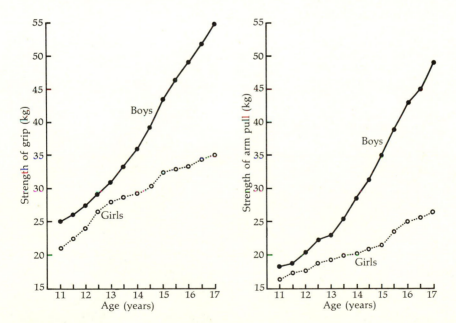

FIGURE 2.11
Increase in muscle mass as reflected in the amount of creatinine excreted. [Redrawn from J. M. Tanner, *Growth at Adolescence*, 2d ed., Oxford: Blackwell, 1962.]

FIGURE 2.12
Differences in muscular strength between boys and girls. [Redrawn from F. A. Beach, in *Reproductive Behavior*, ed. W. Montagna and W. A. Sadler, Plenum, 1974.]

stronger hand grip of boys is in part due to their larger forearms, a difference that is present at birth. The greater ability exhibited by boys in arm pull and arm thrust is the result of stronger arm, shoulder, chest, and back muscles.

Growth in musculature consists of an increase in the number of muscle cells and in their size. In males, there is a fourteenfold increase in the number of muscle cells between the ages of 5 and 16, the maximum gain occurring at the age of $10\frac{1}{2}$. The size of muscle cells continues to increase until the end of the third decade. In females, the increase in the number of cells is tenfold, and maximum muscle cell size is reached by age $10\frac{1}{2}$ (Root 1973a, p. 4; Cheek 1968).

Boys show greater speed and coordination in body movements, whereas girls have greater finger dexterity (Maccoby and Jacklin 1974, p. 38). Between the ages of 14 and 18, male reactions to sudden stimuli also become markedly quicker (Marshall 1973, p. 47).

The image of the lithe, muscular young man has traditionally been celebrated and idealized in works of art (Figure 2.13), whereas in classic depictions the female is usually shown in a static position. But young women are capable of experiencing the physical exuberance of their maturing bodies (Figure 2.14). The physical differences between the sexes that become established in puberty have far-reaching social implications, and their significance will be considered at the end of the chapter.

FIGURE 2.13
Raymond Duchamp-Villon: *The Athlete—Torso of a Young Man,* 1910. [Museum of Modern Art, Paris, Photograph from National Museums.]

FIGURE 2.14
California girls. [Photograph by Co Rentmeester. Time-Life Picture Agency.
© Time Inc.]

The difference in growth rates and proportions of body parts of adolescents has given rise to a number of misconceptions. One is that an adolescent "outgrows" his strength and becomes weak and easily exhausted. There are no grounds for this claim. Puberty is characterized by steady and rapid improvement in physical strength, skill, and endurance. There is no weakening at any time. What does occur is that the growth spurt in height and musculature precedes the peak in strength development. Thus for a year or so, an adolescent is not as strong as an adult of comparable size and muscular development (Tanner 1970, p. 96).

Another notion is that puberty is a period of poor coordination and awkwardness caricatured in the stereotype of the adolescent with what seem to be two left feet. Motor coordination improves as strength develops. So coordination may lag behind growth in stature and musculature, but at no time do coordination and balance deteriorate (Marshall 1973, p. 47). It is also possible that such apparent awkwardness has nothing to do with puberty. "According to the longitudinal data," writes Tanner (1962, p. 205), "a clumsy boy in late adolescence is likely to have been a clumsy child before adolescence and short of and possibly despite special measures is liable to end up a clumsy man." Conceivably, chronic fatigue during puberty may be due to psychological malaise and the appearance of awkwardness a reflection of the adolescent's self-consciousness of his growing body.

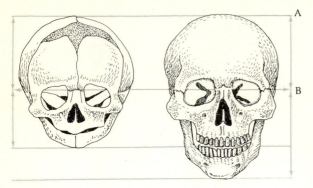

FIGURE 2.15
Growth of the face. The newborn skull and the adult skull have been drawn so that the height of the cranial vault (the distance between the planes A and B) is the same. Notice the great relative increase in the length of the facial skeleton in the adult. [Redrawn from D. Sinclair, *Human Growth After Birth,* 2d ed., Oxford University Press, 1973.]

Body Proportions

The proportions of the body are steadily changing during the entire developmental period (Figure 2.3). Some of these changes may be considered general rules (Sinclair 1973, pp. 106–107). For example, at all ages, the dimensions of the head are nearer maturity than are those of the trunk, which are in turn ahead of the limbs. In the growth spurt, the feet and hands grow larger first, followed by the hips, the chest, the shoulders, and finally the length of the trunk. Because the head develops early, its size relative to the rest of the body becomes progressively smaller. (Compare the younger with the older figures in Figure 2.3.)

The bones of the face grow faster than those of the cranial vault, and at puberty the face is said to "emerge from under the skull" (Figure 2.15). The profile becomes straighter, the nose more projecting, and the jaw more prominent (Bergerson 1972). All of these changes are more marked among males. Facial appearance is further altered by the recession of the hairline, which occurs in all males and in many females but is more distinct in the former. The lips become fuller and, along with other subtle changes, contribute to the emergence of the adult face.

Some skeletal sex differences are present at birth and become greater at puberty. As mentioned earlier, the male forearm is larger relative to height than that of the female. It is common for the index finger to be as long or longer than the ring finger in females, but rarely in males. Other differences emerge at puberty—most notably the broader shoulders of males, their relatively narrower hips, and their larger legs relative to trunk length. In contrast, females have narrower shoulders, wider hips, and shorter legs relative to trunk length. Late-maturing children of both sexes tend to be long-legged and have narrower hips, whereas early maturers tend to have a more stocky physique.

INTERNAL CHANGES

There are additional changes taking place during puberty that are internal and thus hardly realized by the person undergoing them. Apart from the important changes in the reproductive system, which will be discussed separately, these changes involve the structures of various organs of the body as well as their physiological functions.

The study of these internal changes is more recent and more problematic than, for example, the assessment of growth in height. It is more problematic because physiological measurements tend to vary considerably even over short periods in response to factors that may be transient or irrelevant to the process of puberty. The illustrative examples that follow are meant to emphasize the fact that much more is happening during puberty than meets the eye.

Starting with the cardiovascular system, the heart—which is a muscular organ—participates in the growth spurt like the other muscles of the body, and its weight nearly doubles. Like that of other muscles, this growth is more pronounced in boys (Maresh 1948). Systolic blood pressure rises steadily throughout childhood but increases at an accelerated rate during puberty, especially among boys, and soon attains adult values (Figure 2.16). The heart rate is high in childhood but decreases with growth. This decrease is checked during puberty, and there may even be a slight increase in the resting heart

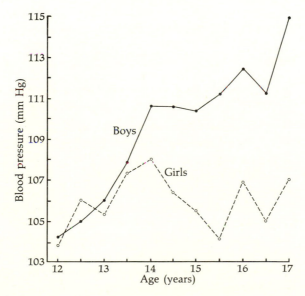

FIGURE 2.16
Differences in systolic blood pressure between boys and girls at puberty. [Redrawn from F. A. Beach, in *Reproductive Behavior*, ed. W. Montagna and W. A. Sadler, Plenum, 1974.]

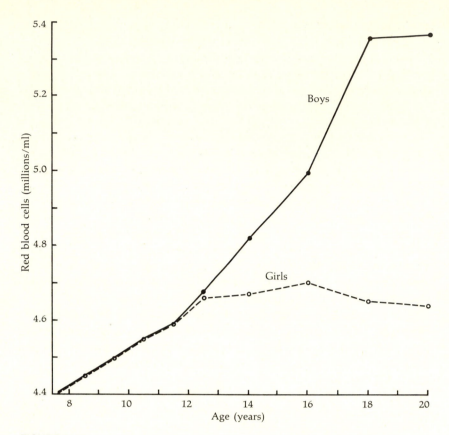

FIGURE 2.17
Differences in the number of red blood cells between boys and girls at puberty.
[Redrawn from F. A. Beach, in *Reproductive Behavior,* ed. W. Montagna and
W. A. Sadler, Plenum, 1974.]

rate (Shock 1944; Iliff and Lee 1952). Puberty also entails changes in the
number of red blood corpuscles, in blood hemoglobin, and in blood volume
(Figure 2.17), and there are significant differences in this regard between the
sexes. Blood volume, hemoglobin, and red blood cells increase markedly in
boys, but not in girls. Adult women have about one million fewer red cells per
milliliter of blood than do men.

The respiratory system undergoes changes similar to those of the cardiovascular system. Both the size of the lungs and respiratory capacity increase
during puberty—more markedly among boys (Shock and Soley 1939; Iliff and
Lee 1952; Ferris, Whittenberger, and Gallagher 1952; Ferris and Smith 1953).
The rate of respiration decreases throughout childhood and puberty in both
sexes, but the amount of air that can be taken in at a single breath or in a

given time increases markedly in adolescent boys but barely in girls. The exchange of oxygen in the lungs is also more efficient in boys.

The basal body temperature gradually decreases with age in both sexes, reaching adult values by age 12 in girls but continuing to drop in boys for a while longer. Similarly, the basal metabolic rate decreases from birth on and into old age. But, during puberty, there is a temporary slowing of this decline. This relative stabilization in the basal metabolic rate in both sexes coincides with the growth spurt and is a reflection of the intensified physiological activities at this time.

The physiological responses to exercise also change at puberty, particularly in boys. Because the heart and lungs have become larger and more efficient, the body can handle the demands placed on it by exercise more effectively. When the body is subjected to severe physical exertion, muscles can continue to function while incurring an "oxygen debt." This capacity improves throughout adolescence until the end of the second decade.

The net effect of all these changes is to increase a person's capacity for physical exertion, to allow quicker recovery from its effects, and thus to improve "exercise tolerance." These gains are definitely more pronounced in males.

The development of the brain during puberty remains something of a mystery. Despite the strides made in the maturation of thinking during adolescence, there is little evidence of gross changes in the brain. As shown in Figure 2.1, the growth of the brain progresses ahead of other systems. The brain has already attained 25 percent of its adult weight at birth; 50 percent at 6 months; 75 percent at $2\frac{1}{2}$ years; 90 percent at 5 years; and 95 percent at 10 years. (In contrast, body weight at birth is only 5 percent and at age 10 only 50 percent of that of a young adult.) Whether the brain itself participates in the growth spurt is not certain. Electroencephalograms show a change in brain waves from childhood (waves of low frequency) to adulthood (alpha rhythm). However, this seems to be a gradual alteration, and it is unclear whether significant changes specifically occur during puberty.

Given the cognitive differences between children and adults and the sequential development of cognition, surely something other than the meager gain in brain size must account for the biological changes that underlie and limit the psychological gains. Because most, if not all, nerve cells in an adult were already formed in the first 20 to 30 weeks of intrauterine life, the answer must be sought in increased "connectivity" or communicative linkages between cells. There is, in fact, for the first several years of life, and possibly longer, a progressive increase in the number and size of dendrites in all layers of the cortex. Dendrites occupy very little space—even millions of them could be accommodated within the modest increase of a few percent in brain size—but the gains in the complexity of communicative networks and hence cognitive functions are immense (Tanner 1970, pp. 118–124).

Although most systems increase in size during puberty, there is at least one that undergoes regression. That is the lymphoid system, which includes the thymus gland and lymphatic tissues (such as the tonsils and adenoids). As mentioned earlier, these structures are in fact larger in childhood and, because they are frequent sites of infection, such regression results in a lowered susceptibility to certain respiratory ailments after puberty.

Unfortunately, not every change in puberty is for the better. Children who are near-sighted (myopic) become more so with puberty, and many new cases of myopia develop at this stage. The visual problem can be easily corrected by prescription glasses, but this in turn may create aesthetic and other concerns.

THE SIGNIFICANCE OF PHYSICAL DIFFERENCES BETWEEN THE SEXES

As mentioned in the introductory remarks concerning the somatic changes of puberty, these biological events result in two major outcomes: the body of the child becomes transformed into that of the adult and the physical differences between the two sexes become more distinct. Both outcomes have profound psychological and social repercussions.

Transformation into adulthood is negotiated relatively easily. Various cultures have evolved definitions of adulthood that take into account the somatic changes of puberty. There may be a great deal that is idiosyncratic in those definitions, but inevitably the somatic changes assert their presence and are recognized. Reproductive capacity in particular—not mere sexual interest or competence—plays a central role in the transition to adulthood.

The gulf that puberty creates between male and female was accepted for a long time, and still is in many cultures, as part of a ''natural'' process. The physical differences that have always characterized the sexes continue of course to do so, but the cultural assumptions of sexual identity and the acceptance of sex roles based on them are currently being questioned. In the polarization of opinion that has resulted, there are some who continue to cling to the traditional biology-is-destiny viewpoint and ascribe much to ''nature'' that has no demonstrable biological basis. At the other extreme, there are those who deny the relevance of any basic physical sex difference (apart from reproductive functions) either out of ignorance or for political ends.

There is a fundamental genetic difference between male and female, which is irrevocably established at conception. As development proceeds through embryonal and fetal stages, sex differences become apparent within the reproductive system. At the time of birth, male and female are quite distinct genetically, hormonally, and anatomically. The differences are most marked in the reproductive system but not restricted to it. For example, newborn male infants are generally heavier by about 0.2 pound and taller by 0.3 inch than females (Barnett and Einhorn 1972, pp. 1921–1922). However, from the moment of birth, girls and boys are treated differently in numerous subtle and not so subtle ways. This differential treatment is so pervasive and persistent that very soon it becomes difficult to tell whether manifest differences in behavior are due to inborn or external influences.

The nonreproductive physical sex differences that become established at puberty can be meaningfully expressed only as averages for large populations, and there is much overlap between the two sexes: There are many women who are taller, heavier, and more muscular, and have longer forearms, higher exercise tolerance, and so on, than the average man. If shoulder and hip measurements alone were used to classify adults, 10 percent would be assigned the wrong classification. If only the ratio of trunk length to leg length were used, 6 percent would be misclassified. The only way in which men and women are normally unique is in reproductive function.

The various physiological differences that characterize the two sexes at the end of puberty add up to the generally superior ability of males for intense physical exertion and recovery from its effects. Because of their skeletal size, proportions, and muscular development, males are able to exert greater force with better coordination. Their cardio-respiratory systems sustain such physical efforts more effectively. The net effect is that, after puberty, males generally excel in activities like lifting, throwing, hitting, running, jumping, and so on. This advantage has tended to become generalized into a conception of all-encompassing male "physical superiority," which is quite unwarranted. In the last analysis, the ability to survive is the critical overall index of physical fitness, and the death rate for women is lower than that for men in every decade of life.

Even within the limits of acknowledged male physical superiority, social factors should not be disregarded. Physical prowess depends to a large measure on exercise and training, which in turn depend on personal motivation, social expectations, and practical opportunities. Males have received more encouragement in this regard, which has contributed greatly to the gap that exists in physical ability between the two sexes. Women are unlikely ever to beat men at the Olympics, but Olympic performance requires exceptional ability for either sex. In everyday life, sex differences do not affect the health benefits and enjoyment derived from active play (Figure 2.18).

The relevance of physical sex differences to occupational choice is also becoming subject to reappraisal. It is one thing to acknowledge that males generally have stronger muscles and quite another to conclude that women should not therefore drive tractors or become engineers.

The human growth curve is a primate characteristic, and somatic sex differences long antedate man. They can be observed readily in other primates

FIGURE 2.18
Co-ed touch football. [News and
Publications Service, Stanford
University.]

among which males are bigger and stronger and have greater physical endurance than females (Tanner 1970; Gavan 1953; Grether 1940). Behaviorally,
males are also more aggressive, dominant, daring, and venturesome. These
traits are not lacking in female primates, but they are less pronounced. Early
man was heir to these primate characteristics and in evolutionary terms they
seem to have served him well, just as other functions more prominent in females
have insured human survival.

Differences in roles that have emerged through time must also be viewed
in evolutionary and historical terms (Beach 1974). To understand these differences requires examining the time when man was a hunter and gatherer
because the entire evolution of man took place in that preagricultural period.
Agriculture has dominated less than 1 percent of the history of man, and there
is no evidence that any major biological changes occurred during that time
(Washburn and Lancaster 1968).

When hunting big game, the male's physical characteristics were a distinct
advantage. Throughout much of history, when muscle and metal determined
the outcome of combat, this advantage has helped man to retain social dominance. But of what relevance are these physical advantages in today's world,
and what is it that justifies preconceived occupational role definitions on the
basis of sex? If men and women were free to choose their own modes of work
and play, they would sort themselves out according to a variety of determinants
of which physical characteristics would be one in relation to some activities.
But such free choices are as yet neither generally available nor widely availed
of. In some ways, society is still organized as if we were hunters. Failure to
recognize the exigencies of the world in which man evolved and those of

FIGURE 2.19
Wilhelm Lehmbruck: *Standing Youth,* 1913, and *Kneeling Woman,* 1911. [Collection, The Museum of Modern Art, New York. Gift of Abby Aldrich Rockefeller.]

the world in which he now lives may be causing more grief than we realize (Hamburg 1962).

The somatic differences between the sexes find eloquent expression in such works of art as those shown in Figure 2.19. But more than broad shoulders and curving hips set these figures apart, for they also reflec. cultural ideals: Observe the man—erect, powerful, and pensive; the woman—submissive, gentle, and beguiling. There are no reasonable grounds to deny or decry the basic sexual dimorphism between Lehmbruck's young man and young woman. But there are good reasons to consider whether this dimorphism has been socially misused to determine what people should or should not do with their bodies and their lives.

Chapter 3

Reproductive Maturation and Factors Affecting Puberty

It is customary to discuss the maturation of the reproductive system separately from the other somatic changes in the rest of the body. This is useful to the extent that it facilitates description, provided that it does not imply a rigid distinction between what is ''sexual'' and what is not. For example, the development of the genitals or of pubic hair is of obvious erotic significance. But such features as stature, musculature, and fat distribution, which may seem sexually neutral, are components of a person's sexual profile that are just as significant. In most cultures, erotic attractiveness, provocativeness, or ''sexiness'' depends more on general physique and the constituent sizes, shapes, and proportions of body parts than on the genital organs as such.

The first part of this chapter treats of the development of the reproductive system as it pertains both to the sexual organs and to the emergence of secondary sexual characteristics. The second part examines factors that affect the onset and course of puberty.

DEVELOPMENT OF
THE REPRODUCTIVE SYSTEM

The pubescent growth spurt in height and musculature is paralleled by the rapid development of the reproductive system (refer to Figure 2.1 on page 25). But there is an additional aspect that is unique, namely, the emergence of reproductive maturity. All of the other manifestations of puberty involve quantitative changes as exemplified by the skeleton, musculature, or the sexual organs becoming larger. Even sexual functions like orgasmic capability may antedate puberty. But the capacity to reproduce is a qualitative change that has no prepubescent counterpart. In this sense, reproductive maturity could be considered the primary criterion of biological adulthood.

All that was said in the preceding chapter concerning the variability in the timing, sequence, and duration of somatic changes of puberty is equally applicable to the maturational events in the reproductive system. Consideration was also given to the timetables of growth of the breasts, penis, testes, and pubic hair, and to the onset of menarche in relation to the height spurt (refer to Figure 2.2 on page 28). Table 3.1 further details the sequence of these events.

Most of the conspicuous changes of puberty that contribute to sexual dimorphism are referred to as the "secondary sex characteristics." They include such features as breast development and fat deposition in females, growth of the beard and deepening of the voice in males, and sprouting of pubic and axillary (armpit) hair in both sexes. Many sources also include the growth of the external genitals (Falkner 1972; Williams 1974), and some add the internal reproductive organs as well (Brobeck 1973). These changes are "secondary" to, or are caused by, the primary pubertal hormonal changes that initiate them. In a more restrictive sense, secondary sex characteristics constitute nongenital characteristics that distinguish between male and female members of a species. Human beards are comparable in this regard to the combs of roosters, the antlers of deer, or similar marks that play a central role in the courting and mating behavior of animals (Tepperman 1973). Human sexual behavior is regulated by far more complex psychological and social variables, but these do not exclude the residual factors from our primate heritage.

As discussed in the preceding chapter, differences between the sexes are produced by the somatic changes of puberty. Even more striking is the diversity that emerges as a result of reproductive development. That is why it is necessary to discuss the reproductive maturation of each sex separately. However, we should not lose sight of the fundamental similarities that combine to link the complementary developmental patterns of males and females. Table 3.1 is particularly useful in correlating the concurrent maturational events in the two sexes.

Table 3.1. Average approximate age and sequence of appearance of sexual characteristics in both sexes.

Age (years)	Boys	Girls
9–10		Growth of bony pelvis Budding of nipples
10–11	First growth of testes and penis	Budding of breasts Pubic hair
11–12	Prostatic activity	Changes in vaginal epithelium and the smear Growth of external and internal genitalia
12–13	Pubic hair	Pigmentation of nipples Mammae filling in
13–14	Rapid growth of testes and penis Subareolar node of nipples	Axillary hair Menarche (average: $13\frac{1}{2}$ years; range: 9–17 years.) Menstruation may be anovulatory for first few years.
14–15	Axillary hair Down on upper lip Voice change	Earliest normal pregnancies
15–16	Mature spermatozoa (average: 15 years; range: $11\frac{1}{4}$–17 years)	Acne Deepening of voice
16–17	Facial and body hair Acne	Arrest of skeletal growth
21	Arrest of skeletal growth	

Source: L. Wilkins, ed. *The Diagnosis and Treatment of Endocrine Disorders in Childhood and Adolescence,* Charles C Thomas, 1957.

Note: The age of menarche given here is later than that given in the text because it is based on older data.

FEMALE REPRODUCTIVE MATURATION

Breasts

The first visible sign of puberty in a girl is the growth of her breasts. It usually starts between the ages of 8 and 13 years (on the average at about 11) and is usually completed between the ages of 13 and 18 (on the average at about 15), as shown in Figure 2.2 on page 28. Breast development follows a predictable sequence, which can be divided into stages that are useful as developmental landmarks (Figure 3.1).

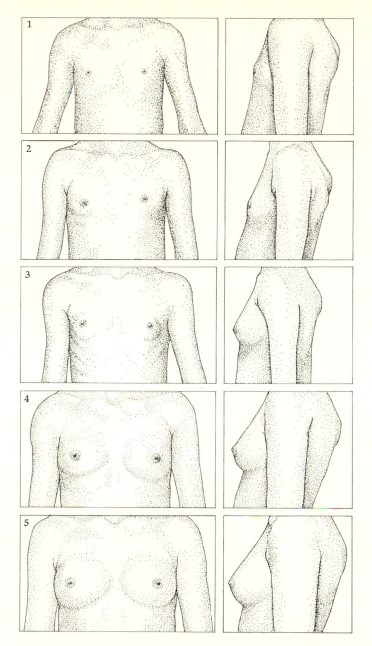

FIGURE 3.1
Stages of breast development in adolescent girls: (1) prepubertal
flat appearance like that of a child; (2) small, raised breast bud;
(3) general enlargement and raising of breast and areola; (4) areola
and papilla (nipple) form contour separate from that of breast;
(5) adult breast—areola is in same contour as breast. [Redrawn from
J. M. Tanner, *Growth at Adolescence*, 2d ed., Oxford: Blackwell, 1962.]

The transition from prepubescent breasts (stage 1 in Figure 3.1) begins with the appearance of a slight protuberance under the nipples (stage 2). This early growth is referred to as "budding" of the breasts. It is followed by the development of mammary glands, which produce milk during lactation, and the deposition of adipose tissue, which gives breasts their adult shape (stage 5).[1] The breasts undergo further modification in adulthood: they become larger during pregnancy and lactation, and smaller and less firm with age, particularly after menopause. Their size and shape are also affected by nutrition and other factors.

Given the aesthetic and erotic appeal of a woman's breasts, their development may be of considerable psychological importance to a young woman. A common concern is whether they will attain the right size and shape.[2] Because it is not unusual for one breast to develop faster than the other, an adolescent girl may worry about the asymmetry that results, especially if she does not know that the difference is usually corrected by the time development is completed. In rarer cases, the breasts overgrow to become extremely large and a possible source of embarrassment. This condition is sometimes referred to as "virginal hypertrophy" to distinguish it from the hypertrophy that accompanies pregnancy.

Most teen-age girls take the development of their breasts in stride, but a certain amount of preoccupation and self-consciousness is quite common nevertheless. Should the breasts fail to develop adequately and symmetrically or should they be deformed, there are safe and effective plastic surgical procedures (as well as some that are not) to correct them after the young woman has attained adulthood. In cases of endocrine deficiency, hormonal treatment may be effective, but if there are no hormonal abnormalities and a young woman is menstruating normally, hormonal treatment will not enlarge breast size (Williams 1974, p. 511). The important fact to remember is that the size and shape of the breasts have no bearing on their capacity to respond to erotic stimulation or to nurse infants.

Pubic Hair

The second sign of puberty in a girl is usually the appearance of pubic hair. However, it can appear before budding of the breasts. Pubic hair begins to grow between the ages of 11 and 12 on the average, and the adult pattern is

[1]The average ages that correspond to the stages of breast development are indicated in Figure 2.2 on page 28. For further descriptions of the individual stages of breast development, see Tanner (1962).

[2]These judgments are relative and matters of fashion. In one study, breasts were classified according to shape—conical (20 percent); round (60 percent), and flat (20 percent); and size—small (38 percent); medium (34 percent); and large (28 percent). These criteria were then used to categorize breasts into several types (small and round, conical and large, and so on) (Reynolds and Wines 1951).

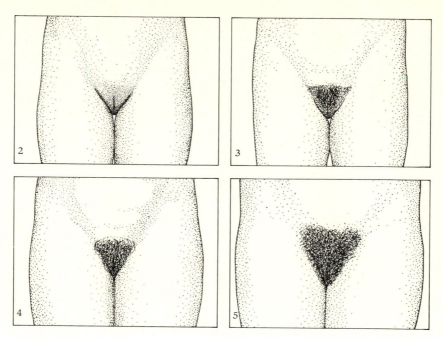

FIGURE 3.2
Stages of pubic-hair development in adolescent girls: (1) prepubertal (not shown) in which there is no true pubic hair; (2) sparse growth of downy hair mainly at sides of labia; (3) pigmentation, coarsening, and curling with an increase in the amount of hair; (4) adult hair, but limited in area; (5) adult hair with horizontal upper border.
[Redrawn from J. M. Tanner, *Growth at Adolescence*, 2d ed., Oxford: Blackwell, 1962.]

established by age 14 (refer to Figure 2.2 on page 28). Its appearance precedes that of axillary hair by more than a year (Table 3.1).

Pubic hair is imbued with erotic significance, and since Paleolithic times its triangular distribution has been used to protray female genitalia and as a fertility symbol (Giedion 1957). For clinical purposes, it provides useful indexes of development (Figure 3.2).[3] Figure 3.3 shows how the parallel stages of breast and pubic-hair development alternate and how they relate to other pubertal events such as menarche and peak velocity of growth in height.

External Sexual Organs

The female genitals are referred to either as the vulva (covering) or as the pudendum (a thing of shame). They include the mons pubis, or mons

___
[3]The average ages that correspond to the stages of pubic-hair development are indicated in Figure 2.2 on page 28. For descriptions of these stages, see Tanner (1962).

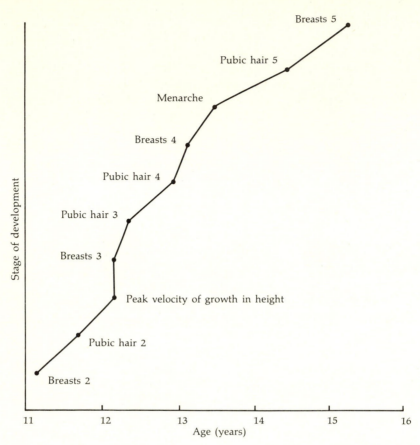

FIGURE 3.3
Sequence of breast and pubic-hair development in adolescent girls. The numbered
stages of development correspond to those illustrated in Figures 3.1 and 3.2. [Redrawn
from A. W. Root, Endocrinology of Puberty. 1. Normal Sexual Maturation, *J. Pediatr.*
83(July 1973):4.]

veneris (the mount of Venus), which consists of the soft protuberance over
the pubic bone. Especially after it is covered with pubic hair, the region of the
mons becomes the most prominent aspect of the female genitals. Somewhat
less visible are the major lips (labia majora), located below the mons, which
enclose the minor lips (which remain free of hair); the clitoris; and the vaginal
opening, which is usually partly covered by the hymen in virgins. The urethra,
though opening into the same general area, is not part of the reproductive
system.[4]

───────────

[4]For further details on sexual anatomy, see Katchadourian and Lunde (1975). A briefer account may
be found in Katchadourian (1972). For more specialized sources, see standard texts on anatomy and
Dickinson (1949).

All these structures undergo significant changes during puberty. They become enlarged and their erotic sensitivity is heightened, especially that of the clitoris. Because the female external genitals are more concealed, changes in them are less noticeable than those in the male external genitals. Nevertheless, young women may be quite sensitive about these transformations. Psychological factors and social attitudes can determine whether they think of their maturing genitals with pride and a sense of satisfaction or with apprehensive self-consciousness.

Because of the anatomy of the female external genitals, changes in them are not as useful as pubic-hair growth or changes in the male external genitals in supplying indexes of development for clinical use.

Internal Sexual Organs

The female internal sexual organs consist of paired ovaries (which produce ova, or eggs, and a number of hormones), the uterine, or fallopian, tubes, the uterus, the vagina, and a few minor, accessory structures.

The internal sexual organs rapidly increase in weight by a considerable amount, as shown in Figure 3.4. The muscular wall of the uterus becomes larger, and elaborate cyclical changes occur in its inner lining (endometrium). To accommodate a fetus during pregnancy as well as effectively force it out during birth, the uterus develops an intricate and powerful musculature. Its inner lining is also critical for successful pregnancy because it is where the fertilized egg is implanted and develops to maturity.

The vagina also becomes larger and its lining (epithelium) thicker. Cytological changes of the vaginal epithelium in fact constitute the first clear indication of impending puberty and antedate the development of breasts or pubic hair (Marshall and Tanner 1974). Another important change is that the vaginal contents, which are alkaline at the beginning of puberty, become acidic.

The growth curve for the ovaries is less spectacular than that of the uterus. A human ovary is in fact already a fairly complete organ at birth. It contains about half a million immature ova (oocytes), each one capable of maturing into an egg. Therefore, a woman is born with all of the eggs that she is ever going to develop—usually about four hundred. The follicles remain immature until puberty when ovulation begins. At puberty, they start maturing into eggs in monthly cycles.

Menarche

The monthly cycle, in which one or more eggs mature, culminates in menstruation, which is a quintessential function of the reproductively active woman and an event of much physiological and psychological significance.

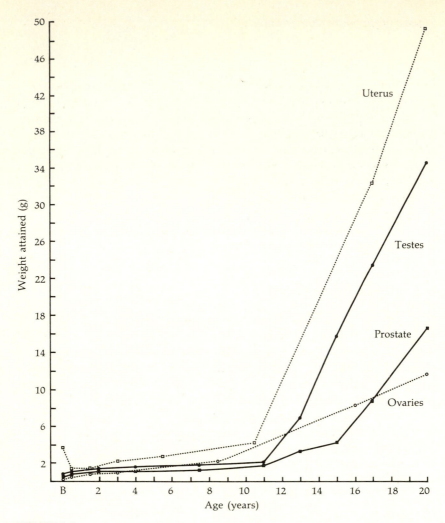

FIGURE 3.4
Growth in weight of the internal sexual organs. [Redrawn from J. M. Tanner, *Growth at Adolescence,* 2d ed., Oxford: Blackwell, 1962.]

Because of its sudden and unmistakable onset and its reproductive implications, the first menstrual period, or *menarche,* has been widely regarded in many cultures as the transitional step to womanhood.

Many rituals and customs concerning menarche have evolved in various cultures (Ford and Beach 1951; Van Gennep 1960). In Western societies, it is a more private event, usually known only to the girl's immediate family and friends. Many uninformed pubescent girls have had the unsettling experience of suddenly bleeding from the vagina (see Box 3.1), but, currently, most teenagers probably receive at least a modicum of information and guidance about what to expect.

One lingering misconception is that menarche marks the onset of puberty; in fact, it is one of the later events to characterize this stage of life. Menarche

BOX 3.1
Experiences of menarche.

What an adventure going out to Illinois at the age of thirteen. . . . But I felt awfully upset, which I supposed was just my excitement at going away. Then of course it proved to be the Curse, for the first time. I thought I was dying of tuberculosis, which in a vague way I knew caused hemorrhages. It must be a serious case because the hemorrhage had gone the wrong way. I wondered if they'd find me dead in the car the next morning. I guess they must have told the porter to take special care of me, because though I'd rather die than call for help, presently he asked through the curtain if I was all right. I said, "I guess I'm sick." "What seems to be the trouble lady?" To that I made no answer at all. I couldn't. With the intuition of a great gentleman he must have guessed, for soon after a large black hand came through the curtains and handed me a package.

Christopher Morley
Kitty Foyle

We were staying with friends . . . I awoke horror-stricken one morning: I had soiled my nightdress. I washed it and got dressed: again I soiled my underclothes. I had forgotten Madeleine's vague prophecies, and I wondered what shameful malady I was suffering from. Worried and feeling somehow guilty, I had to take my mother into my confidence: she explained to me that I had now become "a big girl," and bundled me up in a very inconvenient manner. I felt a strong sense of relief when I learned that it had happened through no fault of my own; and as always when something important happened to me, I even felt my heart swell with a sort of pride. I didn't mind too much when I heard my mother whispering about it to her friends. But that evening when we joined my father in the Rue de Rennes, he jokingly made reference to my condition: I was consumed with shame. I had imagined that the monstrous regiment of women kept its blemish a secret from the male fraternity . . . . I felt as if I could never hold up my head again.

Simone de Beauvoir
Memoirs of a Dutiful Daughter

Wednesday, 5 January, 1944
Yesterday I read an article about blushing by Sis Heyster. This article might have been addressed to me personally. Although I don't blush very easily, the other things in it certainly all fit me. She writes roughly something like this—that a girl in the years of puberty becomes quiet within and begins to think about the wonders that are happening to her body.

I experience that, too, and that is why I get the feeling lately of being embarrassed about Margot, Mummy, and Daddy. Funnily enough, Margot, who is much more shy than I am, isn't at all embarrassed.

I think what is happening to me is so wonderful, and not only what can be seen on my body, but all that is taking place inside. I never discuss myself or any of these things with anybody; that is why I have to talk to myself about them.

Each time I have a period—and that has only been three times—I have the feeling that in spite of all the pain, unpleasantness, and nastiness, I have a sweet secret, and that is why, although it is nothing but a nuisance to me in a way, I always long for the time that I shall feel that secret within me again.

Anne Frank
The Diary of a Young Girl

usually occurs two years after the start of breast development (Marshall and Tanner 1969) and after the peak of the growth spurt in height. In the United States, the average age at which menarche occurs at present is about 12.8 years (Zacharias, Rand, and Wurtman 1976), but the range is normally from 9 to 18 years.[5]

As indicated in Table 3.1, there is a lag of a few years between the onset of puberty and the attainment of reproductive maturity when the processes of ovulation and spermatogenesis become well established. This lag is known as the period of relative sterility of puberty. During this phase, adolescents are less likely to impregnate or become impregnated, but this does not amount to contraceptive security.

MALE REPRODUCTIVE MATURATION

Testes

The onset of puberty in boys is marked by the initial enlargement of the testes (Table 3.1). This usually starts between the ages of 10 and $13\frac{1}{2}$. Testicular development remains in progress throughout most of puberty and is accomplished sometime between the ages of $14\frac{1}{2}$ and 18 (see Figure 2.2 on page 28).

Compared with a girl's breasts, the testes are more hidden from view and their increase in size is not as dramatic. Thus, in addition to the fact that boys enter puberty about two years later than girls, even after they have become pubescent their development is less noticeable initially.

The testes are the male reproductive glands that produce sperm and the male hormones. In this duality of function, they are identical with the ovaries. They are somewhat larger and heavier than ovaries and have a very different internal structure, even though originally both are derived from the embryonal undifferentiated gonads.

Unlike ovaries, infantile testes do not contain all the sperm that they are ever going to produce. Instead, they are a conglomerate of solid threadlike cords called "seminiferous tubules" without sperm. During puberty, these tubules increase in size, and the cells in the lining of the tubules pass through a succession of stages to become differentiated into sperm, which are discharged into the newly formed lumen. From puberty on, the testes more or less continuously produce sperm, generating billions in the course of an adult lifetime.

Like the uterus, the testes gain most of their bulk during puberty, as indicated in Figure 3.4. An important difference between male and female gonads—that

---

[5]The physiology of menstruation is discussed in Chapter 4 and the disorders in Chapter 5.

is, the testes and ovaries—is that the ovaries become nonfunctional at menopause, whereas the decline in testicular function is far more gradual in terms
of both sperm and hormone production (Bermant and Davidson 1974).

Other reproductive structures develop concurrently with the testes. The
male reproductive system is best understood as consisting of three parts:
testes, which produce sperm and hormones; a set of tubes (epididymis, vas
deferens, ejaculatory duct, and urethra), which convey sperm; and the penis,
which delivers the ejaculate (Katchadourian and Lunde 1975).

In addition there are a number of accessory sex glands such as the prostate
gland, the seminal vesicles, and other less significant structures. The prostate
gland enlarges markedly during puberty (Figure 3.4), and its secretions account
for much of the volume of semen and its characteristic odor. In spite of their
enormous numbers, sperm make up a very small fraction of the ejaculate. Thus,
the capacity to ejaculate semen is a direct result of the prostate having become functional.

Ejaculation

Sexuality does not begin with puberty. The capacity for orgasm is present
at birth, is manifested by some children of both sexes, and is retained by both
sexes throughout life. But following puberty, orgasm in males is normally
accompanied by ejaculation. Orgasm is a neuromuscular event. Ejaculation is
the discharge of semen during orgasm, the semen consisting of sperm from the
testes and the secretions of the accessory sex glands. Women produce vaginal
fluids during sexual arousal that may be quite profuse, but they do not ejaculate
during orgasm.[6]

The capacity for ejaculation is a key physiological development of male
puberty. Nothing comparable separates adult female orgasm from prepubescent female orgasm. A reproductively mature woman can conceive with or
without orgasm, but male ejaculation is necessary for fertilization. Furthermore, this process has psychological consequences as well. If a man has
ejaculated, he hardly needs to wonder whether he has attained orgasm, as
some women do.

For a pubescent boy, the first ejaculation is an impressive event and may
be just as startling as menarche can be for a girl (see Boxes 3.2 and 3.3).
It usually occurs about a year after testicular growth, but its timing is highly
variable. Among males in the Kinsey sample, the earliest first ejaculation
remembered was at about 8 years of age, and the latest was at age 21. About
90 percent of all males had had this experience between the ages of 11 and

---

[6]For a detailed consideration of the physiology of orgasm, see Masters and Johnson (1970). A more
concise discussion may be found in Katchadourian and Lunde (1975).

BOX 3.2
Nocturnal emissions. [From G. Stanley Hall, *Life and Confessions of a Psychologist*,
D. Appleton, 1924.]

So great was my dread of natural phenomena that in the earliest teens I rigged an apparatus and applied bandages to prevent erethism while I slept, which very likely only augmented the trouble. If I yielded to any kind of temptation to experimentation upon myself I suffered intense remorse and fear, and sent up many a secret and most fervent prayer that I might never again break my resolve. At one time I feared I was abnormal and found occasion to consult a physician in a neighboring town who did not know me. He examined me and took my dollar, and laughed at me, but also told me what consequences would ensue if I became unchaste. What an untold anguish of soul would have been saved me if some one had told me that certain experiences while I slept were as normal for boys in their teens as are the monthly phenomena for girls. I did not know that even in college and thought myself secretly and exceptionally corrupt and not quite worthy to associate with girls. This had probably much, if not most, to do with my abstention from them and was, I think, the chief factor that brought about my "conversion" in my sophomore year, although this made the struggle for purity far more intense, though I fear but little more successful.

I fear the good Lord on whom I was told, and tried, to cast my burden did not help me much here. Indeed, perhaps in transferring and committing all to Him I trusted my own powers less. Perhaps, again, my profound sense of inferiority here prompted me to compensate by striving all the harder for excellence in other lines, although there was always a haunting sense that if I succeeded in making anything of myself it would be despite this private handicap. I should certainly never dare to marry and have children. It was ineffable relief, therefore, to learn, as I did only far too late, that my life in this sphere had, on the whole, been in no sense abnormal or even exceptional.

15 years. It is interesting that, even in this primarily physiological event, socioeconomic circumstances seemed to make a difference. In the group with the least advantageous socioeconomic background, the mean age for first ejaculation was 14.6 years, almost a year later than in the most advantaged group. Such differences could be due to physiological factors such as the age at reaching puberty, which in turn could be dependent on nutrition and the like. Sexual behavior is also heavily subject to cultural influences. In addition, there are marked individual differences between boys in all socioeconomic groups.

In two out of three cases in the Kinsey sample, the first ejaculation was achieved through masturbation. Nocturnal emissions accounted for only one out of eight, and homosexual contacts for one out of twenty cases. These data contradict the popular belief that pubescent sexuality is usually ushered in by nocturnal emissions. In most cases, the first ejaculation through nocturnal emission occurred almost a year after ejaculatory ability had been achieved (Kinsey, Pomeroy, and Martin 1948).

Another interesting finding of the Kinsey survey was an apparent sex difference in the correlation of pubescent change and sexual function. Assuming

BOX 3.3
"It" by Edward Field. [Reprinted with the permission of the author.]

When her breasts started growing
she bound them down with a strap.
She was ashamed to have them stick out
so people could tease her—
even if she had always looked forward to having them
and stared at the brassiere ads.

It's harder (so to speak) for boys.
Suddenly it is sticking out in front of you
what nobody had ever mentioned,
and even a jockstrap doesn't help much.
And even worse, maybe, is the come.
What do you do with the stuff when it spurts out?

My mother always said how important it was
to prepare girls for what was about to happen
so they shouldn't pick up wrong ideas
from other girls like she did,
or think they were dying
when they woke up one day in a pool of blood.

I was always listening while she taught my sisters
what to expect from nature and to say no until marriage.
Of girls you could speak; boys were unmentionable.
She must have believed about boys
that if you train them not to touch it
and don't ever mention it, it doesn't exist.

But it did: I woke up one morning
with a hard-on that wouldn't go down,
come all over the sheets and no way to wipe it up
and the whole family around and nowhere to hide.
This was unthinkable, and I prayed and prayed
for it to go away forever.

And the terrible act I couldn't help doing although I vowed
   to stop
and half-losing consciousness in the pleasure:
How to remember to think of the gooey mess, and watch out?
Does it show? Can they smell it? Did I make any noise?
You must control yourself, I ordered desperately,
or your life will be ruined like it says in the handbook.

I couldn't control it nor did it go away:
Too bad there wasn't the horrible exposure I dreaded
because as it was I kept it secret—
I was alone in the whole world with it,
and while trying to destroy it, I almost destroyed myself.
Only now, after years of struggle,
I face the simple facts of nature
and think how useless to have suffered.

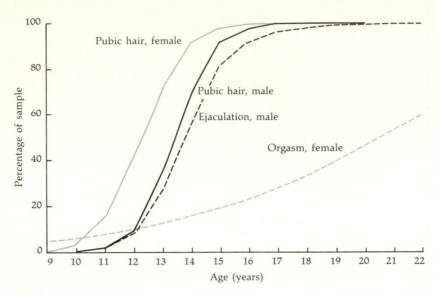

FIGURE 3.5
Onset of puberty and sexual response. [Redrawn from A. C. Kinsey, W. B. Pomeroy,
C. E. Martin, and P. H. Gebhard, *Sexual Behavior in the Human Female*, Saunders, 1953.]

the appearance of pubic hair to signify the onset of puberty and orgasm or
ejaculation to represent specific evidence of erotic response, Kinsey and his
associates demonstrated a number of interesting sex differences in the emergence of pubescent sexuality. As illustrated in Figure 3.5, the development of
pubic hair in boys parallels that in girls, but girls mature earlier than boys by a
couple of years. There is also a close association between the appearance of
pubic hair in boys and experiencing the first ejaculation. These two curves rise
very steeply beginning with age 12, and by age 17 or 18 almost all males in the
sample had developed pubic hair and shown evidence of orgasmic response.
The curve for female orgasm climbs gradually so that even by age 22 only
60 percent of women attain orgasm (Kinsey et al. 1953).

These findings raise the interesting question of whether the difference in
maturational rates between the sexes is due to biological factors or to cultural
conditioning. There are currently no formal data to adequately clarify this issue.
Available evidence as well as general observation would indicate that, since
Kinsey's survey, sexual activity among teen-age girls has risen significantly,
thus narrowing the apparent sex difference in this regard.

Pubic Hair

The appearance of pubic hair in boys is usually an early event of puberty
but may normally be any time between the ages of 10 and 15 (refer to Figure

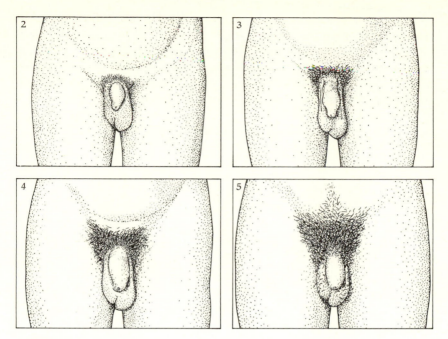

FIGURE 3.6
Stages of pubic-hair development in adolescent boys: (1) prepubertal (not shown) in
which there is no true pubic hair; (2) sparse growth of downy hair mainly at base of
penis; (3) pigmentation, coarsening, and curling with an increase in amount of hair;
(4) adult hair, but limited in area; (5) adult hair with horizontal upper border and
spread to thighs. [Redrawn from J. M. Tanner, *Growth at Adolescence,* 2d ed., Oxford:
Blackwell, 1962.]

2.2). Like that of female pubic hair, its progressive growth provides useful
developmental landmarks (Figure 3.6). A prepubescent boy may have some
finely textured hair but no true pubic hair. Long strands of slightly curly hair
then appear at the base of the penis; the pubic hair becomes darker, coarser,
and more curly as it spreads over the scrotum and higher up the abdomen.

Among women, the triangular pubic-hair pattern established during puberty
persists in adulthood. But, among males, pubic hair continues to spread up
the center of the abdomen until about age 25, producing a pubic hairline that
is less sharply defined.

External Genitalia

The penis and scrotum are the external genitals of the male. The testes,
which are enclosed in the scrotal sac, are considered to be internal sexual
organs even though located outside of the abdominal cavity.

During adulthood there is some growth in the size of the penis and scrotum,
but their general appearance changes very little during prepubescence. The

penis begins to grow markedly a year or so after the onset of testicular and pubic-hair development, usually between the ages of 10 and 13½. Growth continues until sometime between the ages of 13½ and 16½ (as shown in Figure 2.2 on page 28). For descriptive purposes, genital growth has also been divided into five stages (Figure 3.7). Stage 1 is the prepubertal stage, in which the size of the penis and testicles is much the same as that in early childhood. In stage

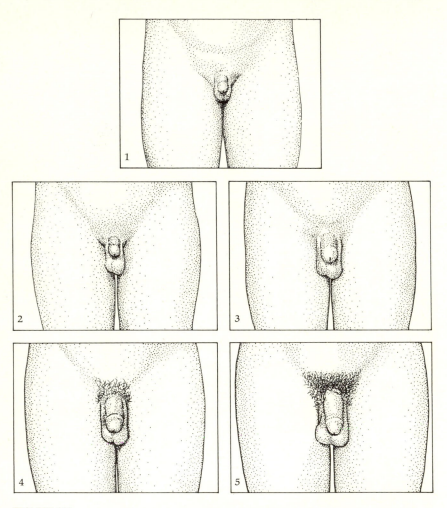

FIGURE 3.7

Stages of male genital development: (1) prepubertal in which the size of the testes and penis is similar to that in early childhood; (2) testes become larger and scrotal skin reddens and coarsens; (3) continuation of stage 2, with lengthening of penis; (4) penis enlarges in general size, and scrotal skin becomes pigmented; (5) adult genitalia. [Redrawn from J. M. Tanner, *Growth at Adolescence*, 2d ed., Oxford: Blackwell, 1962.]

2, the testes become larger and the scrotal sac becomes redder and coarser. These changes continue in stage 3 and are accompanied by lengthening of the penis. In stage 4, the penis enlarges further, and the scrotal skin becomes pigmented and darker. In the last stage, the genitalia have attained maturity. In rating a boy developmentally, the genitalia and pubic hair are used together and in the same order. For example, a boy may be categorized as: Age 12 years, 3 months, puberty rating 2:2 (Falkner 1960). Figure 3.8 shows the sequence of the stages of genital and pubic-hair development and their interrelationships.

Beyond its obvious importance for reproductive and erotic purposes the penis has been the object of much preoccupation. Phallic worship is one of

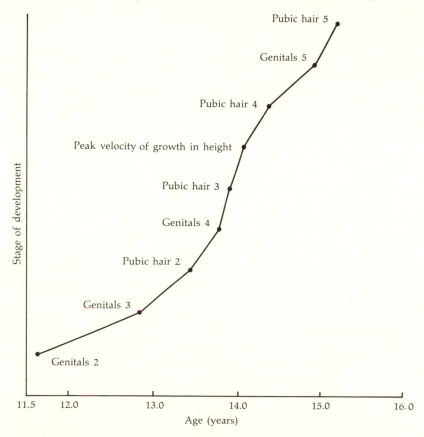

FIGURE 3.8
Sequence of genital and pubic-hair development in adolescent boys. The numbered stages of development correspond to those of Figures 3.6 and 3.7. [Redrawn from A. W. Root, Endocrinology of Puberty. 1. Normal Sexual Maturation, *J. Pediatr.* 83(July 1973):2.]

the oldest religious practices known. It existed in Greek and Roman times, as well as in such disparate cultures as Japanese and American Indian. Phallic worship is no longer practiced, but there are ample linguistic references and symbolic representations of the penis as a source of power and virility.

An adolescent boy's views of his developing sex organs are likely to be influenced by such pervasive cultural attitudes. As a result, the size of his penis, for example, may become a source of preoccupation and anxiety. These concerns tend to persist into adult life and may greatly affect sexual functions.

The size and shape of the penis are not related to a man's physique, race, virility, or ability to give or receive pleasure. Like any organ, penises differ in size, but the differences tend to diminish in the erect state (Masters and Johnson 1970). The penis neither atrophies with lack of use nor enlarges through frequent use.

Voice Changes

Deepening of the voice is a well-known pubertal event that results from the enlargement of the larynx. Girl's voices change to some extent, but the change is more marked in boys. It is a late development in puberty and may occur either gradually or rather abruptly. It is not unusual for a pubescent boy to go through an awkward period in which his voice is neither here nor there —his newly acquired baritone periodically breaking into a high-pitched voice.[7]

If a boy fails to go through normal puberty, the pitch of his voice remains high in adulthood. In the sixteenth century, the practice of castrating boys who had musical ability became established to secure soprano voices for choirs because women were barred from active participation in church services and on the stage. Some of these *castrati* attained great prominence in seventeenth- and eighteenth-century Italian opera.

Facial and Axillary Hair

The growth of facial hair is an important event because of its social implications as a badge of manhood. Axillary and facial hair usually appear about two years after the growth of pubic hair. The first facial hair to grow is that at the corners of the upper lip; it then spreads to form a mustache over the entire upper lip. The next facial hair to appear is that on the upper part of the cheeks and the area under the lower lip; it eventually spreads to the sides and lower border of the chin and the rest of the lower face. Body hair first appears

---

[7]Using data on voice-breaking among members of J. S. Bach's choir, an attempt has been made to assess the age of puberty of boys between 1729 and 1749 (Daw 1970). For a study of voice breaks in young female public speakers, see Duffy (1970).

concurrently with axillary hair but continues to spread for a while after puberty. The hairline of the forehead begins to recede with puberty among males, but not females, as already indicated in the previous chapter.

In addition to the growth of facial and body hair, the skin of a pubescent boy undergoes other alterations. For example, the scrotal sac becomes more pigmented and wrinkled. The more striking and problematic skin changes, however, are due to the growth of sebaceous glands. These glands are associated with hair follicles; if a follicle opening becomes plugged, the result is a comedo, or blackhead, which is the primary lesion of acne, the bane of puberty (see Chapter 5).

Breasts

Breast development in boys does not match that in girls, but nevertheless there is some growth in males, which usually takes the form of a hard node under the nipple and its surrounding area—the areola (Figure 3.9). In a study of a large number of 10- to 16-year-old boys, close to 40 percent (30 percent among blacks) showed breast enlargement. The peak incidence was in the 14- to 14½-year-old group (65 percent). In many cases the enlargement disappeared within a year; in a third of the cases, in two years; and, in about 8 percent, in three years (Nydick et al. 1961). The areolar enlargement that occurs in puberty is permanent (Roche, French, and Da Vila 1971).

Boys and their parents, if not aware of the normality and transient nature of this change, may be concerned about its "feminizing" aspects. Only in rare cases is breast enlargement pathological (gynecomastia). Obese boys also appear to have enlarged breasts because of the extra layers of fat.

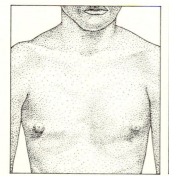 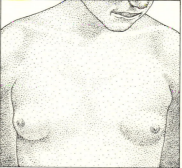 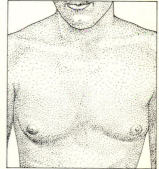

FIGURE 3.9
Varying degrees of breast development among normal pubescent boys. [Redrawn from A. Prader, *Growth and Development*, in *Clinical Endocrinology*, ed. A. Labhart, Springer-Verlag, 1974.]

FACTORS AFFECTING PUBERTY

The discussion so far has concerned the orderly changes of puberty, with only occasional references to its variabilities. The sequence of these events is in fact quite orderly in both males and females and, given sufficiently large populations, individuals in general develop in accord with these schedules. Against this predictable background, we must now examine the wide range of normal variability that exists among individuals and consider the factors that account for it.

The striking differences in maturational level that may exist for chronological peers is illustrated in Figure 3.10. Each of the three girls represented is precisely the same age ($12\frac{3}{4}$ years), but the girl on the left has not yet reached puberty, the girl in the middle is part way through it, and the one on the right has completed her development. The boys illustrated are also the same age ($14\frac{3}{4}$ years) and show a similar variation in stage of development. The variability shown is perfectly normal.

Equally striking are the data in Figure 3.11. Although most boys seem to go through puberty in eighth and ninth grade, there are boys who are pubescent in the first and second grades, and some in the tenth grade or higher who are not. Most educational and athletic programs in schools are organized on the basis of chronological age with little attention paid to physiological age, which may be entirely out of phase. The confusion and incongruities that can result from this situation deserve reflection.

The fact that the physical changes of puberty are orderly without being rigid implies that there are both powerful factors determining their constancy and other forces affecting individuals differently.

The factors affecting puberty consist of complex, interacting forces. Therefore, it is convenient to divide these factors into two groups: genetic and environmental. However, it should be kept in mind that a given genetic pattern may itself have been selected in response to environmental pressures and that environmental forces may affect individuals differently because of differences in genetic makeup.

To further complicate matters, the genetic and environmental factors that determine rate of growth are distinct from those that determine body size and shape. And body size and shape are subject to independent influences. Intricate correlations may link some of these determinants but not others. Body shape, but not size, tends to be linked with the rate of growth. For example,

---

FIGURE 3.10 (opposite)
Variations in pubescent development. All three girls are $12\frac{3}{4}$ years and all three boys are of $14\frac{3}{4}$ years of age but in different stages of puberty. [Redrawn from Growing Up by J. M. Tanner. Copyright © 1973 by Scientific American, Inc. All rights reserved.]

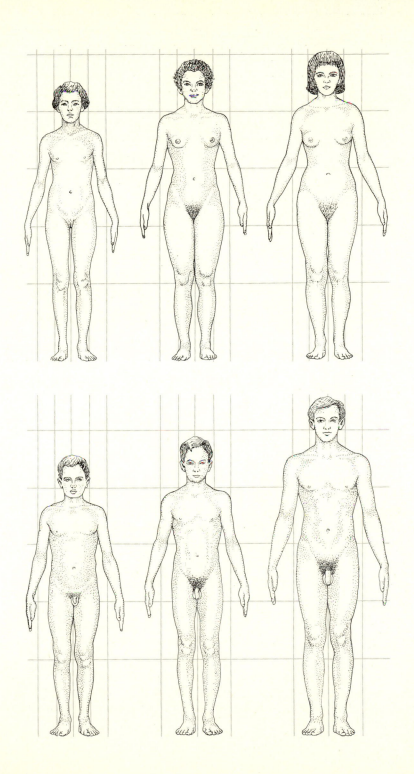

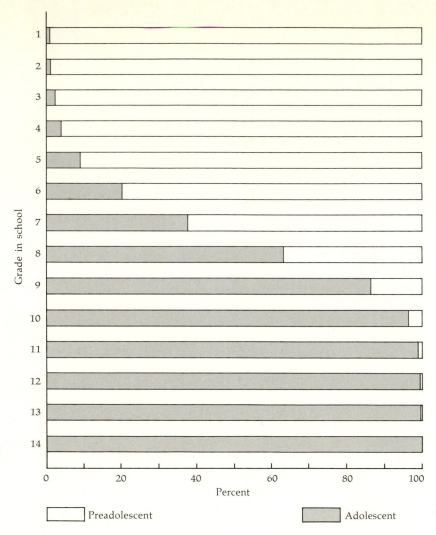

FIGURE 3.11
Percentage of boys who are adolescent (pubescent) in each grade of primary and secondary school. [Redrawn from A. C. Kinsey, W. B. Pomeroy, and C. E. Martin, *Sexual Behavior in the Human Male*, Saunders, 1948.]

people with linear, *ectomorphic* physiques—that is, of slender build—tend to mature late. This brief discussion does not allow a thorough examination of all the details, but one should not lose sight of the complexity of the matter.

GENETIC DETERMINANTS

The effect of heredity in shaping our bodies is self-evident in the way we resemble each other as members of the same species, of a particular race, and, most specifically, of an individual family. Such resemblance is epitomized by identical siblings.

The effect of puberty is important, but our physical "mold" is cast basically at conception, is already visible in childhood, and by and large persists through life. For the developmental process to unfold itself, satisfactory environmental conditions are essential, and external factors can drastically alter the orderly and predetermined course of events. But, under ordinary circumstances, how tall one grows to be, the color and density of pubic and facial hair, the size and shape of breasts, and other somatic and sexual characteristics are largely determined by heredity. Genetic factors also influence the timing and tempo of the changes taking place during puberty.

Evolutionary Considerations

To place the matter in an evolutionary framework, let us first consider the extent to which puberty is an exclusively human attribute. This is difficult to determine because we do not have adequate information about the rate of physical change that is manifested by "pubescent" animals. Whatever information is available mostly pertains to growth in body weight, which in contrast to measurements of height serves less well as a basis for comparison for reasons discussed earlier.

Despite these limitations, the evolutionary path of growth patterns can be traced (Tanner 1962, 1970). Among such mammals as mice and rats, the interval between birth and puberty is short. The velocity of growth during this period does not markedly slow down and there is no growth spurt at puberty. The growth curve for man therefore is not characteristic of all mammals. Rather, it is a primate characteristic, which so far has also been documented for the chimpanzee and the rhesus monkey. As shown in Figure 3.12, growth of the chimpanzee is remarkably similar to that of man: a long period intervenes between birth and puberty during which the velocity of growth is steadily on the decrease, but at puberty it markedly accelerates, particularly in males (Tanner 1962; Grether and Yerkes 1940; Young and Yerkes 1943; Gavan 1953). The growth curve of the rhesus monkey is similar to that of the chimpanzee, but puberty occurs sooner.

It seems clear that the human pattern of puberty is the culmination of an evolutionary step taken by the primates and successively carried further by monkeys, apes, and man. Because the onset of puberty is triggered in the brain, the explanation for this phenomenon must be sought in the central nervous system, despite the fact that the brain matures early relative to the general growth pattern (see Figure 2.1). It is as if the part of the brain that initiates puberty is being held back, whereas the part that deals with the complex tasks of learning and human interaction goes on developing while the person remains relatively immature both physically and sexually. It has been suggested that this discrepancy is advantageous because it allows the prolonged period of learning to proceed when a child is docile and not in aggres-

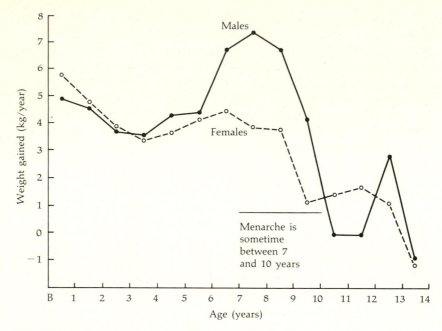

FIGURE 3.12
Curve showing velocity of weight gain in chimpanzees. [Redrawn from J. M. Tanner, *Growth at Adolescence,* 2d ed., Oxford: Blackwell, 1962.]

sive sexual competition with adults (Tanner 1970). In any event, the pattern of puberty in humans probably evolved with early man and, except for such minor changes as time of onset, it has basically remained the same.

Racial Differences

The issue of racial differences is complex and politically sensitive. Some racial characteristics are clearly indisputable. Striking differences also exist intraracially: for example, African Dinkas are tall and Pygmies are short.[8] Similar contrasts exist for other aspects of body build.[9]

Differences in pubertal patterns between races are less distinct. For example, there are vast differences in nutrition, which by itself demonstrably affects

---

[8]The reason for the Pygmy's smaller size is the relative unresponsiveness of tissues to the effects of growth hormones rather than the levels or chemical properties of these hormones (Sinclair 1973, p. 123).

[9]For a review, see Tanner (1966).

growth and development between populations that are considered racially separate. Thus, what may appear to be a racial difference may be simply a difference in affluence between countries or social classes within a country (Weir, Dunn, and Jones 1971).

In recent years, extensive information has been gathered on the age of menarche around the world (Table 3.2). The difference in age is impressive, ranging from an average of 12.4 years for Cuban blacks in the first study to an average of 18.8 years for the Bundi highlanders of New Guinea. However, this difference does not seem to be linked to race: blacks account for both the earliest and the latest maturers; blacks, whites, and Chinese are included in the groups having the lower median ages. We must conclude therefore that racial factors, though conceivably significant, do not determine the onset of menarche on their own.

Other evidence shows that significant differences exist within a given race or ethnic group. For example, in an Israeli study, the age of menarche was found to be significantly different for women who were born in Europe or the United States, or whose fathers came from those parts of the world, and for

Table 3.2. Median age at menarche in several populations.

Population or Location	Median age (years)*	Population or Location	Median age (years)*
Cuba		Tel Aviv, Israel	13.0‡
Negro	12.4	London, U.K.	13.1
White	12.4	Assam, India (city dwellers)	13.2
Mulatto	12.6	Burma (city dwellers)	13.2
Cuba		Uganda (wealthy Kampala)	13.4
Negro	12.9†	Oslo, Norway	13.5
White	13.0†	France	13.5
Mulatto	13.0†	Nigeria (wealthy Ibo)	14.1
Hong Kong (wealthy Chinese)	12.5	USSR (rural Buriats)	15.0
Florence, Italy	12.5	South Africa (Transkei Bantu)	15.0
Wroclaw, Poland	12.6	Rwanda	
Budapest, Hungary	12.8	Tutsi	16.5§
California, U.S.A.	12.8	Huru	17.1§
Colombo, Ceylon	12.8	New Guinea (Bundi)	18.8
Moscow, USSR	13.0		

Source: Jean Hiernaux, Ethnic Differences in Growth and Development, *Eugen, Q.* 15:12–21. Copyright © 1968 American Eugenics Society.

*Data from Tanner (1966b) unless otherwise indicated.

†Pospisilova-Zuzakova, Stukovsky, and Valsik (1965).

‡Ber and Brociner (1964).

§Hiernaux (1965).

those from Asia and North Africa (Halbrecht, Sklorowski, and Tsafriv 1971). Environmental factors, such as nutrition, could also be the basis of differences between subcultures within a country.

Familial Tendencies

The effect of genetic factors is far more clearly evident within the confines of familial tendencies. That tall parents are likely to have tall children is self-evident. The heights of mothers and daughters correlate better than the heights of mothers and sons at all ages up to puberty. Father-offspring correlations have not been as reliably ascertained, but it seems that the heights of fathers and sons may be better correlated than those of fathers and daughters (Tanner and Israelsohn 1963).

The manifestation of genetic influences can also be seen in correlations between the age of menarche and kinship. Randomly chosen and unrelated girls have their first menstrual periods at ages that differ on the average by 19 months. For sisters, this difference is 13 months; for nonidentical twins, it is 10 months; and only 2.8 months for identical twins who are growing together under average Western European economic conditions (Tanner 1962). This familial genetic effect also applies to skeletal maturation at all ages (Reynolds 1943).

Because sex also is genetically determined, it, too, ought to be included here. As we have seen, a person's sex markedly affects the events of puberty.

Another indication of the role of genetic factors is the relationship between physique, which is constitutionally determined, and age at menarche. There is consistent evidence that girls who have a linear build (who are leptosomic) mature later than girls who are short and stocky (pyknic) (Widholm and Kantero 1971). But it is as yet unclear whether the tendency for short stature precipitates early menarche or early maturation shortens the growing period, resulting in shorter stature (Daly 1966). Boys who are linear in build also mature later than boys who are short and stocky.

ENVIRONMENTAL EFFECTS

Environmental effects operate at a number of levels. Over long periods, they govern the selection of certain genetically determined characteristics over others. For example, the tall, lean physique of a Nilotic is understandable in terms of its adaptive value in the environment where it originated, and it will persist through countless generations of blacks wherever they live whether it makes adaptive sense or not. But it is the immediate impact of the environment on puberty that we will be concerned with here.

Climate and Season

For years, it was thought that children living in hot and humid climates "ripened" sooner, and, as early as the fourth century B.C., Hippocrates referred to the late advent of puberty in colder climates. In fact, there is no convincing evidence that climate exerts a significant influence on the time of onset of puberty. Boys in Nigeria and in England, for example, are reported to go through puberty on comparable schedules. Nor are there significant differences in puberty between girls living in central India, which is hot and humid, and those living in northern Nigeria, where the climate is also hot but dry (Tanner 1962). Similar discrepancies may be noted in the countries included in Table 3.2. Where differences in climate have been reported as significant, insufficient precautions have usually been taken to control for important factors like nutrition.

The season of the year, on the other hand, has a well-documented effect on the velocity of growth: height increases twice as fast in the spring, and growth in weight is four or five times as fast in the autumn (Sinclair 1973, p. 135). This is true not only for puberty, but for all growing periods. During spring, there is a significant reduction in the incidence of menarche (Zacharias, Rand, and Wurtman 1976).

Figure 3.13 illustrates a standard pattern of seasonal variation in the growth in height of German cadets in 1902. Note that the seasonal difference is most marked during the adolescent growth spurt (Thompson 1942). The physio-

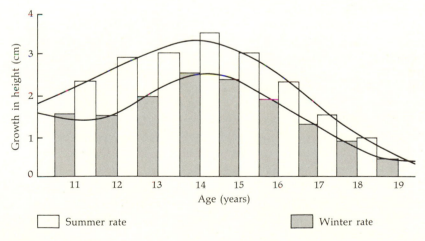

Summer rate   Winter rate

FIGURE 3.13
Effects of season on growth. [Redrawn from D'Arcy W. Thompson, *Growth and Form*, 2d ed., Cambridge University Press, 1942.]

logical mechanism responsible for seasonality of growth is unknown, but presumably it is based on hormonal factors. In countries where food is scarce, seasonal changes may mainly reflect the availability of food (Billewiez 1967).

The onset of menarche is also linked to season, especially in countries with marked seasonal variations. Thus, in Finland, the incidence of menarche is highest in the summer months and then in December and January (Kantero 1971).

Nutrition

Because the growth of the body depends on the intake of nutritional raw materials, malnutrition stunts growth. When this occurs during prepuberty, the onset of puberty may be interfered with.[10] There are important differences in this regard in the vulnerability of physiological systems.

Caloric requirements vary with age, but, generally, the earlier malnutrition occurs the more deleterious are its effects. Figure 3.14 shows the average total calories normally required from the first to the eighteenth year. Relative to body size, the caloric requirements for children are higher than those for adults. For example, a 3-week-old baby quietly sleeping a good deal of the time has a caloric requirement per unit of body weight that is more than twice that for an adult engaged in moderately heavy labor. During the first month of life, caloric requirements are highest—from 100 to 120 calories per kilogram of body weight. These figures decline slowly until age 16 in boys and 13 or 14 in girls, and more rapidly thereafter until the adult requirement of 40 to 50 calories per kilogram is reached (Holt 1972, p. 130).

In absolute terms (rather than relative body weight), the need for food is greatest during puberty. Peak caloric requirements for girls are reached between ages 12 and 15, usually coinciding with menarche. For boys, they are reached somewhat later, concurrently with the growth spurt, or between 14 and 17 years. More calories are needed by youth than by adults engaged in physical labor or by nursing mothers. Apart from growth needs, a person's caloric requirements are affected by climate, physical activity, and so on. (For a more extensive discussion of adolescent nutrition, see Heald [1969].)

The deleterious effects of malnutrition depend on not only severity, but also chronicity. Retardation of growth due to acute malnutrition is readily corrected: when adequate nutrition is provided, the body catches up in growth (Prader, Tanner, and von Harnack 1963). It is severe and protracted malnutrition that causes permanent stunting, and entire populations of children have been

---

[10]The raw materials for growth consist of five classes of chemical substances: proteins, fats, carbohydrates, vitamins, and minerals. Proteins are the most critical to growth because they are the main constituent of protoplasm—the ''stuff'' that cells are made of.

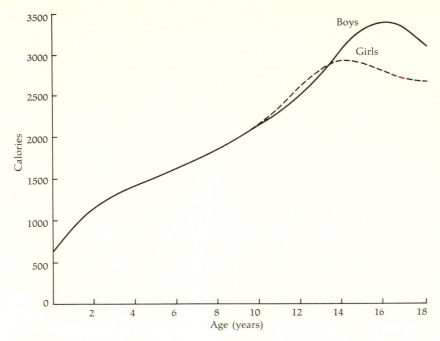

FIGURE 3.14
Daily caloric requirements for both sexes from birth to 18 years. [Redrawn from
H. L. Barnett and A. H. Einhorn, eds., *Pediatrics*, 15th ed., 1972. Courtesy of Appleton-
Century-Crofts, Division of Prentice-Hall, Inc., New York.]

noted to be thus affected by famine resulting from major wars or from prolonged severe poverty.[11] In the United States, the average amount of protein
in an adolescent's diet is generally well above recommended allowances
(Heald 1969).

The effect of malnutrition on growth is relatively selective. For example, size
and rate of growth are far more easily affected than shape and tissue composition. Contrary to earlier claims, there is no evidence that malnutrition in
humans causes short legs in relation to trunk length as it does in cattle. Japanese children reared in California are taller at all ages than those in Japan, but
the ratios of leg length to height are essentially the same (Greulick 1957). (The
Japanese tend to have relatively shorter legs, which is a genetically determined
characteristic.)

Undernutrition tends to exaggerate the differential rates of growth of tissues,
and priorities are given to some tissues over others. Thus, under poor dietary

---

[11]See, for example, a study of the heights of children in Stuttgart between 1910 and 1950, which
encompassed both world wars (Howe and Schiller 1952).

conditions, the growth of teeth takes precedence over the growth of other bones, which in turn suffer less than muscle and fat. The growth of sexual organs at puberty is relatively less retarded than that of other tissues and organs. Boys are generally more vulnerable to the effects of malnutrition than girls.

The differences in the age of menarche in various countries are due at least in part to differences in nutrition. Within the same country, differences can often be seen between urban and poor rural areas. For example, in Rumania, the average ages for menarche are 13.5 years in towns and 14.6 years in villages. Corresponding discrepancies have been reported from the USSR (13.0 and 14.3 years), India (12.8 and 14.2 years), and other diverse parts of the world (Tanner 1970, pp. 146–147). Menarche tends to be delayed in girls who have many siblings and may also be caused by nutritional deficiencies if there is a scarcity of resources.

For the sake of simplicity, caloric requirements have been used here as the nutritional yardstick, although nutrition includes far more than mere caloric intake. For example, there must be an adequate supply of protein. The absence of any of the essential amino acids will stunt growth, and protein deficiencies will delay puberty. Similarly, vitamins (especially vitamins A, B_2, C, and D) and minerals are quite essential. Although not a nutritional factor, there is also the role of oxygen: children with congenital heart defects have stunted bodies; yet when the defect is surgically corrected normal growth follows. Factors other than oxygenation must also be involved because heart defects that do not interfere with oxygenation may also stunt growth (Sinclair 1973, p. 131).

Finally, it must be noted that our knowledge of the effects of malnutrition on growth and maturation is so far mostly restricted to severe types of damage. The possibility of more subtle impairment of the brain, which as yet cannot be ascertained, remains to be determined.

Illness

The effects of illness on growth are similar to those of nutrition and are sometimes confused with it. Retardation of growth depends on the severity, duration, and nature of the illness. The effect of heart defects has already been noted. Chronic kidney disease similarly retards growth, as does a long list of other conditions (Falkner 1972, pp. 248–250). In contrast, blind children tend to reach menarche sooner than usual (Magee et al. 1970; Zacharias and Wurtman 1964).

Fortunately, most childhood illnesses, such as measles, upper respiratory infections, and even pneumonia, cause no apparent retardation of growth

(Meredith and Knott 1962). Other illnesses that keep a child in bed for several months may retard growth temporarily, but after recuperation the growth process catches up (Prader, Tanner, and von Harnack 1963). Girls are more resilient in this regard than boys.

There are other diseases that specifically disturb growth and the process of puberty. They will be dealt with in more detail in Chapter 5.

The specific mechanisms by which illness retards growth are insufficiently known and probably vary from one disease to another. The neural and endocrine mechanisms regulating growth and puberty can be disrupted at various levels. For example, the hormone cortisol participates in reactions to stress and has a demonstrable retarding effect on growth when administered to children for therapeutic purposes (Tanner 1970, p. 114). Cortisol can also suppress reproductive hormones.

Socioeconomic Class

Socioeconomic class, which is determined by a cluster of variables, has a demonstrable impact on development. For example, a British study revealed a difference of about 2 inches in height between the children of professionals and managers and those of unskilled laborers at puberty.[12] This is probably due in large part to the nutritional, health, and other advantages that accompany a higher standard of living. But there is also a curious correlation between height and social status and mobility. For example, studies conducted in Scotland revealed that, regardless of the occupations of their fathers, taller women held jobs requiring greater skills than those held by shorter women. Further, whatever their earlier occupations, taller women generally married men who held skilled jobs, whereas shorter women had husbands whose jobs required fewer skills (Scott, Illsley, and Thomson 1956; Thomson 1959).

Socioeconomic status is also related to age at menarche, which is probably a reflection of variation in nutrition. In Hong Kong, the age at menarche is 12.5 years for the rich, 12.8 years for the average, and 13.3 years for the poor (Tanner 1970, p. 146). In European countries, the difference is from two to four months. Yet, in other studies, no correlation is found between age at menarche and social class despite correlations between the latter and height within the same groups (Douglas and Simpson 1964). The lack of consistency may be due to social class distinctions being relative: the "poor" in one country may be starving, and in another they may be in a reasonably good nutritional state.

-----

[12]Tanner (1970). For India, see Prabhaker et al. (1970).

Emotional Factors

Everyone knows that happy children thrive better than unhappy ones. Currently, much remains to be learned about the specific manner in which emotional states affect growth and maturation, but formal documentation of the fact that they do is not lacking.

Among the serious effects of emotional deprivation in early life is retardation of growth (Patton and Gardner 1969; Powell, Brasel, and Blizzard 1967). Recently, a syndrome of "psychosocial dwarfism" has been described, which correlates the stunting of growth in children with eating disorders and other reactions to emotional disturbances in the parents. These children revert to a normal growth pattern when removed from the adverse environment (Blizzard 1972a; Powell, Brasel, and Blizzard 1967).

An inadvertent discovery of the effect of emotional factors on growth rate was made in a German orphanage in 1948. Children who were getting a food supplement initially thrived better than the control group but then did worse despite the extra food after a harsh supervisor moved into the institution and proceeded to ruin the children's mealtime atmosphere by delivering public rebukes. The supervisor's favorites, who were spared such abuse, continued to show the benefits of the food supplement (Widdowson 1951).

There is increasing documentation about the interaction of emotional factors and their effects on the manifestations of puberty. The hormones active during this period may have profound effects on mood and behavior, as well as on such physiological functions as menstruation. This will be discussed further in Chapter 4.

THE SECULAR TREND

Another example of the impact of various interrelated factors on puberty can be observed in the West: successive generations have been generally getting taller and attaining puberty at progressively earlier ages. This is referred to as a "secular" trend because the phenomenon is manifested through many generations spanning many years. (The term in this context has no connotation of being the opposite of religious.)

Reliable records from different countries show that since 1900 children of preschool age have been taller on the average by 1.0 centimeter and heavier by 0.5 kilogram per decade. The gains during puberty are 2.5 centimeters and 2.5 kilograms, and for adults 1.0 centimeter per decade (Falkner 1972, p. 239; Bakwin, 1964). The significant change is mainly in earlier maturation. Because growth also stops earlier, the increase in adult size is not as spec-

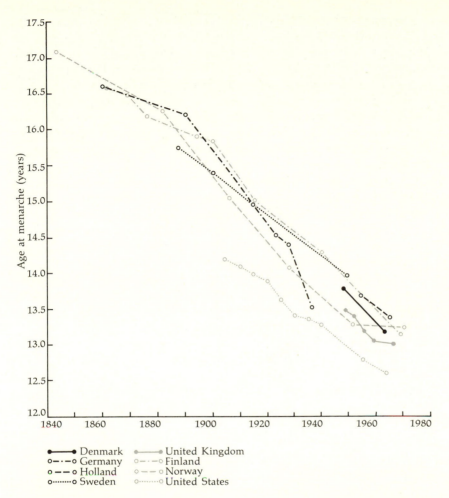

FIGURE 3.15
Declining age of menarche. [Redrawn from Growing Up by J. M. Tanner. Copyright ©
1973 by Scientific American, Inc. All rights reserved.]

tacular (Bakwin and McLaughlin 1964; Maresh 1972). New evidence shows
this trend to have stopped.

Figure 3.15 illustrates the secular trend of declining age at menarche—
another index of earlier maturation. In 1840, Norwegian girls reached menarche
at about 17 years; now they do so four years earlier on the average. The
general rate of decline has been approximately four months per decade. Some
of the grandmothers of today's American teen-agers reached puberty in 1900
at about age 14: their granddaughters now do so about a year or two younger.

If this trend is extrapolated into the past, women in the Middle Ages would presumably have reached menarche in their thirties, for which there is no evidence. If it is projected into the future, girls will be menstruating in childhood which is unlikely. As evident in Figure 3.15, some curves have already begun to flatten out. More recent data show that the age of menarche has not changed in the West in the past 30 years; nor has height or weight at specified ages (Zacharias, Rand, and Wurtman 1976). A report issued recently by the National Center for Health Statistics indicates that the trend toward a steady increase in the size of American children has virtually come to an end in the last decade.

The decline in age of menarche is generally attributed to environmental factors like better nutrition (especially higher caloric and protein intake in infancy) and improved health. It has also been suggested that were the age of menarche to be plotted for several centuries, the resulting curve might show the secular trend to be part of an undulating phenomenon with no simple all-encompassing cause (Falkner 1972).

Because boys do not manifest a sharply defined and widely recognized pubertal event like menarche, there are no comparable data for them. It is assumed, however, that a secular trend for earlier reproductive maturation has also been in progress for males.

Chapter 4

Hormonal Regulation of Puberty

Hormones are chemical substances secreted directly into the blood stream by the endocrine, or ductless, glands. They are specific in their effects on many tissues and functions of the body throughout its life. Even though the concept of remote chemical control can be traced to ancient notions of body humors, the modern science of endocrinology is quite young: the term *hormone* (from the Greek word for "excite") was first used at the turn of this century. Since then, about two dozen hormones have been discovered. Many of them have a bearing on puberty, and some are directly responsible for bringing about its changes.[1]

Hormones begin to play a decisive role very early in prenatal life. For example, those secreted by the embryonal testes have a directive effect on the

---

[1]Many college biology texts contain introductory discussions of general endocrine functions. See, for example, Keeton (1972) and Wilson et al. (1973). For more specialized reading, see such endocrinology texts as Williams (1974) and Tepperman (1973).

subsequent development of the reproductive system. In addition, maternal hormones cross the placenta and affect the fetus. Therefore, the hormones that are critical during puberty have functional antecedents operating in earlier phases of development.

Given the many and profound biological changes of puberty, it will hardly come as a surprise that there are complex processes initiating and governing them. This discussion will be limited primarily to hormonal influences in this regard, but hormones are by no means the only agents that may affect these changes. There is usually no discernible difference between the hormonal functions of a person who grows to be 6 feet tall and of another only 5 feet tall. Even giants and dwarfs may have no demonstrable hormonal discrepancies. We attribute such differences to hereditary factors that exert their effect through nonhormonal means, although other genetic influences operate through hormones. Likewise, many environmental factors, some of which were discussed earlier, may greatly affect growth and puberty without necessarily involving the actions of hormones directly.

These qualifications notwithstanding, the role of hormones in the growth spurt as well as the other changes of puberty can hardly be overemphasized. Growth depends on metabolism, and hormones regulate metabolic processes. Therefore, in this general sense, many hormones contribute in some way to growth. But some hormones have specific growth-regulating functions, and it is with these, together with the hormones that regulate sexual maturation, that we shall be concerned here.

The hormones to be discussed first are those that act directly on tissues and bring about the changes that have been described. With one exception, they are produced by the ovaries, testes, thyroid glands, and the adrenal cortex. These endocrine glands are in turn controlled by the hormones of the pituitary gland. The one exception is the *growth hormone,* which is produced by the pituitary itself and acts directly on body tissues without benefit of known intermediaries. The tissues that hormones act on are called *target tissues.* If the impact is on another gland, that gland is referred to as the *target gland* for that particular hormone.

HORMONES REGULATING GROWTH

The Growth Hormone

The primary hormone regulating growth before puberty is the growth hormone (somatotropin), which is produced by the anterior pituitary, an endocrine gland of great importance that will be discussed in more detail later in this chapter.

The existence of a growth-promoting factor in the pituitary was suspected at the turn of the century. When subsequent research confirmed its presence, it was called "the growth hormone." Although the name retains its legitimacy, we now know that the growth hormone is merely one of several hormones that promote and regulate growth. Nevertheless, it has many claims to distinction. It is the most abundant of the active principles of the anterior pituitary. Its molecular structure has been elucidated. But the molecule is so complex that it is still not possible to synthesize the substance. For research as well as therapy, one must rely mainly on extracts from human pituitaries.[2]

The primary but not the sole function of this hormone is to stimulate growth, and its impact is best seen in its effect on overall body size. Its influence on a growing child is much more marked than are its effects on an adult.[3]

Growth hormone causes the body to retain nitrogen and other constituents of tissue, such as sodium, chlorine, potassium, phosphorus, and calcium. It increases the transport of amino acids into tissues and enhances their incorporation into protein. It plays a significant role in the increase of muscle cells (Cheek et al. 1966). It also affects the metabolism of fat and carbohydrates by switching over the source of fuel for the body from carbohydrates to fat. The secretion of somatotropin constantly fluctuates in response to internal factors and conditions like physical exercise and emotional states.

The precise role of growth hormone at puberty is unclear. It has been reported to increase during puberty by some investigators but not others. Growth hormone loses its primacy in the control of growth at puberty to the gonadal hormones, but it may continue to be important for the growth spurt and the development of secondary characteristics by its complementary and facilitating effects on testosterone and estrogen (Root 1972, 1973a).

Thyroid Hormones

Other hormones that have a life-long effect on growth are produced by the thyroid gland, which is located in the neck, in front and on the sides of the trachia. Thyroid activity gradually decreases during childhood until puberty when this trend either slows down or is reversed.

The effects of thyroid deficiency are most marked during the earlier years of life. In addition to their influence on growth in stature, thyroid hormones are necessary for developing normal skeletal proportions, for converting cartilage into bone, for forming and erupting teeth, and for developing the brain (Heald and Hung 1970, pp. 31 and 35; Rivlin 1969).

There are many unanswered questions about the role of the thyroid gland in puberty. Its hormones do not seem to play a primary role in muscle growth.

---

[2]This is easier said than done, because only about 4 mg of growth hormone can be obtained from each pituitary gland, and to treat a child who lacks this hormone for five years requires processing 650 glands removed soon after death (Tanner and Taylor 1969, p. 166).

[3]Abnormalities in growth-hormone production have dramatic effects, which are discussed in Chapter 5.

They are necessary for skeletal maturation and affect linear growth somewhat, but probably are not critical to the growth spurt (Tepperman 1973).

The two primary thyroid hormones (thyroxine and triiodothyronine) are iodine-containing amino acids. Their structural formulas and methods for synthesis have been available since the late 1920s. Preparations of thyroid hormone are plentiful, inexpensive, and widely used in medicine.

When the thyroid was first described in the seventeenth century, the observation that it was larger in women than in men led to some ingenious explanations. Some proposed that its purpose was to add grace to the female neck. One authority suggested that the gland acted as a vascular shunt for the brain. Because women had "more numerous causes of irritation and vexation of mind" than men, they obviously needed a larger shunt to prevent their brains from getting excessively congested as a result! Still other scientists decided that the gland served no useful function. The real function of the thyroid gland has become established only in the past century (Goodman and Gilman 1975).

There are other hormones that affect growth, but their precise roles during the adolescent growth spurt are unknown. An example is insulin, which is produced by the pancreas. Experimental work indicates that optimal growth occurs only if both growth hormone and insulin are present (Cheek 1967). Another example is cortisol (hydrocortisone), which is discussed in the next section. It is produced by the adrenal cortex and may play a role in terminating the growth spurt (Kenny et al. 1966). It definitely retards growth if administered in substantial doses.

Of great importance to pubertal growth and maturation are the steroid hormones produced by the testes and the ovaries. Because of their central role in reproductive maturation, they are considered separately and in greater detail in the following section.

HORMONES REGULATING SEXUAL MATURATION

All of the known hormones produced by vertebrate gonads (including human testes and ovaries), as well as the hormones of the adrenal cortex, belong to a group of closely related chemical compounds known as steroids, which have in common a basic molecular structure (the cyclopentanophenanthrene ring) (Bermant and Davidson 1974; Fieser 1955).

As discussed earlier, the gonads have a dual function: they produce germ cells (sperm and ova) and secrete hormones. The major ovarian hormones belong to two classes: estrogens, which include a number of compounds (estradiol-17β being the most important); and progestational compounds of which the only one with physiological significance is progesterone. The major hormones produced by the testes are called androgens, the main one being testosterone.

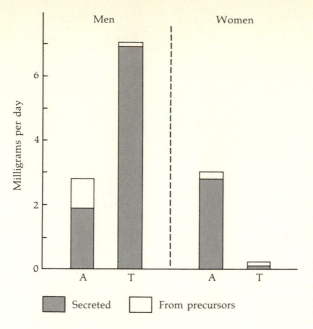

Men   Women

Milligrams per day

6

4

2

0

A   T   A   T

■ Secreted   □ From precursors

FIGURE 4.1
Daily production of androstenedione (A)
and testosterone (T) in men and women.
Some is secreted directly by the adrenal
glands, the ovaries, or the testes, and
some is produced in the bloodstream
from precursors secreted by the
endocrine glands. [Redrawn from
D. Baird, R. Horton, C. Longcope,
and J. F. Tait, *Perspectives in Biology and
Medicine*, vol. 2, University of Chicago
Press, 1968.]

Sex hormones are also produced in both sexes by the adrenal glands, which are located just above the kidneys. The cortex, or outer part, of the adrenal produces a number of steroid hormones in both sexes, including androgens and small amounts of estrogen. The other adrenocortical hormones (such as cortisone) are very important in stress reactions and in a number of other physiological functions, but these are not of concern here.

Because testosterone, estrogen, and progesterone are produced mainly by the gonads and are responsible for the final maturation of the reproductive system and the development of secondary sexual characteristics, they are commonly referred to as the "sex hormones."

The nomenclature of sex hormones can be confusing. For example, the male hormones are collectively called androgens, but there is no comparable general term for the female hormones. Estrogens and progestins are often referred to simply as estrogen and progesterone. Testosterone is frequently used as a synonym for androgen because it is the main androgen produced by the testes. Thus, the use of the term *testosterone* for the androgens produced by women may seem inappropriate. There are numerous synthetic chemical substances structurally related (and some unrelated) to the naturally occurring hormones that have androgenic, estrogenic, and progestational properties. For the sake of simplicity, the sex hormones will be referred to as testosterone, estrogen, and progesterone in this book, but we should not lose sight of the foregoing qualifications.

"Male" and "female" sex hormones exist in both sexes but in different concentrations (Figures 4.1 and 4.2).[4] All the steroid hormones are linked

---

[4]Estrogen has been extracted from the testes of bulls, and the grand champion of estrogen production is the stallion, which is not exactly the most effeminate creature by most conventional standards (Goodman and Gilman 1975, p. 1538).

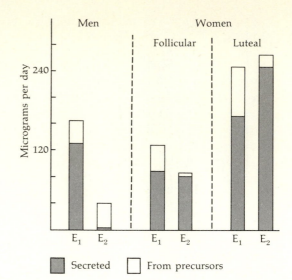

FIGURE 4.2
Daily production of estrone (E₁) and
estradiol-17β (E₂) in men, and in women
during the follicular and luteal phases of the
menstrual cycle. Some estrogens are secreted
directly by the adrenal glands, ovaries, or
testes, and some are produced in the
bloodstream from precursors secreted by the
endocrine glands. [Redrawn from D. Baird,
R. Horton, C. Longcope, and J. F. Tait,
Perspectives in Biology and Medicine, vol. 2,
University of Chicago Press, 1968.]

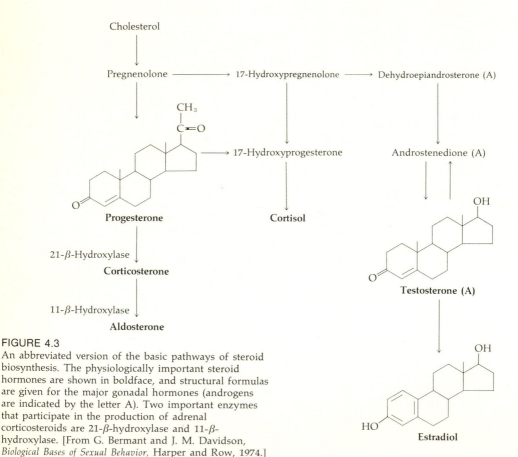

FIGURE 4.3
An abbreviated version of the basic pathways of steroid
biosynthesis. The physiologically important steroid
hormones are shown in boldface, and structural formulas
are given for the major gonadal hormones (androgens
are indicated by the letter A). Two important enzymes
that participate in the production of adrenal
corticosteroids are 21-β-hydroxylase and 11-β-
hydroxylase. [From G. Bermant and J. M. Davidson,
Biological Bases of Sexual Behavior, Harper and Row, 1974.]

through biosynthetic pathways that are part of a common manufacturing process taking place in the gonads and the adrenal cortex. Figure 4.3 shows several of the major steps in this process. Note that estradiol (an estrogen) is made from testosterone, which in turn can be derived from progesterone. Steroid-producing glands thus can shift "emphasis" in production from one end product to another. This is known to occur in pathological conditions and perhaps goes on normally as well (Tepperman 1973).

Testosterone

Endocrinology is sometimes claimed to have originated in antiquity with observations of castrated men. In the fourth century B.C., Aristotle wrote about the effects of castration in birds and men. In 1771, a London surgeon named John Hunter demonstrated that male characteristics could be induced in the hen by the transplantation of testes from the cock, and, in 1849, Arnold Berthold showed that by transplanting testes into castrated roosters the effects of castration could be prevented (Tepperman 1973). This work is generally regarded as the first scientific demonstration of endocrine function.

Scientists began investigating androgenic substances in urine as well as the effects of testicular extracts in the early 1930s. The isolation of an active male hormone from the urine took extraordinary effort: Adolf Butenandt had to process 15,000 liters of male urine to obtain between 15 and 25 milligrams of androsterone, which is one of the urinary products of testosterone (Goodman and Gilman 1975). The chemical structure of testosterone has been known and methods of synthesis have been available for many years. But testosterone research was handicapped until recently by a lack of adequate methods for the determination of hormone levels in blood.[5]

In males, androgens are produced in the testes by the interstitial, or Leydig, cells that are interspersed between the seminiferous tubules. Ordinarily, a relatively small quantity is produced in the adrenal cortex so that castration results in gross androgen deficiency. In females, androgens do come mainly from the adrenal cortex. The ovaries produce certain androgens that can be converted into testosterone.

Embryonal and fetal counterparts of adult androgen are at work in prenatal life, and testosterone is present in low concentrations during childhood (Beach 1974, p. 336). During puberty, this concentration increases markedly in boys in response to stimulation by a pituitary gonadotropic hormone (LH) (Figure 4.4) that will be discussed further on. In one study, the pubertal increase in testosterone has been shown to be tenfold (Gandy and Peterson 1968). Between 10 and 17 years, plasma testosterone increases twentyfold (Faiman

---

[5]The traditional method of assessment was to measure the urinary-excretion products of androgens, collectively known as 17-ketosteroids. At persent, through the use of more sophisticated techniques, blood levels of the hormone can be determined directly (Hasan et al. 1973).

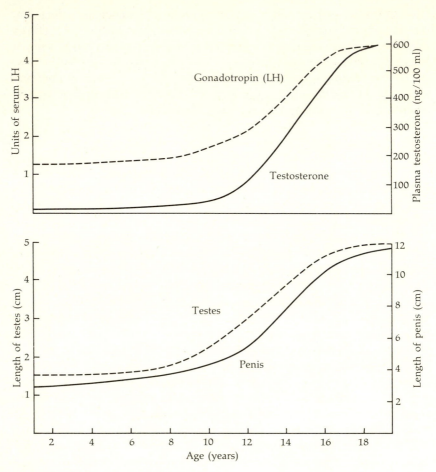

FIGURE 4.4
Serum gonadotropin and testosterone levels and testes and penis measurements through childhood and adolescence. As the gonadotropin level rises, the testes enlarge and produce more testosterone, which, in turn, enlarges the penis. [Redrawn from J. S. D. Winter and C. Faiman, Pituitary–Gonadal Relationships in Male Children and Adolescents, *Pediatr. Res.* 6(1972):126.]

and Winter 1974, p. 36). Evidence from animal research indicates that at puberty the Leydig cells increase the capacity to manufacture testosterone from existing precursors (Lindner 1961).

The adrenal androgenic hormones also show a marked increase at puberty in both boys and girls. One adrenal androgen (dehydroepiandrosterone, DHA) is detectable in the urine of boys between 6 and 9 years of age and rapidly increases in amount after age 10. Testosterone of adrenal origin may be detected in the urine of girls by 5 or 6 years of age, increasing after age 11

(Root 1973a, p. 5). Dehydroepiandrosterone sulfate may be the primary androgen produced by the adrenals at menarche (Drucker et al. 1972). Other adrenocortical hormones, such as cortisol, do not manifest increased production at puberty.

The mechanism of increased androgen production by the adrenal glands at puberty is unknown. A gonadotropic hormone may stimulate androgen synthesis. Or it may be initiated by an as yet unidentified pituitary "adrenarche hormone" (Root 1973a, p. 6).[6]

The primary effects of testosterone in the male at puberty are to promote the growth and development of the reproductive system and to enhance the development of certain other body tissues, such as muscles. Testosterone thus acts both as a sex hormone and as a growth hormone, and is the main agent for bringing about the biological changes of puberty in boys (Figure 4.5) (Knorr et al. 1974; Weiland, Yen, and Pohlman 1970).

The effect of testosterone on the reproductive system is visible in the enlargement of the testes and the growth of the penis. But internal changes within the testes are responsible for the development of fertility, in the course of which the nonfunctioning solid seminiferous tubules of the child become active sperm-producing structures. Testosterone brings about the change in voice and the development of pubic, axillary, facial, and body hair. Its effects predispose the skin to acne.

The growth-promoting activities of testosterone are known as its anabolic (i.e., constructive) effects and include the acceleration of growth in height and an increase in the number and size of muscle cells. In this regard, the effects of testosterone are similar to those of somatotropin, including the retention of nitrogen, which is used in the building of proteins.

Androgens greatly contribute to the growth spurts, but may not be solely responsible for it. They also hasten the closure of the epiphyseal growing ends of long bones, thus "breaking" linear growth. This seemingly paradoxical effect may be related to the amount of testosterone present: small doses promote linear growth and maturation, but large doses stimulate epiphyseal maturation and closure (Heald and Hung 1970, pp. 330–335).

Adrenal androgen enhances growth of pubic and axillary hair in girls, as well as development of the clitoris. It also contributes to the general growth spurt. The sexual differences in adult physique are thus largely attributable to the presence of androgens in higher concentrations in males.[7] This is true of

---

[6]For further studies of androgens in puberty, see Frasier and Horton (1966); Tanner and Gupta (1968); Frasier, Gafford, and Horton (1969); Weiland, Yen, and Pohlman (1970); Forest and Migeon (1970); Gupta, McCafferty, and Rager (1972); Winter and Faiman (1972); and August, Grumbach, and Kaplan (1972). For more specialized sources of the study of androgens, see Dorfman and Shipley (1956) and Wolstenhome and O'Connor (1967).

[7]In adult males, plasma testosterone levels are more than tenfold higher than in females. Adrenal androgen levels are about the same in both sexes (Root 1973a, p. 7). See Figure 4.6.

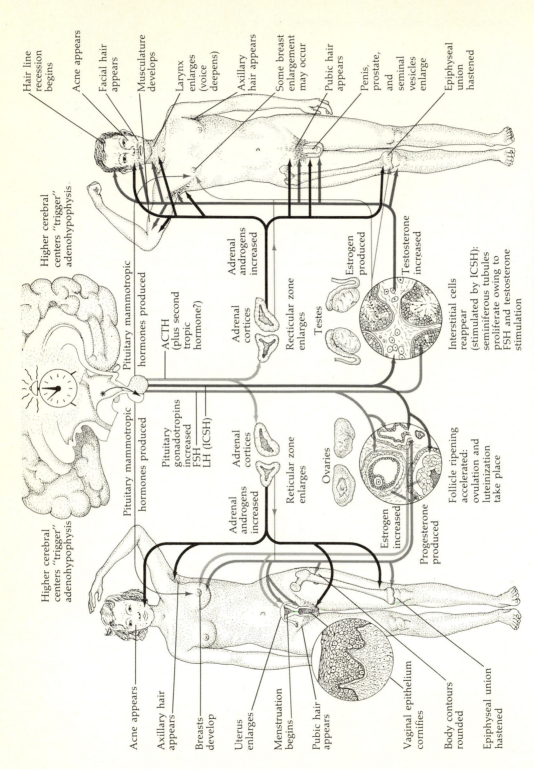

EFFECTS OF SEX HORMONES ON DEVELOPMENT AT PUBERTY

other animals as well. If the testes of young male guinea pigs are removed, the animals do not develop the normal large musculature. If testosterone is injected into female or castrated male guinea pigs, marked muscular development promptly ensues.

Behavioral Effects of Sex Hormones

Most people consider it self-evident that puberty entails behavioral as well as physical changes. A common theme is the awakening of sexuality during adolescence. This notion of a pubescent instinctual upsurge has also characterized the thinking of many students of human behavior. Concepts like "instincts" and drive behavior are complex and controversial enough to preclude their consideration here in any detail. What will be considered here, if only briefly, are the possible roles of sex hormones in mediating sexual and aggressive behavior.

A great deal of research has been undertaken pertaining to the relationship of sex hormones and behavior among animals (Bermant and Davidson 1974). Information about the correlation of endocrine secretions and human behavior at puberty is more equivocal and meager (Hamburg 1974, p. 107).

Hormones influence behavior in two ways. They play an organizational role before and just after birth and an activational role in puberty and adulthood (Bermant and Davidson 1974, p. 232). What concerns us here is their activational role.

Androgens are clearly responsible for the maturation of the reproductive system and the development of adult sexual functions in the form of ejaculatory orgasm in boys. But do androgens affect sexual behavior? Figure 4.6 seems to show convincingly that they do, but such claims should be examined with caution.

The onset of nocturnal emissions during the period of rapid increase in testosterone levels is just another facet of ejaculatory competence. But boys are capable of orgasm earlier even though they do not ejaculate and may well have experienced nonejaculatory orgasm nocturnally before puberty. Orgasmic experience is probably far less frequent before puberty than after it.

The same is true for masturbation. If culmination in ejaculation is considered a necessary condition for masturbation, then it does in fact start in puberty.

FIGURE 4.5 (opposite)
Effects of sex hormones on development at puberty. [Adapted from an original painting by Frank H. Netter, M.D., from The CIBA Collection of Medical Illustrations, vol. 4, 1965. Copyright by CIBA Pharmaceutical Company, Division of CIBA-GEIGY Corporation. All rights reserved.]

However, boys manipulate their genitalia for pleasure and very frequently attain erection, and sometimes orgasm, long before puberty.

The correlation of testosterone elevation with "dating" and "first infatuation" are more problematic. Prepubescent children are capable of strong emotional attachments with romantic and erotic overtones, and the age at which young people start to date is in large measure a function of social convention.

These remarks do not invalidate the central message of Figure 4.6. The real issue is not the onset but the nature and intensification of sexual behavior concomitant with rising levels of hormones, and intensification of sexual behavior during and following puberty clearly does occur (Kinsey, Pomeroy, and Martin 1948, 1953).

That testosterone is associated with increased sexual activity can be substantiated by the effects of castration. Males castrated before puberty are almost invariably impotent. For those castrated after puberty, failure of sexual functions is more variable, though generally quite serious. Of 157 men who were castrated for medicolegal reasons, almost half lost their potency and sexual desire shortly after castration; such loss was delayed for a year in about

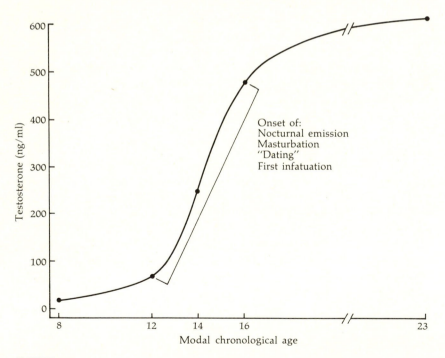

FIGURE 4.6
Amount of testosterone in the plasma of human males at different ages. [Redrawn from F. A. Beach, in *Reproductive Behavior*, ed. W. Montagna and W. A. Sadler, Plenum, 1974.]

20 percent; the rest were able to function sexually for more than a year but not quite adequately (Bremer 1959). Further evidence linking testosterone with potency and sexual drive is that hypogonadal males who are treated with testosterone exhibit improvement (Miller, Hubert, and Hamilton 1938).

The administration of testosterone has no proven effect in heightening the sexual responsiveness of healthy males; most cases of impotence have no known hormonal basis but are psychogenic. We can therefore conclude that, although the presence of an adequate amount of androgen does not ensure sexual adequacy, a substantial lack of the hormone will certainly hamper it.

There is evidence that adrenal androgens enhance libido in women: it has been claimed that frigidity can be treated with testosterone, that sexual desire and responsiveness decrease after hypophysectomy or adrenalectomy, and that there is an incidental increase in libido in women treated with testosterone for other medical purposes (Salmon and Geist 1943; Schon and Sutherland 1960). Although others disagree with these claims (see Bermant and Davidson [1974, p. 241]), it is provisionally assumed that androgens enhance sexual drive and responsiveness in women as well as in men (Money 1961). They presumably do this by heightening susceptibility to psychic and somatic stimulation, by increasing sensitivity of the external genitalia (causing clitoral hypertrophy), and by inducing greater orgasmic responsiveness (Greenblatt, Jungck, and Blum 1972). The fact that the administration of androgen enhances the female libido does not necessarily imply that the normally present and much lower levels of androgen are responsible for it.

The relationship of testosterone to aggression is equally fascinating. As with sexuality, biological variables alone are unlikely to explain the many facets of this complex issue, but that does not detract from their potential relevance.

It has been well known in animal husbandry that castration renders young males less aggressive. Research using laboratory animals has amply substantiated this effect (Hellyer, Corning, and Corning 1975). Specific correlations have been made between testosterone levels and aggressive behavior in monkeys (Rose, Holaday, and Bernstein 1971).[8] Preliminary studies of humans tend to indicate a similar association.

The effect of female sex hormones in regulating the sexual behavior of mammals is unequivocally established. Animals copulate only when the female is in "heat" (estrus), which is closely tied to ovulation. "Spontaneous ovulators" are receptive shortly before ovulation, and ovulation is precipitated by coitus itself in "reflex ovulators" (Bermant and Davidson 1974, p. 134). When the ovaries are removed from subprimate mammals, sexual receptivity and hence sexual activity cease to exist.

---

[8]For further considerations of the biological aspects of aggressive behavior, see Hellyer, Corning, and Corning (1975); Hamburg (1971); and Wolstenholme and O'Connor (1967).

The sexual behavior of subhuman primates seems to be less dependent on hormones, and that of the human female is apparently completely independent of ovarian control (Beach 1947). Women are potentially sexually receptive any time during the ovarian cycle; surgical removal of the ovaries or cessation of their functions following the menopause does not result in loss of sexual interest or responsiveness. These considerations and related ones have led to the hypothesis that, with increasing development of the neocortex during evolution, the hormonal control of behavior has progressively declined.

This is not to say that there is no hormonal influence in this regard. Some studies indicate that there is a correlation between the incidence of coitus and the phase of the menstrual period: the highest rate (42 percent) of intercourse occurs at about the time of ovulation, indicating perhaps a higher receptivity on the part of the female at that time (Udry and Morris 1968; Moos and Lunde 1969). However, the results of such studies are not always consistent (Bermant and Davidson 1974; O'Connor, Shelley, and Stern 1974). In studying the sexual behavior of humans, we must allow for considerable variability because much of it is psychosocially controlled.

Ovarian hormones also affect emotions. It is common knowledge that many women undergo changes in mood during the menstrual period. Several decades ago, researchers reported that changes in mood occurred throughout the monthly cycle rather than only at the time of menstruation (Benedek and Rubinstein 1939a, 1939b). More recent studies have tended to substantiate this. Women have rated themselves as being more pleasant, active, and sexually responsive during the first half of the cycle, which is dominated by estrogen. But, in the second half, in which progesterone predominates, pleasantness, activity, and sexual arousal decrease. During the few days preceding the menses, when both hormones drop sharply, there is an increased likelihood of irritability, anxiety, and depression (Moos 1969). (Menstrual distress will be discussed in the next chapter.)

Estrogen and Progesterone

Our knowledge of the two principal female sex hormones has a shorter history but in the past century we have learned a great deal about estrogen and progesterone. The major discoveries have been made since the early 1930s, when the molecular structures and methods of synthesis of these hormones were discovered. Because the ovaries are not exposed like the testes, experimentation by removal was not possible in former times (Tepperman 1973; Goodman and Gilman 1975).

Testosterone has relatively few worthwhile uses in medicine, but estrogen and progesterone are used by many women: birth control pills consist of various combinations of estrogen and progesterone. Estrogenic compounds retard the aging effects of the menopause; they are far more effective in the retention of youthfulness in women than testosterone is in men.

Estrogen and progesterone are secreted by the cells of the ovarian (graafian) follicles. The immature and maturing follicles mainly produce estrogen, whereas the remains of the follicles (corpus luteum) produce progesterone, for the most part, after the egg has been discharged (Kase 1969). During pregnancy, the placenta takes over the production of female hormones.

The prenatal differentiation of the female reproductive tract seems to be primarily determined by the absence of testosterone rather than the active participation of female hormones (Money and Ehrhardt 1972, p. 45). A small amount of estrogen is present in children of both sexes, and the amount increases with age and maturation (Pennington and Dewhurst 1969; Winter and Faiman 1972). At puberty, the production of estrogen accelerates in girls, the amount multiplying several times from age 7 to age 12 (Root 1973a, p. 8; Kelch, Grumbach, and Kaplan 1972; Jenner et al. 1972; Saez, Morera, and Bertrand 1972). Estrogen levels continue to increase after menarche until full reproductive maturity is attained.

The amount of estrogen in boys also increases at puberty but much less so than in girls (Winter and Faiman 1972). Adult males continue to excrete small amounts of estrogen, probably produced by the adrenal cortex and the testes (O'Connor, Shelley, and Stern 1974, p. 310), but its function in males is unclear.

The overall effect of estrogen on the pubescent development of the female is in many ways similar to that of androgen in the male (see Figure 4.5). Namely, by a direct action, it causes growth and development of the reproductive organs—the ovaries, uterus, and vagina. It is responsible for the enlargement of the breasts and contributes to the growth of the skeleton and the molding of body contours through fat distribution. Its actions are like those of androgens in males in the development of axillary and pubic hair and the darkening of the skin of the nipples, the areola, and the genital region. Yet estrogen is a weak anabolic agent and does not promote growth to the extent that androgens do.

The role of estrogen in the growth spurt is obscure. This event in females is presumably controlled by adrenal androgens or other factors. All growth at the epiphyseal plates depends on somatotropin, thyroid hormones, insulin, androgens, and other factors (Heald and Hung 1970, p. 33). Estrogen, like androgen, promotes epiphyseal maturation, inhibiting the growth of long bones after puberty. Because excessive height in women can be objectionable for aesthetic reasons, estrogen has been used in selected circumstances to inhibit growth in adolescent girls (Wettenhall and Roche 1965).

Progesterone has a much more limited range of effects than does estrogen, but its functions are not trivial. It controls the fundamental mechanisms of ovulation and the sustenance of the embryo.

During puberty, the production of estrogen and progesterone begins to follow a cyclical pattern. This mechanism is the key regulator of the menstrual cycle. Figure 4.7 shows the relation of hormone levels to changes in the ovarian follicles, the uterine lining (endometrium), the cervix, and the vaginal epithelium in a monthly cycle. (Disregard for now the part of the diagram dealing with the gonadotropic hormones FSH and LH, which will be discussed further on.)

Menstruation consists of the shedding of the uterine lining, which is rich in blood vessels; hence, the presence of blood in the menstrual discharge. Right after this has occurred, increasing levels of estrogen cause a new ovarian follicle to begin to mature and a new uterine lining to begin to form. This process continues for about two weeks, or the first half of a 28-day menstrual cycle, and is known as the *follicular phase.* Concurrently, the vaginal epithelium thickens, and there are changes in the mucous glands of the cervix.

Ovulation occurs midcycle when the increasing amount of fluid within the ovarian follicle ruptures it and the mature egg is extruded from the ovary. The remainder of the ovarian follicle is transformed into the corpus luteum ("yellow body"). The corpus luteum produces progesterone, which with estrogen further enhances endometrial development. The endometrial glands then begin to secrete a nutrient fluid. The physiological importance of this development is that, should the ovum get fertilized, the zygote will reach the uterine lining when it is optimally ready to accommodate and sustain it. The second half of the menstrual cycle is thus referred to as the *postovulatory, secretory,* or *luteal phase.*

If the ovum has not been fertilized or the zygote fails to become implanted, the production of estrogen and progesterone decreases rapidly. The uterine lining loses its hormonal sustenance and sloughs away, resulting in the menstrual flow. If, on the other hand, the ovum has been fertilized and implantation takes place, then the corpus luteum is sustained, estrogen and progesterone production continue, and in several months this function is taken over by the placenta.

As indicated earlier, menstrual cycles are normally quite irregular during puberty. Even after they become regularized in young adulthood, they can vary in length to some extent. Cycles on the average are completed in 28 days, but many are as short as 26 days or as long as 34 days. The differences are usually due to the length of the preovulatory phase, which tends to be more variable. The postovulatory phase is quite constant, usually lasting from 12 to 14 days. The period of actual menstrual bleeding is from a few days to a week during which about two ounces of blood is lost. Healthy women on adequate diets regain this loss readily.[9]

Progesterone probably has some effect on the development of the breast during puberty, but its role in this regard is not entirely clear. Its importance in

---

[9]For further discussion of the menstrual cycle, see Katchadourian and Lunde (1975).

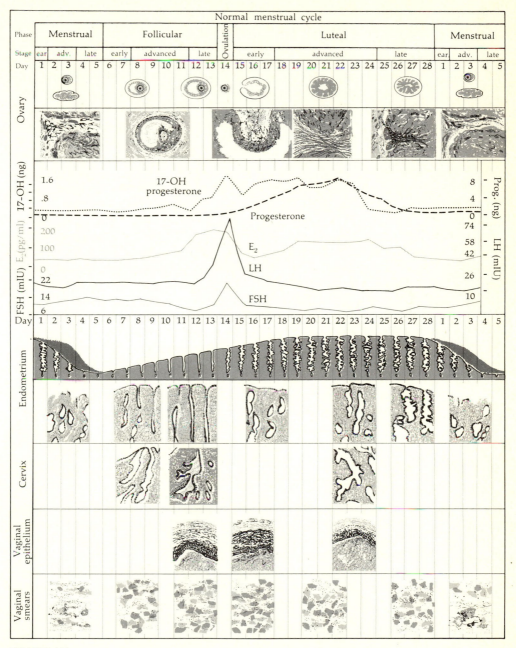

FIGURE 4.7
Hormone levels and changes in the reproductive organs during ovulatory menstrual cycles: mIU = milli international unit; pg = picogram (grams × 10⁻¹²). [Redrawn from R. H. Williams, *Textbook of Endocrinology,* Saunders, 1968.]

the development of the mammary gland during pregnancy is much better established. The slight rise in temperature that women experience at midcycle, which correlates with the event of ovulation, is caused by progesterone. This is the basis of the rhythm method of birth control; knowing the time of ovulation allows a woman to determine the "safe period" (Katchadourian and Lunde 1975, pp. 164–165). The same thermogenic effect is also produced when nonovulating women or even men are given the hormone.

PITUITARY
AND HYPOTHALAMIC CONTROL

Hormones course through the bloodstream day and night, influencing various functions of the body. They are produced and released by endocrine glands many of which are under the control of a single tiny structure called the pituitary.

Despite its grandiloquent titles ("the master gland," "the leader of the endocrine orchestra"), the historical origins of the pituitary gland are quite humble. The pituitary derived its name from the Latin word for "phlegm" because the gland was thought to be the source of the mucus that moistens the nose. It was not until the latter part of the nineteenth century that its function as a master gland began to be recognized. Since then, its many functions were identified one after another. In the late 1920s, a number of hormones were attributed to it that subsequently turned out to be nonexistent (Tepperman 1973; Goodman and Gilman 1975). Even so, the pituitary gland was thought to control the entire endocrine system until about a decade or two ago when it was realized that, although the pituitary was indeed master of many other endocrine glands, it was not its own master; rather, it was controlled by the hypothalamus.

The pituitary is a pea-sized organ located on the underside of the brain at the level of the eyes (Figure 4.8). It is also called *hypophysis cerebri* (i.e., outgrowth of the brain) because it appears to be an extension of brain tissue. In terms of its origin, this is true only for the posterior part of the gland, which during embryological development begins to grow downward from the brain as a tiny fingerlike projection while an outpouching of the primitive foregut moves upward to develop into the anterior pituitary. These two structures come to rest in a bony cavity called the *sella turcica* (so named because to an early anatomist it resembled a Turkish saddle). Thus, what appears to be a single gland actually consists of two separate glands with widely different functions that are under the control of the hypothalamus.

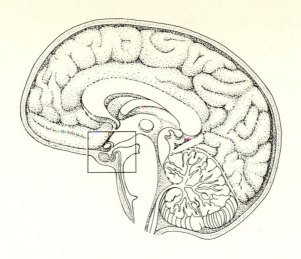

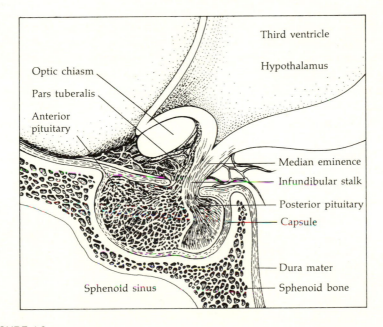

FIGURE 4.8
The bony receptacle that encloses the pituitary gland is a cavity in the sphenoid bone, on which the base of the brain rests. The outlined section in the upper illustration is detailed below. The hypothalamus and pituitary are connected by a stalk that passes through the membranous cover of the receptacle in the sphenoid bone in which the pituitary rests. The double embryological origin of the two lobes of the pituitary is reflected in their differing tissues and functions and in the way that each is connected to the hypothalamus. [Adapted from The Hormones of the Hypothalamus by R. Guilleman and R. Burgus. Copyright © 1972 by Scientific American, Inc. All rights reserved.]

PITUITARY HORMONES

The two glands of the pituitary are called the anterior pituitary, or *adeno-hypophysis,* and the posterior pituitary, or *neurohypophysis* (Figure 4.9). The hormones of the posterior lobe do not concern us here.[10]

The names of the six hormones of the anterior lobe are derived from the names of their target glands or tissues, to which the suffix *tropic* (Greek for "being drawn to") is added. (In some of the literature, the suffix *trophic* [to feed upon] is used.) Thus, the pituitary hormone that controls the thyroid gland is called the thyrotropic hormone, or thyrotropin. The others are the somatotropic, or growth, hormone (GH), which was discussed earlier; the adrenocorticotropic hormone (ACTH); two gonadotropic hormones (FSH and LH); and the mammo- or lactotropic hormone (LTH), which is more commonly called prolactin (PRL).

A small organ like the anterior pituitary is able to produce so many substances because of the high degree of specialization of its cells. Endocrine glands are typically composed of masses of secretory cells arranged in clusters. The anterior pituitary probably contains specific cells for producing each of the six hormones (four such cell types have already been identified, by means of electron microscopy, on the basis of the size of the granules they contain). In functional terms, the anterior pituitary is not a single endocrine gland, but rather a group of six separate glands, which helps to explain why crude methods of study, such as using extracts of the gland for determining its effect, are likely to give bewildering results. The preferable approach is to isolate and synthesize the specific hormones, but this is a formidable task, given the fact that the pituitary hormones are proteins, which are large molecules enormously more complex than the steroid hormones (Figure 4.3).

The Gonadotropins

Two two anterior pituitary hormones that act on the gonads are essentially the same chemical substances in males and females. One is called the follicle stimulating hormone (FSH) for the very good reason that it stimulates the maturation of the ovarian follicles. This same hormone in the male promotes spermatogenesis, but it is still called FSH. The second gonadotropin is called the luteinizing hormone (LH) because it promotes the formation of the corpus luteum; LH is also referred to as the interstitial cell stimulating hormone (mer-

---

[10]One of these hormones (oxytocin) stimulates the contraction of the muscles of the uterus in childbirth and of the duct of the mammary gland in lactation. The second hormone (vasopressin, or antidiuretic hormone) participates in the control of water excretion by the kidney and in the regulation of blood pressure.

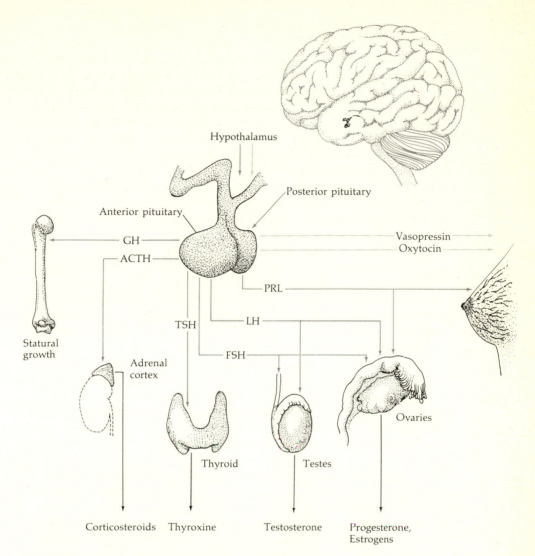

FIGURE 4.9
Hormones of the pituitary and their targets. [Redrawn from The Hormones of the
Hypothalamus by R. Guillemin and R. Burgus. Copyright © 1972 by Scientific
American, Inc. All rights reserved.]

cifully abbreviated to ICSH) because that is precisely what it does in males,
but LH is the more commonly used abbreviation.

The pituitary gonadotropins perform two functions in both sexes: they control
the production of steroid hormones (testosterone, estrogen, and progesterone);
and they maintain the structure of the gonads, promoting their gametogenic

functions (production of sperm and ova).[11] Their role at puberty is crucial (Bearwood and Russell 1970; Blizzard et al. 1972; Faiman and Winter 1974).

In prepubescent girls, only small amount of FSH and LH are produced by the pituitary. The amount of serum FSH increases gradually between 2 and 8 years of age, as does the amount excreted in the urine between 5 and 8. Serum FSH levels further increase between 9 and 12 years and in the early stages of adolescent development. The amount excreted in the urine more than doubles from childhood to adulthood (Lee et al. 1970, 1974; Rifkind, Kulin, and Ross 1967).

The amount of LH in females increases similarly. It is low in children, but gradually increases between 2 and 10 years of age, especially after age 8 and in the early phases of puberty. The amount excreted in the urine after puberty is eleven times as great as that excreted before puberty (Rifkind et al. 1970; Kulin et al. 1967).

Gonadotropins have been detected in boys in early childhood, FSH having been present in the urine of one in five subjects being studied between the ages of about 5 and 11 (Fitschen and Clayton 1965; Kulin et al. 1967). Levels increase between the ages of 5 and 10 and continue to do so until age 16. The amount of LH also increases gradually in childhood and more sharply at puberty: there is a threefold increase in the amount excreted in the urine from age 9 or 10 to age 11 or 12, with a further fivefold increase by age 18. Serum ICSH levels increase gradually between birth and age 8 and more sharply between the ages of 9 and 12 (Rifkind et al. 1970; Blizzard et al. 1970, 1972).

Studies have been reported that contradict some of the quantitative details of the preceding statements. But the main facts to note here are that gonadotropins exist in childhood and that sharp increases in amount herald puberty and trigger the chain of events discussed so far. (For a review of the literature, see Root [1973].)

We should now return to Figure 4.5 to examine the role of gonadotropins in the overall scheme of pubertal changes and to Figure 4.7 to see the relationship of these hormones to the menstrual cycle.

In females, FSH promotes the growth of the ovarian follicles (Gemzell and Roos 1966). These follicles are generally dormant during prepubescence, but because of the increased levels of FSH and perhaps because of their increased sensitivity to its effects, they begin to mature and produce estrogen, which in turn enhances the physiological effects of FSH (Goldenberg, Vaitukaitis, and Ross 1972).

---

[11]The anterior pituitary is the exclusive source of gonadotropins in nonpregnant females and in males. But, during pregnancy, the placenta is also active in this regard and its hormones are called *chorionic gonadotropins*. Their actions are similar to those of the pituitary hormones but not identical with them in all their biological properties. Chorionic gonadotropins have nothing to do with the changes of puberty.

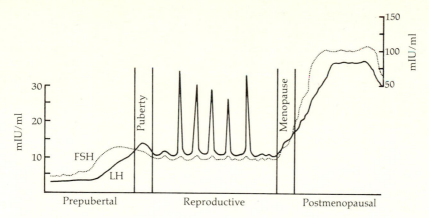

FIGURE 4.10
The life cycle of gonadotropin secretion in the human female. [Redrawn from M. Ferin,
F. Halberg, R. M. Richart, and R. L. Van de Wick, *Biorhythms and Human Reproduction,*
Wiley, 1974.]

The actions of LH in females are closely coordinated with those of FSH. The
response of the developing follicle to FSH is very much enhanced by the
presence of LH. But the more specific role of LH is in causing ovulation and
the formation of the corpus luteum, which in turn produces progesterone. There
is some evidence that LH also stimulates progesterone secretion from other
parts of the ovary as well (Bermant and Davidson 1974, p. 128). In postpubescent females, the level of FSH fluctuates cyclically, regulating the tempo
of the menstrual cycle. After the menopause, the levels of FSH and LH remain
stable at a relatively high level for reasons to be explained further on. These
changing patterns of gonadotropin secretion throughout a woman's life cycle
are shown in Figure 4.10.

The relationship of FSH and LH levels to those of estrogen (E_2) and progesterone (and hydroxy-, or 17-OH, progesterone) shown in Figure 4.7 is more
complex than that illustration indicates. The extent to which the levels of these
hormones fluctuate can be seen in Figure 4.11. The key event is the sudden
increase in the secretion of FSH and LH at midcycle. The pronounced secretion
of LH results in ovulation within 24 hours (Odell and Mayer 1971).[12]

As it does in females, FSH promotes gametogenesis in males. Increased
levels of FSH cause the seminiferous tubules to mature and to begin to produce
sperm (see Figure 4.5) if concentrations of thyroid hormone and testosterone
are adequate and the temperature is optimal.[13] Unlike that of females, FSH

---

[12]For further discussion of the relationship of pituitary hormones to those secreted by the gonads in
girls, see Sizonenko et al. (1970) and Adamopoulos (1974).

[13]Undescended testes will not produce fertile sperm because the temperature within the abdomen is
higher than in the scrotal sac. However, potency and testosterone production are unaltered.

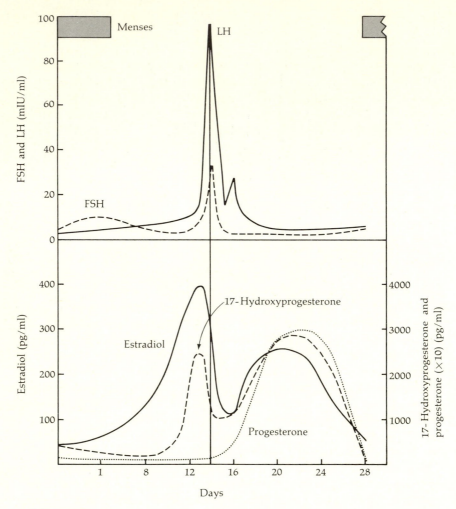

FIGURE 4.11

Changes in the amount of circulating follicle stimulating hormone (FSH), luteinizing hormone (LH), and several steroid hormones during a normal menstrual cycle. Because progesterone levels are much higher than those of other steroids, their concentrations were divided by 10 in this diagram. [Adapted from W. D. Odell and D. L. Moyer, *Physiology of Reproduction,* St. Louis, 1971, The C. V. Mosby Co.]

secretion does not lead to the production of steroid hormones by the gonads in males.

In males, ICSH affects the interstitial, or Leydig, cells by causing them to start producing testosterone. Therefore, FSH initiates puberty in females by triggering the production of estrogen, whereas ICSH does so in males by triggering that of testosterone. These hormones, in turn, bring about the physical changes. The close correlation between the increased amount of LH (i.e., ICSH) and testosterone and the growth of the testes and penis is clearly evident in Figure 4.4.

The two gonadotropic hormones in males may not be as independent of each other as our discussion would imply. Just as LH is the major ovulatory hormone, so it may also be the most important in spermatogenesis. FSH has been isolated from human and animal pituitaries. It is a protein whose molecular structure is being elucidated (Hafer and Evans 1973). Recently, potent preparations of human FSH (and the drug clomiphene) have become available; they are used in treating infertility and account for a large number of multiple births. Such treatment causes sluggish ovaries to become extraordinarily active: multiple ova reach maturity at the same time and, in some cases, are simultaneously fertilized.

Other Pituitary Hormones

The thyrotropic, or thyroid-stimulating, hormone (TSH) regulates the output of the thyroid gland. The adrenocorticotropic hormone (ACTH) controls the secretions of the adrenal cortex, including androgens.

Prolactin performs important functions in rodents, but its significance in other mammalian species is not clear, although it has been shown to be a distinct hormone of the human pituitary (Hwang, Guyda, and Friesen 1971). It has no established role in puberty, but it does function in lactation.

HYPOTHALAMIC HORMONES

The nervous and endocrine systems constitute the two major communicative systems of the body. It has been known for some time that these two systems closely interact and influence each other. However, only in the past several decades has the field of neuroendocrinology taken shape, and a great deal of the research has focused on the interrelationship of the hypothalamus and the pituitary, each of which is a relay station of central importance within its own system. The hypothalamus and pituitary interrelate on such vital functions as sexual activity.[14]

The hypothalamus is not an anatomically discrete organ like the pituitary; rather it is a part of the brain (refer to Figure 4.8). It is therefore much more difficult to characterize its shape and size. There are regions in the hypothalamus that contain cell clusters specifically concerned with the control of pituitary activity.

---

[14]For further reading on general hypothalamic functions, see Haymaker, Anderson, and Nauta (1969); Martini, Motta, and Fraschini (1970).

Hypothalamic control of the pituitary has been demonstrated by various experimental techniques, including the classical methods of localized destruction and electrical stimulation. If small electrodes are inserted into certain areas in the hypothalamus, resulting in tiny lesions due to electrocoagulation, the anterior pituitary stops producing hormones even though it has not been tampered with directly. Conversely, if the nerve cells in the same areas of the hypothalamus are electrically stimulated, without getting damaged, the anterior pituitary responds by greatly increasing its output of hormones (Figure 4.12).[15] Such experiments suggest that there are nerves connecting the hypothalamus to the anterior pituitary (as there are to the neurohypophysis), but, in fact, no nervous connections between these two structures exist. Vascular connections were evident in early experiments, but this knowledge did not help initially because the hypothalamus, being a part of the nervous system and not an endocrine gland, was not expected to produce hormones. Now we know that this is exactly what it does: Nerve cells in certain regions in the hypothalamus secrete hormones just like an endocrine gland, but, unlike other hormones, which act through the general bloodstream, the hypothalamic hormones travel through the local portal veins to the anterior pituitary and regulate its actions (Porter, Kamberi, and Grazia 1971) (Figure 4.13). It was only late in 1969 that the first of these hypothalamic hormones was definitively identified—that which controls the release of thyrotropin.[16]

It is now generally accepted that the hormones produced by the hypothalamus are specifically linked to each of the six hormone-producing systems of the anterior pituitary. Most of the hypothalamic hormones cause the anterior pituitary to release its own hormones; therefore they are known as *releasing factors*.[17] The hypothalamic hormones that are pertinent to this discussion are: FSH-releasing factor (FRF); LH-releasing factor (LRF); (adrenal) corticotropin-releasing factor (CRF); thyroid-stimulating-hormone-, or TSH-, releasing factor (TRF); and growth-hormone-releasing factor (GRF). The sixth hypothalamic hormone inhibits the release of prolactin by the pituitary and is called the prolactin-inhibitory factor (PIF). In other words, the only time that the pituitary starts producing prolactin is when the hypothalamus stops telling it not to. Another hypothalamic substance called somatostatin has been shown to have an inhibitory effect on the secretion of growth hormone (Brazeau et al. 1973).

---

[15]For a review of the methodologies, see Bermant and Davidson (1974, pp. 99–102) and Davidson (1974, pp. 82–84).

[16]To obtain 1 milligram of this substance, about 5 million hypothalamic fragments dissected from 500 tons of sheep brain tissue had to be processed, an endeavor that took four years to accomplish (Guillemin and Burgus 1972).

[17]The releasing factors are short-chain polypeptides and may be the same in all mammalian species (Austin and Short 1972, vol. 3, p. 36). See also McCann and Porter (1969); Kastin et al. (1972); and Donovan (1972).

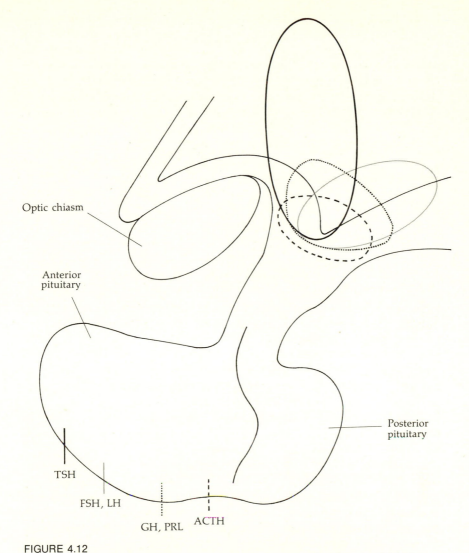

Optic chiasm

Anterior
pituitary

Posterior
pituitary

TSH

FSH, LH

GH, PRL   ACTH

FIGURE 4.12
The relation between the hypothalamus and anterior pituitary has been established
experimentally. Lesions in specific regions of the hypothalamus interfere with the
secretion of specific hormones by the anterior lobe, whereas electrical stimulation of
those regions enhances their secretion. Each region and its associated hormone are
delineated in the same way. [Redrawn from The Hormones of the Hypothalamus by
R. Guillemin and R. Burgus. Copyright © 1972 by Scientific American, Inc. All rights
reserved.]

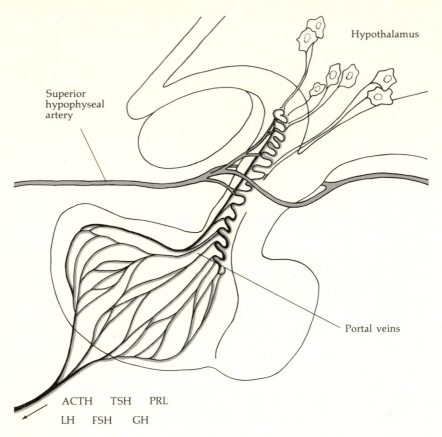

FIGURE 4.13
Vascular connections between the hypothalamus and the anterior lobe of the pituitary.
[Redrawn from The Hormones of the Hypothalamus by R. Guillemin and R. Burgus.
Copyright © 1972 by Scientific American, Inc. All rights reserved.]

Because some hypothalamic hormones may have an inhibitory rather than
releasing effect on the pituitary, a more accurate but less often used term for
the hormones is *hypophysiotropic factors.*

Having traced the course of events as far back to their origins as is currently
possible, we can now reconsider Figure 4.5 in full. The alarm clock shown in
the brain is a confession of ignorance. It suggests that somewhere in the brain
a "trigger" is set off that initiates activity in which the releasing factors in the
hypothalamus prompt the anterior pituitary to release its gonadotropic hormones in response to which the ovaries and testes produce the sex hormones
with the resultant physical changes in sexual maturation during puberty. These
events are regulated by an intimate system of neuroendocrine relays.

NEUROENDOCRINE
RELAY SYSTEMS

The discussion so far has followed a hierarchic model in which the peripheral hormones do the footwork, the hypothalamus controls the headquarters, and the pituitary hormones are the intermediaries. Actually, instead of such a chain of command, the neural and endocrine centers are linked in self-regulating relay systems. Cybernetic models have become increasingly useful in medicine and are particularly suitable to neuroendocrine regulatory systems.[18]

A central concept in such systems is that of "feedback," and the most common example used to illustrate it is the household thermostat. When the temperature of a room falls below that for which the thermostat has been set, a sensing device causes the furnace to work. When the temperature of the room reaches that indicated on the thermostat, the furnace is shut off. The thermostat and furnace are thus linked in a communication system in which the temperature of the room acts as a signal, or basic information unit. The information is fed back and forth so that the furnace and the thermostat mutually control each other. Theoretically, the thermostat could be dispensed with if all the factors that affect the temperature of the room were known and could be controlled, in which case the furnace could simply be set to work at a given rate that would keep the temperature constant. But, in practice, a great deal is unpredictable. Therefore, the advantage of feedback systems is that they preclude the need for prediction and operate not on the basis of expected conditions but on the basis of actual conditions as they occur. This enables us to set the thermostat and go to bed at night without worrying about how the weather will turn out. Because of similar but more complex feedback mechanisms in our bodies, we are able to carry out our daily activities without being concerned with all that it takes to maintain the homeostasis of our internal environments.

The concentration of hormones in the bloodstream is analogous to the temperature of the room. Just as heat is continuously lost on a cold day and the furnace must keep working to keep the room warm, hormones are continuously used up by the body and must be replenished. The mechanism by which they are used up is the metabolic transformation or destruction of these compounds primarily by the liver. Such losses must then be offset by further production of the hormone by the endocrine gland.

To maintain a reasonably steady balance, hormones in circulation and the gland that produces them (their controller) keep correcting each other: when

---

[18]The term "cybernetics" was first used by Norbert Weiner (derived from the Greek for "steersman" or pilot); it was applied to certain concepts in theories of communication (Weiner 1950).

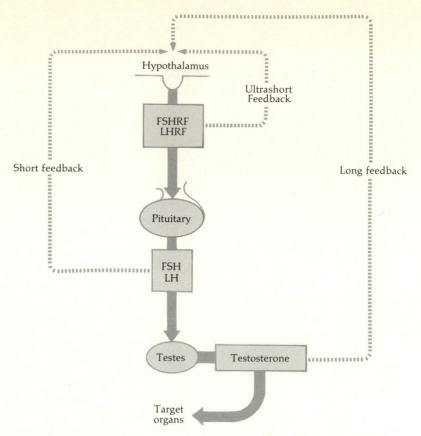

FIGURE 4.14
Interactions of the hypothalamus, the pituitary gland, and the testes. Gonadotropin-releasing factors (FSHRF, LHRF) cause the anterior lobe of the pituitary to discharge FSH and LH into the blood, stimulating the testes and promoting the production of testosterone by interstitial Leydig cells as well as spermatogenesis. The concentration of releasing factors, gonadotropins, and testosterone regulates the output of hypothalamic gonadotropin-releasing factors by feedback mechanisms. [Redrawn from E. S. E. Hafez and T. N. Evans, eds., *Human Reproduction: Conception and Contraception,* Harper and Row, 1973.]

the concentration of hormones falls below a "set" point, the gland produces more; when the concentration returns to that point, the gland is "turned off," or decreases its rate of production. This is an example of feedback inhibition, or *negative feedback.* In *positive feedback,* the hormones that are released by the endocrine gland stimulate further production—a mechanism that can operate only for short periods, otherwise the gland would rapidly become depleted. The levels at which feedback mechanisms operate also vary. Three such levels have been described for the interactions of the hypothalamus, the pituitary gland, and the gonads (Root 1973a; Hafez and Evans 1973; Grumbach et al., 1974, pp. 115–181). Figure 4.14 illustrates these levels in males.

Long feedback regulates the interactions between the gonads and the hypothalamus-pituitary complex. Hypothalamic releasing factors stimulate the production of FSH and LH, which, in turn, increase the production of gonadal hormones. When the gonadal hormones reach a certain concentration, the pituitary and hypothalamus are inhibited through negative feedback. As a result, levels of releasing factors, gonadotropins, and gonadal hormones successively decline, eventually removing the inhibitory effect on the higher centers and prompting the hypothalamus to increase its output of releasing factors, thus renewing the cycle.

More specifically, estrogen reduces, through negative feedback, the secretion of FSH and LH by inhibiting the hypothalamus and the pituitary (Franchimont 1971). Progesterone inhibits LH production, but has no effect on FSH secretion unless combined with estrogen (Wallach, Root, and Garcia 1970).

Birth-control pills work on this principle. Because they consist of estrogen and progesterone, they increase the concentration of these hormones, which causes the pituitary (and hypothalamus) to suppress the midcycle surge of gonadotropin production. Regardless of the source of the sex hormones —whether from the pharmacy or the ovary—the net effect is the same: less FSH and LH, no ovulation, and no baby.

Estrogen stimulates the sudden secretion of LH at midcycle through positive feedback (Figure 4.11). As the amount of estrogen increases, so does that of LH, culminating in the high concentration necessary to produce ovulation (Abraham et al. 1972). This process is not endless—if the amount of estrogen were to continue to increase for a long period, the negative feedback mechanism would take over and inhibit LH production. Thus, the negative and positive feedback systems work in a coordinated fashion.

In males, testosterone has been shown to inhibit the secretion of LH, but how FSH secretion is regulated is not known (Root 1973*a*; Franchimont 1971).

Short feedback is demonstrated by the regulatory effect of FSH and LH on the hypothalamus. Evidence for this comes from the finding that the production of gonadotropic-releasing factors can be inhibited by implanting FSH or LH into the appropriate hypothalamic areas (Motta, Fraschini, and Martini 1969).

Ultrashort feedback allows the hypothalamus to regulate itself. This model is based on experimental work. The physiological roles of short and untrashort feedback are not yet established.

Feedback mechanisms regulate the production of gonadal hormones in females in a similar way (Figure 4.15), but there are two important differences between the female and male systems. The first is cyclicity. Hormone production in postpubescent women fluctuates cyclically (as shown in Figure 4.10), resulting in the phases of the menstrual cycle (Figure 4.7) unless interrupted temporarily by pregnancy (Figure 4.15). The production of testosterone in men

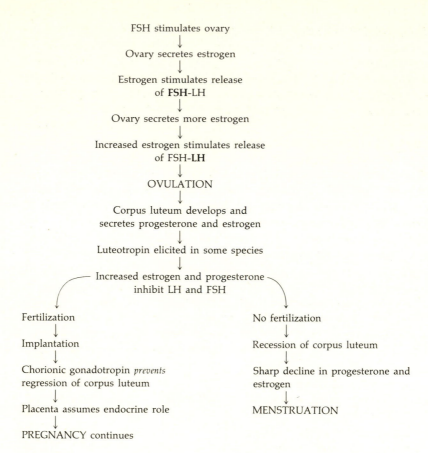

FSH stimulates ovary
↓
Ovary secretes estrogen
↓
Estrogen stimulates release
of **FSH**-LH
↓
Ovary secretes more estrogen
↓
Increased estrogen stimulates release
of FSH-**LH**
↓
OVULATION
↓
Corpus luteum develops and
secretes progesterone and estrogen
↓
Luteotropin elicited in some species
↓
Increased estrogen and progesterone
inhibit LH and FSH

Fertilization   No fertilization
↓   ↓
Implantation   Recession of corpus luteum
↓   ↓
Chorionic gonadotropin *prevents*   Sharp decline in progesterone and
regression of corpus luteum   estrogen
↓   ↓
Placenta assumes endocrine role   MENSTRUATION
↓
PREGNANCY continues

FIGURE 4.15
Summary of the hormonal control of ovulation, menstruation, and pregnancy. [From
Metabolic and Endocrine Physiology, by Jay Tepperman. Copyright © 1968, Year Book
Medical Publishers, Inc. Used by permission of Year Book Medical Publishers.]

is more steady, being controlled by the feedback mechanisms just described.
Although testosterone levels fluctuate daily (Corker and Exley 1968), there
is only a weak diurnal rhythm.

The second difference is the status of the sex hormones in midlife. Testosterone levels decline gradually with age in men, but usually without the abrupt
interruption of sex-hormone production that occurs at menopause in women.
The high levels of gonadotropin in postmenopausal women (as shown in Figure
4.10) are caused by the failure of the ovaries to sustain the production of
estrogen and progesterone. Uninhibited by these hormones, the pituitary
goes on producing larger amounts of gonadotropin.

CONTROL OF THE ONSET OF PUBERTY

The presence of a "sexual centrum" in the brain that triggers the onset of puberty was postulated in 1932, but its location has remained elusive. Extra-hypothalamic influences from other areas of the brain such as the limbic system and the pineal body have been postulated.

Much of this research is still in the experimental stage and the precise mechanism for the control of puberty is unknown (Grumbach et al. 1974). The hypothalamus, the pituitary, the gonads, and body tissues can be stimulated into adult function long before the normal ages of puberty. Furthermore, the hypothalamic-pituitary-gonadal axis is functional not only before puberty, but in fetal life (Donovan and Van der Werff Ten Bosch 1965). So the onset of puberty is due to the further activation of an already functional system rather than the sudden awakening of a previously dormant one. There is a change in the sensitivity of the hypothalamic "gonadostat" (Figure 4.16). The dominant

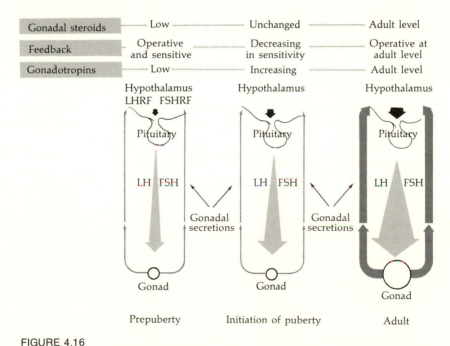

FIGURE 4.16
Changes in the sensitivity of the hypothalamic "gonadostat." Before puberty, the concentration of sex steroids and gonadotropins is low; the hypothalamic "gonadostat" is functional and very sensitive to sex steroids. With the onset of puberty, the sensitivity of the hypothalamus to negative feedback by sex steroids decreases, the production of LH-releasing factor increases, and the secretion of gonadotropins is enhanced. [Redrawn from M. M. Grumbach et al., in *Control of the Onset of Puberty*, ed. M. M. Grumbach, G. D. Grave, and F. E. Mayer, Wiley, 1974.]

theory[19] explaining how this occurs is summarized by Root (1973a, p. 14):

> These data are consistent with the hypothesis that as the child matures the sensitivity of the hypothalamic receptor sites to inhibition by gonadal steroids declines; consequently, larger amounts of gonadotropins are secreted until increased gonadal function reestablishes an equilibrium between pituitary and gonadal activities. Readjustment continues until the quantities of gonadal steroids required for hypothalamic suppression exceed the sensitivity of the peripheral tissues to these materials, at which point the physical signs of puberty appear. Reequilibration continues until the adult relationship between hypothalamic-pituitary and gonadal activities is established.

Why the sensitivity of the hypothalamic receptor sites, which mediate the suppressive effects of the gonadal sex hormones, declines remains a mystery. One hypothesis is that there is a direct relation between a critical body weight and the onset of puberty. It has been found that the mean weights of 30 kg at the initiation of the growth spurt in girls, 39 kg at the time of peak velocity of weight gain, and 47 kg at menarche do not differ for early and late maturing girls. Thus, puberty seems to be related more to body weight than chronological age. The explanation is that "the attainment of the critical weight causes a change in metabolic rate per unit mass (or per unit of surface area), which in turn affects the hypothalamic-ovarian feedback by decreasing the sensitivity of the hypothalamus to estrogen. The feedback is then reset at a level high enough to induce maturation, which results in menarche" (Frisch 1974, pp. 406–407).[20]

There is far more to the underlying physiological processes of puberty than is known, and what has been described herein only touches on what is known. But it should be quite clear that the processes are complex and that many forces affect the events in an integrated and interdependent manner. It is also futile to set up hierarchies of eminence between parts of the brain and the body. One is reminded in this connection of the story about a Roman general who claimed that his youngest son was the most powerful figure in the world, because Rome controlled the world, the Emperor controlled Rome, the general controlled the Emperor, the general's wife controlled the general and was in turn controlled by the little boy!

---

[19]For a critique of this theory, see Davidson (1974).

[20]See also Frisch and Revelle (1970); Frisch and Revelle (1971); and Johnston, Malina, and Galbraith (1971).

Chapter 5

Disturbances of Puberty and Common Physical Ailments

Children who reach puberty considerably earlier or later than most deviate from the usual maturational pattern only in a statistical sense. Such variation is normal. But the events of puberty can be abnormal in a pathological sense. One kind of abnormality is precocious puberty, in which the onset is strikingly early and for which there is often some demonstrable cause. For example, a child of age 3 or 4, or even younger, who begins to grow pubic hair or shows some other unmistakable manifestation of puberty is outside the range of normal variation. Precocious puberty is easily distinguished from early maturation if there is an identifiable pathological cause, such as a hormone-producing tumor. Otherwise the distinction is more arbitrary.

Early and late maturation are relatively common conditions whose effect on the health of the person affected is in terms of the psychological reactions they may elicit. The pathological disturbances of puberty are rare, but their effects on health are much more serious; in some cases, the condition may be fatal.

Disturbances in puberty can be due to malfunction at any of the levels that control the process. The problem may be in the hypothalamus or at any point "down the line" that disrupts the neuroendocrine relay system. Such disorders are generally divided into two categories: those due to the hypoactivity of endocrine sources (usually as a result of destructive lesions) and those due to their hyperactivity or to abnormal sources of hormones, such as hormone-producing tumors. Thus, there are conditions known as hypo- and hyperpituitarism or hypo- and hypergonadism, which refer to the under- or overactivity of the various levels of the system. As a general rule, the "higher" the level of disturbance, the more far-ranging are its effects. For example, pituitary malfunction may affect gonadotropins, as well as other pituitary hormones, so that not only sexual maturation but other functions will be disturbed, whereas gonadal disturbances do not affect these other functions.

DISTURBANCES OF GROWTH

Because growth is controlled by the complex interactions of genes, hormones, and environmental factors, there are many possible causes of its disturbance. For growth to proceed normally, nutritional building materials of adequate quality and quantity must be available; these materials must be properly absorbed, transported,and assimilated; neuroendocrine regulation of growth must function adequately; and the end organs—that is, the tissues to grow—must possess a normal growth potential. These conditions are, in turn, influenced by a host of factors ranging from the genetic to the psychological (Prader 1974).

Some disturbances of growth were discussed in Chapter 3. Additional ones that are primarily of hormonal origin will be briefly considered here. More comprehensive treatment is beyond the scope of this book.

Most disturbances of growth become apparent before puberty and are more properly regarded as problems of childhood rather than the second decade of life. But their effects persist into puberty and sometimes become manifest during it.

The two main types of disturbance are insufficient and excessive growth, and persons so affected are commonly referred to as dwarfs and giants. In both medical and popular usage, these terms have a certain arbitrariness that must be made explicit. It is self-evident that there are normal variations in stature both within and between racial and ethnic groups. Sometimes the variations are so extreme that some individuals and groups can be considered statistically deviant, that is, shorter or taller than most people.

Pygmies (from the Greek word for "dwarf"), for example, consist of unrelated groups of people who live in isolated parts of Africa, India, and Melanesia and who never grow taller than $4\frac{1}{2}$ feet. This fact is not explained by environmental factors. Nor are these people physically abnormal. Their condition is presumably the result of chance mutations preserved by inbreeding. Some anthropologists suggest that they represent an early model of *Homo sapiens* that has managed to survive (Tanner and Taylor 1969).

There are also people within the U.S. population whose stature is markedly shorter or taller than that of the majority. They, too, may not be physiologically abnormal, although such extreme variation may become a source of psychological conflict or a social handicap. On the other hand, some manage to use it to great advantage, such as jockeys or basketball players.

In clinical practice, the terms short and tall stature are used to designate children whose height deviates by more than 20 percent from the norm. If the deviation exceeds 40 percent then ''dwarfism'' and ''gigantism'' become applicable. If the same criteria are applied to adults, men and women who are shorter than 165 cm and 155 cm, respectively, would be of *short stature,* and those shorter than 145 cm and 135 cm would be *dwarfs.* Conversely, those taller than 185 cm and 170 cm would be of *tall stature,* and those taller than 200 cm and 185 cm would be *giants* (Prader 1974, p. 1027).

Causes of Short Stature

Table 5.1 lists the causes of short stature and Table 5.2 presents the relative frequency of their occurrence in a group of patients. These data are presented to convey an idea of the wide range of conditions that may underlie

Table 5.1.   Causes of short stature.

Familial short stature	

Constitutional slow growth
  with delayed adolescence
	Primordial dwarfism (intrauterine dwarfism)
	  Dwarfism without congenital anomalies
	  Dwarfism with congenital anomalies
	  Dwarfism with intrauterine infection

Chromosomal disorders
  Trisomy syndromes
  Gonadal dysgenesis
	Endocrine disorders
	  Primary hypothyroidism
	  Anterior pituitary insufficiency

Metabolic disorders
  Inborn errors of metabolism
  Renal tubular defects
	Organic hypopituitarism
	   Idiopathic hypopituitarism
	   Familial hypopituitarism
	   Psychosocial dwarfism

Skeletal disorders
  Chondrodystrophies
  Epiphyseal dysplasias
  Metaphyseal dysplasias
  Diseases of the spine
  Pseudo- and pseudopseudohypoparathyroidism
	Excessive androgen or estrogen production
	   with early epiphyseal fusion
	  Glucocorticoid excess
	  Insulin deficiency

Source: R. H. Williams, ed., *Textbook of Endocrinology,* 5th ed., Saunders, 1974.

Table 5.2.   Incidence of causes of short stature.

Cause	Male		Female		Total	
	No.	%	No.	%	No.	%
Constitutional delay	173	35	15	6	188	25
Familial short stature	43	9	38	15	81	11
Familial short stature and constitutional delay	32	6	—	—	32	4
Idiopathic hypopituitarism						
Multiple tropic hormones	40	8	10	4	50	7
Isolated growth hormone	8	2	—	—	8	1
Organic hypopituitarism	14	3	6	2	20	3
Gonadal dysgenesis	—	—	50	20	50	7
Psychosocial dwarfism	26	5	17	7	43	6
Chondrodystrophy	18	4	5	2	23	3
Primary hypothyroidism	7	1	11	4	18	2
Intrauterine growth retardation	15	3	16	6	31	4
Crohn's disease (+ steroids)	8	2	1	0.4	9	1
Crohn's disease (− steroids)	2	0.4	1	0.4	3	0.4
Steroid-induced short stature without Crohn's disease	4	0.8	—	—	4	0.5
Cushing's syndrome	1	0.2	2	0.8	3	0.4
Prader-Willi syndrome	3	0.6	—	—	3	0.4
Diabetes insipidus	4	0.8	—	—	4	0.5
Diabetes mellitus	1	0.2	6	2.4	7	0.8
Other	94	19	77	30	171	23
Totals	493	100	255	100	748	100

Source: R. H. Williams, ed., *Textbook of Endocrinology*, 5th ed., Saunders, 1974.

short stature. Many of the disorders given in Table 5.1 have their own subsidiary causes. This discussion will be restricted to a brief consideration of some of the more common causes of shortness.[1]

You will note that in Table 5.2 there are almost twice as many male (493) as female (255) cases. This in all likelihood is a reflection of greater parental concern about a boy being too short, because tall stature is more closely associated with images of masculinity. Adolescents themselves worry about stature, boys about being too short and girls about being too tall.

As Table 5.2 shows, a large proportion of children of short stature for whom treatment is sought have no endocrine or other physical abnormality. Twenty-five percent (35 percent of males, 15 percent of females) are short because of *constitutional delay.* In other words, they are late maturers who will catch up with their peers by the end of puberty (see Figure 2.8). Eleven percent are short because their parents and families tend to be short. In another 4 percent, constitutional delay and familial tendencies combine to produce shortness.

[1]For a detailed discussion of these conditions, see Williams (1974, chapter 26).

As a result, fully 40 percent of those seeking treatment are healthy, and nothing should or can be done about their stature.

Among endocrine disorders, the most prevalent cause of short stature is insufficiency of the anterior pituitary. The insufficiency may be organic, such as destructive lesions in the pituitary or hypothalamus, or idiopathic—that is, due to a cause that cannot be determined. Or it may be familial or psychosocial (a condition referred to in Chapter 2). The insufficiency may involve multiple tropic hormones or the growth hormone only (Goodman, Grumbach, and Kaplan 1968).

Pituitary insufficiency is the most frequent disorder underlying short stature in both sexes, but particularly males. Turner's syndrome is a form of gonadal dysgenesis that exclusively affects females and results from a chromosomal disorder that causes stunting of growth in addition to other abnormalities (Federman 1967).

Hypothyroidism, if untreated during the growing period, leads to marked stunting of growth. It also produces other effects, particularly in body proportions, whereas dwarfism due to other causes does not affect proportion (Figure 5.1).

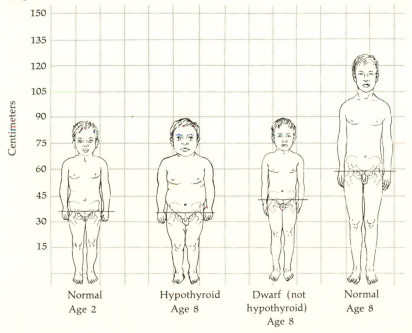

FIGURE 5.1
Comparison of normal boys, 2 and 8 years of age, respectively, with 8-year-old dwarfs. In normal boys, the ratio of upper to lower skeletal segments measured from the pubis symphysis (gray line) is 1.7/1 at birth and 1/1 at 10 years of age. The hypothyroid dwarf has the height and proportions of a 2-year-old, whereas dwarfs of pituitary or primordial types attain the more mature proportions of their chronological age. [Redrawn from L. Wilkins, *The Diagnosis and Treatment of Endocrine Disorders in Childhood and Adolescence*, 3d ed., Charles C Thomas, 1965.]

Most cases of hypothyroidism become manifest in infancy and are a result of iodine deficiency (endemic cretinism), inborn errors in the development of the thyroid gland, or failure to synthesize thyroid hormone (Van Wyk 1972).

There is also a rare, acquired form of juvenile hypothyroidism in which the thyroid gland becomes atrophied during puberty. The young girl portrayed in Figure 5.2 was apparently quite normal until age 9 when her thyroid gland began to fail with a concomitant slowing of growth in height and the gradual development of typical characteristics of severe hypothyroidism, or myxedema (Van Wyk 1972, p. 1075). (Note the response to treatment in the lower right-hand photograph.)

Precocious puberty, which will be discussed further on, also leads to stunting of growth. The excessive production of estrogen and, more important, androgen initially stimulates excessive growth but then enhances the epiphyseal fusion of long bones before adult stature is attained. In other words, when what would normally happen during puberty happens in childhood, the total growing period is accelerated, but also shortened.

Not all disturbances of growth involve disturbances of sexual maturation. For example, so-called primordial dwarfs, whose growth is insufficient for an unknown reason, reach puberty at the usual ages and undergo the normal changes, except to grow adequately in stature.

The treatment of short stature depends on the cause. Most cases either require no treatment or cannot be helped. Human growth hormone, which is in rare supply, is effective in cases of documented pituitary deficiency. Thyroid hormone is useful in primary hypothyroidism and if TSH is deficient in hypopituitarism. There are some cases for which the judicious use of estrogen, androgen, and other hormones may be effective.

The most tragic cause of all, severe malnutrition, which stunts the growth of millions of children in remote and forsaken parts of the world, as well as in metropolitan areas, should be the easiest to eradicate. Unfortunately, the prospects of relieving world hunger seem to grow dimmer with time.

Causes of Overgrowth

Overgrowth, as manifested in extremely tall stature, is usually genetically determined. Persons whose tallness is hereditary are normally proportioned and have no hormonal or other abnormalities related to their size. Because

---

FIGURE 5.2 (opposite)
The progressive effects of hypothyroidism. Height measurements from the school records of this girl show that thyroid malfunction began between age 9 and 10, but the full clinical picture required several more years to emerge. [From H. L. Barnett and A. H. Einhorn, eds. *Pediatrics,* 15th ed., 1972. Courtesy of Appleton-Century-Crofts, Division of Prentice-Hall, Inc., New York.]

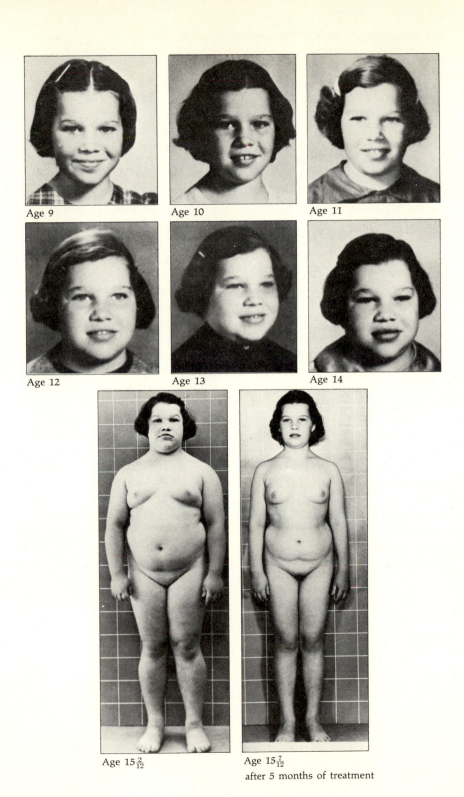

Age 9

Age 10

Age 11

Age 12

Age 13

Age 14

Age $15\frac{2}{12}$

Age $15\frac{7}{12}$

after 5 months of treatment

people tend to marry others of commensurate stature, these genetic traits continue to be perpetuated in families.

Occasionally, parents of ordinary stature will produce a giant. Such a person may be afflicted with *cerebral gigantism* in which the head is disproportionately large, with a high forehead and large eye sockets. Other characteristics of cerebral gigantism are very large, plump hands and feet, clumsy movements because of poor motor coordination, and slight mental retardation. There is no demonstrable hormonal disturbance nor other known cause for this clearly pathological form of gigantism (Prader 1974; Abraham and Snodgrass 1969).

Growth disturbances of pituitary origin are rare and are usually due to a hormone-producing tumor (eosinophilic adenoma). Children suffering from this condition present a very different picture from those who are large for their age for familial or constitutional reasons (de Majo and Onativia 1960).

The effect of excessive growth hormone production depends on whether the person is a child or an adult. Just as a deficiency in childhood results in dwarfism, an excess leads to gigantism. But given the fact that human long bones cannot grow after puberty, no amount of growth hormone will cause an adult to become a giant.[2] If excessive amounts are produced in adulthood, dramatic changes take place in the face, hands, and feet resulting in a condition called acromegaly (large extremities) (Figure 5.3).

The discovery of the role of the pituitary in gigantism is a fascinating story. The eighteenth-century London surgeon John Hunter was very keen on adding to his medical collection the skeleton of a contemporary Irish giant named Charles Byrne (reputedly 8 feet, 4 inches tall, but actually only 7 feet, 7 inches). The giant was horrified to learn of John Hunter's interest and instructed his friends that, on his death, his body be encased in lead and sunk at sea. Hunter nevertheless got the body by reportedly bribing the undertaker and added the skeleton to his collection. In 1909 (126 years later), Harvey Cushing, an eminent American neurosurgeon, examined the skull and, noting the enlargement and deformation of the bony cavity housing the pituitary, inferred that the giant must have been the victim of a pituitary tumor.[3]

PRECOCIOUS PUBERTY

Given the wide range of normal variation in the time of onset of puberty, a chronological definition of precocious puberty is necessarily somewhat arbitrary. Thus, given the fact that sexual development becomes evident in most

---

[2]In this regard, dachshunds are like humans: growth hormone in adults produces only an overgrowth of the skin. On the other hand, rats, which are capable of skeletal growth throughout life, respond with true gigantism even in adulthood.

[3]Another famous medical study is that of the Alton giant. See Behrens and Barr (1932).

FIGURE 5.3
The progression of acromegaly: (upper left) age 9, normal; (upper right) age 16, early coarsening of features; (lower left) age 33, acromegaly well established; (lower right) age 52, acromegaly in final stage, with gross disfigurement. [Clinical Pathological Conference, *Am. J. Med.* 20(1956):133. Photographs courtesy of William H. Daughaday, M.D.]

girls at about age 12 and in most boys at 13, comparable changes at age 8 or younger in girls and at age 9 or younger in boys are considered precocious (Bongiovanni 1972, p. 1122). Specific criteria are breast enlargement before age 8, adult pubic and axillary hair before age 9, and so on (Vaughan and McKay 1975).

For almost all children who undergo precocious puberty, there is no demonstrable abnormality in the nervous or endocrine systems (Wilkins 1965, p. 329). Many of these children are probably experiencing more extreme forms of early puberty. But, in a significant percentage, there are definite and often serious illnesses causing the precocity. In view of this, physicians carefully study all cases of premature sexual development so that pathological causes can be detected early and treated promptly.

Precocious puberty of all types is twice as common in girls as in boys. It is also usually a far less serious condition in girls than in boys: 80 percent of precociously pubertal girls have no concomitant illness, whereas 60 percent of such boys have serious organic disease. There are important differences in the ways in which organic causes are distributed in the two sexes. In girls, ovarian tumors account for 15 percent and intracranial lesions (such as brain tumors) for 4 percent of the cases. In boys, 20 percent are due to intracranial disorders, 25 percent to adrenal disorders, and less than 10 percent to testicular disorders (Reichlin 1974).

Table 5.3 contains a classification of the types of pubertal precocity. The first type is complete precocious puberty, in which the full range of pubertal changes take place, including maturation of the reproductive system with the production of sperm or ova as well as development of secondary sexual characteristics. In other words, pubertal development is complete but at an unusually early age (Figure 5.4). Menarche has been observed in the first year of life[4] and pregnancy has been reported as early as $5\frac{1}{2}$ years of age.[5] Penile development is known to have taken place in 5-month-old boys, and spermatogenesis in 5-year-old boys. In the nineteenth century, a boy reportedly fathered a child before he was 7 years old (Reichlin 1974, p. 812). In these situations, paternity is far more difficult to establish than maternity.

Of all cases of precocious puberty in girls, 85 percent are complete, whereas in boys only 35 percent are complete. In most cases, there is no demonstrable cause other than the presumably early triggering of the pubertal chain of events by the hypothalamus. In some of these cases, abnormal brain waves have been recorded, despite the absence of other neurological symptoms,

---

[4]The youngest case of puberty on record was reported in 1897: the girl had enlarged breasts and pubic hair at birth and menstruated at the age of six weeks (Wilkins 1965, p. 229).

[5]The youngest documented pregnancy is that of a Peruvian girl who started menstruating at 3 years of age, was impregnated at 4 years, 10 months; she delivered (by Caesarian section) a boy weighing $6\frac{1}{2}$ pounds on May 15, 1939, at age 5 years, 7 months [Escomel (1939) quoted by Wilkins (1965, p. 253)]. About eighteen cases of pregnancy have been reported in girls under 10 years of age.

Table 5.3. Classification of pubertal precocity.

Complete precocious puberty
  Activation of all levels, usually idiopathic or organic
  Central-nervous-system lesion

Incomplete precocious puberty
  Pubic-hair development (precocious adrenarche)
  Breast development (precocious thelarche)

Feminization of males
  Gynecomastia with:
    True precocious puberty
    Feminizing adrenal tumor
    Feminizing testicular tumor
    Seminiferous tubule disease (Klinefelter's syndrome)
    Exogenous estrogens

Masculinization of females
  Adrenal tumor or hyperplasia (in males or females)
  Arrhenoblastoma
  Exogenous androgens
  Constitutional (?)

Source: H. L. Barnett and A. H. Einhorn, eds, *Pediatrics,* 15th ed., 1972. Courtesy of Appleton-Century-Crofts, Publishing Division of Prentice-Hall, Inc.

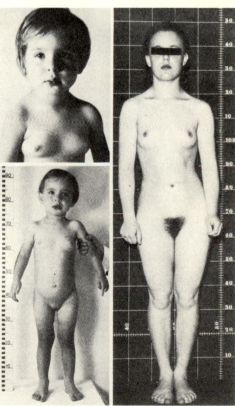

FIGURE 5.4
Idiopathic true precocious puberty in a girl: (left) $2\frac{1}{2}$ years of age (slight breast development, very little pubic hair, menarche); (right) at 13 years, 2 months, growth already terminated (epiphyseal fusion). [Adapted from A. Labhart, in *Clinical Endocrinology,* ed. A. Labhart Springer-Verlag, 1974.]

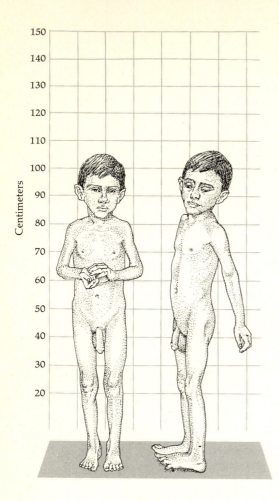

FIGURE 5.5
Precocious puberty due to a brain tumor in a boy aged 4 years, 1 month. [Adapted from L. Wilkins, *The Diagnosis and Treatment of Endocrine Disorders in Childhood and Adolescence,* 3d ed., Charles C Thomas, 1965.]

and there may well be other abnormalities that have not yet been discovered. In other cases, brain lesions have been shown to be the cause of premature stimulation of the hypothalamus. These lesions include tumors (such as hamartomas of the tuber cinereum), congenital brain defects (McCune-Albright syndrome), and postencephalic scarring following inflammatory disorders of the central nervous system (Figure 5.5) (Blunck 1975).

Complete precocious puberty can thus be the outcome of a variety of causes. If it is merely extremely early but normal maturation, the growing spurt is brief and rather short adults result. Such persons suffer from no apparent physical abnormalities, and, at the end of puberty, they may be indistinguishable from other adolescents.

There may well be, however, marked effects on their psychological development. Because they appear to be older than they actually are, more is often expected of them. This can be frustrating because they are not necessarily intellectually precocious as well. Precociously pubertal children may be made to feel like "freaks." Parents and teachers are often uncertain about how to relate to them and may require guidance (Ehrhardt and McCauley 1975). Sexual motivation seems to be rare in precocious girls (Jolly 1955), whereas precocious boys tend to have a greater capacity for sexual fantasy and arousal (Money and Alexander 1969).

Incomplete precocious puberty consists of isolated pubertal changes, such as the development of pubic hair (pubarche) or development of the breasts (thelarche) (Caprano et al. 1971; Altchek 1972; Jenner et al. 1972). Both occur more frequently in girls and are generally benign conditions. The enlargement of the breasts usually takes place between the first and third years of life, and only one of the breasts may develop. Although this may be an early sign of complete precocious puberty, more often it is a benign abnormality that disappears spontaneously. The premature development of pubic hair can be the first of a whole sequence of events, but, if it occurs in isolation, it has no pathological consequences unless the child or the parents become upset by it.

Both the complete and incomplete forms of precocious development described so far are referred to as "true" precocious puberty. They are due to abnormalities in the brain or premature activation of brain centers controlling the onset of puberty. Although anterior pituitary disorders might be expected to contribute to such development because spontaneous activation of gonadotropic production would result in true precocity, there are no known pituitary conditions that trigger these events prematurely. There is a malignant tumor (chorionepithelioma), which may develop almost anywhere in the body, that does produce gonadotropins, but its development in childhood is exceedingly rare.

Another form of disturbance is ovarian or testicular, in which excessive amounts of gonadal hormones are produced. Only the secondary sexual characteristics are affected, without reproductive maturation of the gonads and, hence, without ovulation or spermatogenesis. For this reason, such disturbances are called *precocious pseudopuberty*, or *pseudoprecocious puberty*. The feminization of males and the masculinization of females are of this type (Table 5.3).

In true precocity, the physical changes are always consistent with the person's sex—that is, girls develop breasts and boys grow facial hair as they normally would. The ovary and testes are simply secreting their usual hormones, albeit precociously. This type of precocity is, therefore, always *isosexual*.

In pseudoprecocious puberty, on the other hand, the gonadal sex hormones in prematurely high concentration may come from a variety of hormone-secreting tumors or through the ingestion of hormone-containing medications. The changes can be isosexual, but, because either sex may be subjected to the hormone of the opposite sex, from either an internal or an external source, such precocity can be "heterosexual." (The terms isosexual and heterosexual used in this regard should not be confused with the behavioral terms homosexual and heterosexual.) Thus, pseudoprecocious puberty can be androgenic or of estrogenic origin.

The most common source of excessive androgen production in childhood is the adrenal cortex. This may be due to a congenital condition of adrenal hyperactivity (congenital adrenal hyperplasia) or to androgen-producing tumors. In females, either cause results in heterosexual precocity or virilization consisting of early muscular development, growth of pubic hair, clitoral enlargement, and deepening of the voice. The same changes in males would be isosexual; they would be abnormal only because of their precocity.

Less common sources of abnormal androgen production are testicular tumors in males, which consist of androgen-producing interstitial cells. In females, there is a rare tumor of the ovary (arrhenoblastoma), which also produces androgen and leads to heterosexual precocity.

The accidental ingestion of androgenic hormones by children is unlikely because such compounds are not usually found around the house. But certain medications given to children may have similar effects.

Pseudopuberty of estrogenic origin may arise from estrogen-producing ovarian tumors in girls and from a rare tumor of the adrenal cortex in both sexes. These conditions will produce isosexual precocity in girls and heterosexual, or feminizing, changes in boys.

Estrogen is far more commonly ingested accidentally than androgen. For example, birth-control pills containing estrogen are found in the medicine cabinets of many homes. Exposure to estrogen from the absorption of estrogen-containing cosmetic creams through the skin is also common (Hertz 1958, fig. 3). Vitamin capsules have been found to be contaminated with sufficient estrogen (because of poor manufacturing processes) to produce clinical effects in children. Stilbestrol, which is one of the most widely used estrogens in medicines, typically produces marked pigmentation in nipples, which alerts physicians to its presence.[6]

DELAYED PUBERTY AND SEXUAL INFANTILISM

Whereas precocious puberty is a result of the untimely outpouring of sex hormones, puberty is delayed or even prevented from occurring if these hormones do not appear in sufficient concentrations when they should. As a

---

[6]For further discussion of sexual precocity, see Penny et al. (1970); Money (1970); Cloutier (1970); George (1970); McDonough (1971); and Reiter and Kulin (1972).

Table 5.4. Causes of sexual infantilism.

Hypothalamic lesions (tumors, cysts, congenital defects)
  Sexual infantilism without obesity
  Sexual infantilism with obesity, diabetes insipidus, etc.
    Froehlich's syndrome
    Lawrence-Moon-Biedl syndrome

Pituitary deficiency
  Generalized, with dwarfism
  Specific gonadotropic deficiency (pituitary eunuchoidism)
  Specific deficiency of ACTH

Primary gonadal disorders and gonadal dysgenesis
  Syndrome of gonadal aplasia and stunted growth
  Gonadal hypoplasia
  Gonadal dysplasia
  Primary testicular disorders
    Defective testes with germinal aplasia
    Defective testes with tubular fibrosis
    Anorchia
    Males with webbed neck resembling Turner's syndrome
  Prepubertal castration

Source: L. Wilkins, ed., *The Diagnosis and Treatment of Endocrine Disorders in Childhood and Adolescence,* 3d ed., Charles C Thomas, 1965.

result, most changes of puberty fail to occur when they should, including reproductive maturation and the development of secondary sexual characteristics.[7] If they fail to occur altogether, there is a marked underdevelopment of sexual characteristics in adulthood.

As with precocious puberty, the causes underlying delayed or impeded puberty may be at various levels of the neuroendocrine system and may result from different conditions (Root 1973*b*). But the frequency of interference at each station of the neuroendocrine relay differs for the two types of malfunctions. For example, whereas a pituitary disorder is virtually never the primary cause of precocity, it is a frequent cause of the failure of puberty. Tumors that cause precocity produce hormones, but tumors that lead to infantilism destroy the tissues that normally do so. Table 5.4 lists the causes of sexual infantilism and is presented mainly to convey an idea of the range of disturbances, most of which need not be discussed here.

Disturbances in the endocrine functions of the testes or the ovaries are classified as primary hypogonadism. If the gonads are normal, but the origin of

[7]For clinical purposes, puberty is considered delayed if secondary sexual characteristics have not begun to appear by age 14 in girls and by age 16 in boys (Prader 1974, p. 1054). Puberty is delayed in 25 out of 1,000 children (Illig 1975).

the pathology is in the pituitary or higher centers, it is classified as secondary hypogonadism.

Secondary hypogonadism results in an insufficiency of gonadotropins (Figure 5.6). It may be due to hypothalamic lesions or to primary disturbances of the anterior pituitary itself, including destructive lesions like cancer. In some cases, the pituitary hormones are biologically inactive. The release of normal hormones may be inhibited by emotional disturbances or their production suppressed through negative feedback by peripheral hormones that have been ingested or absorbed. It is also quite common to find no discernable cause for the pituitary malfunction (idiopathic hypopituitarism) (Blizzard 1972a, p. 1052).

Because the pituitary produces so many hormones, its malfunction is usually evident in childhood—one symptom being a failure to grow normally. Only occasionally is the deficiency isolated and found to involve only the gonadotropins, in which case the child appears to be normal until puberty, but fails to exhibit the pubertal changes that are normally effected by the actions of FSH and LH.

Primary gonadal malfunctions may result from various disturbances of the ovaries (Ross and Vande Wiele 1974; McDonald 1972) and the testes (Paulsen 1974). The gonads may have failed to develop, or be congenitally absent (aplasia), their development may be imcomplete (hypoplasia), or it may be abnormal (dysplasia). Genetic aberrations may be the cause of these disturbances. For example, the sex chromosomes of normal males consist of an X and a Y chromosome; the presence of an extra X chromosome (XXY) results in a pathological condition known as Klinefelter's syndrome. Normal females possess two X chromosomes; if one of the X chromosomes is missing (XO), a condition known as Turner's syndrome results. Both syndromes cause sexual infantilism.

Historically, the most famous exemplification of primary hypogonadism is the eunuch, who is a male castrated before puberty. The practice of castrating prepubescent boys goes back to ancient Egypt, China, and Rome (eunuch means "guardian of the bed" in Greek). As mentioned earlier, the castrati of eighteenth-century Italy were also prepubescent castrates.

Without testes, a prepubescent boy fails to undergo most of the changes of puberty, even though androgen is not entirely lacking owing to the production of testosterone by the adrenals. Having bypassed most of the changes of

---

FIGURE 5.6 (opposite)
Hypogonadotropic eunuchoid: (A, B, and C) pubertal development had not progressed past minimal pubic-hair growth by age 22; (D, E, and F) after 6 months of chorionic gonadotropic therapy, facial-hair growth is evident on the upper lip and penile growth has occurred (note the appearance of scrotal rugae); (G, H, and I) after 5 years of intermittent chorionic gonadotropic therapy, full sexual maturation has been achieved (note that testicular size is normal). [Adapted from R. H. Williams, ed., *Textbook of Endocrinology*, 5th ed., Saunders, 1975.]

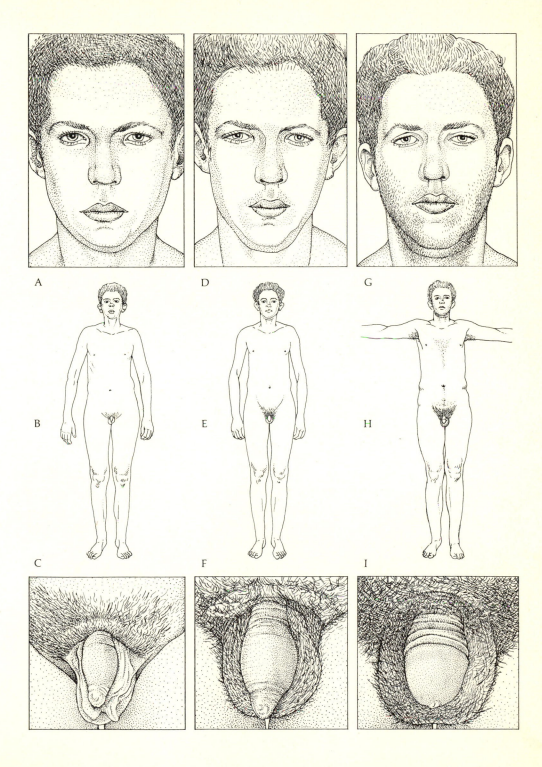

A   D   G

B   E   H

C   F   I

puberty, adult eunuchs tend to be tall men with poor muscular development, high-pitched voices, infantile genitalia, sparse or absent facial and body hair, and scant pubic and axillary hair. The reason they are tall is that the growth of long bones in not inhibited as it normally is by testosterone. The physical features shown in Figure 5.6 are similar to those characteristic of a prepubescent castrate. However, a castrated boy would not respond to treatment with gonadotropins; rather, treatment with testosterone would be required. Castration is no longer legally permitted in prepubescence, but, in adults, it is occasionally resorted to for medical reasons. In experiments with animals, castration has been an important research tool (Bermant and Davidson 1974).

COMMON AILMENTS

Adolescents are variously susceptible to countless ailments that also affect persons of other ages. It is not the purpose of this book to review everything from the common cold to rare and exotic diseases that affect youth. Instead, this discussion will be limited to a relatively small group of physical ailments that are of importance because they constitute particularly significant and common problems during adolescence.[8]

By the time a child reaches puberty, congenital defects he may have been born with have been generally long since apparent. The fact that a person has survived infancy and childhood is testimony to the basic soundness and resilience of his body.

The infectious and parasitic diseases that are common in childhood, especially in communities with inadequate medical facilities, become a far less serious problem during the second decade. A notable exception is tuberculosis, which is a serious health problem in adolescence. Although effective means of prevention and cure make pulmonary tuberculosis much less of a hazard now in developed and affluent countries, it remains a serious public health problem among the poor, particularly in less-developed countries.

Degenerative diseases, cardiovascular ailments, and cancer, which plague adults, do not afflict youth as much. As a result, one would expect the second decade of life to be one of physical rigor and good health and relatively free of illness and disability. This is generally so, except for several serious health problems and hazards: veneral diseases, accidents, and drugs. Venereal diseases in youth have reached epidemic proportions and account for half of

---

[8]For general sources on adolescent medicine, see Levine (1975); Garell (1973); Daniel (1970); World Health Organization (1965); Hambling and Hopkins (1965); Meiks and Green (1960); and Gallagher (1960). For more specialized sources, see Ford (1966) for neurology; Wilkins (1965) for endocrinology; and Altchek (1972c) for gynecology. Other specialized sources treat of particular symptoms: see, for example, Brunswick and Josephson (1972).

all the known cases in the United States today. Accidents, together with suicides and homicides, are the cause of more than 70 percent of all deaths between the ages of 15 and 19. Heroin was the leading cause of death among adolescents in New York City in 1969 and 1970. The major health problems among youth, then, are in a sense mostly self-inflicted. (Venereal and other diseases will be considered in this chapter. Accidents and drugs are dealt with in Chapter 6.)

GYNECOLOGICAL DISORDERS

Reproductive maturation in a young woman entails new physiological functions and malfunctions from which young men are exempt. This section deals, therefore, with physical ailments that affect only women.

Menstrual Dysfunction

Common pubescent menstrual problems are a failure to menstruate, excessive menstrual bleeding, premenstrual tension, and painful menstrual periods.

As discussed earlier, the initiation and sustenance of menstruation involve complex physiological changes and adjustments. Following menarche at age 12 or 13, the menstrual cycle takes a number of years to evolve into an adult pattern, and so a young woman's menstrual cycles are often quite irregular and she is not fully fertile until the end of the second decade. Such irregularities are not usually pathological. Occasionally, however, they are caused by conditions that need medical attention. The normal menstrual flow, which is the shedding of the uterine lining in response to a drop in estrogen and, specifically, progesterone levels, amounts to about 2 ounces. Uterine bleeding can also be caused by other mechanisms. If the endometrium is continually stimulated by an uninterrupted administration of progesterone or estrogen, bleeding will be erratic (progesterone breakthrough bleeding). Similarly, estrogen withdrawal and estrogen breakthrough bleeding may occur, forming the basis of early, nonovulatory (and therefore nonprogesterone-induced) menstrual cycles in pubescent girls.

Estrogen breakthrough bleeding, which can be heavy and prolonged, is the main cause of excessive uterine bleeding in puberty. Tumors of the uterus, although extremely rare in adolescent girls, also result in abnormal bleeding.

Occasional heavy menstrual bleeding does not produce ill effects. But repeated occurrences result in anemia, which must be corrected. Hormonal therapy can effectively check such menstrual dysfunction until the normal maturational process takes over.

Amenorrhea. The failure to menstruate is called amenorrhea. In primary amenorrhea, menstruation fails to occur. Secondary amenorrhea is the cessation of menses in a woman who has previously had normal menstrual periods. The causes of primary amenorrhea are mainly the same as those of sexual infantilism. Primary amenorrhea may also be due to a number of other very rare conditions that do not entail ovarian malfunction or any other disturbances of puberty. They include abnormalities of the genital tract, ranging from congenital absence of the uterus or vagina to simple blockage of the menstrual flow by an imperforate hymen. The virginal hymen normally has an opening to the outside that is large enough to admit a sanitary tampon without tearing. The imperforate hymen has no opening, so that, following menarche, the monthly menstrual discharge accumulates, creating a swelling. The condition is easily corrected surgically (Katchadourian and Lunde 1973, pp. 34–35).

Secondary amenorrhea during puberty results from various ailments that affect ovarian function after menarche. These ailments may be in the ovaries themselves or they may be in response to hypothalamic-pituitary distrubances. The menstrual cycle can also be disrupted by nutritional factors, by illness elsewhere in the body, by the use of drugs, such as tranquilizers, and, of course, by pregnancy.

The menstrual cycle is responsive to emotional states, and amenorrhea due to psychogenic causes is thought to be the most common form of amenorrhea in young women (Rakoff 1968). Acute emotional traumas induced by being raped or the sudden loss of a loved person can disrupt the cycle. Women with chronic psychiatric disturbances have a high incidence of menstrual disorders; the same is true during social upheaval, such as war.

Women who develop the conviction that they are pregnant when they are not will stop having periods. Not infrequently, intercourse without contraceptive protection will lead to a fear of pregnancy and a delay of the menses. Psychogenic factors can be so effective that hormonal abnormalities result, suggesting hypothalamic-pituitary malfunction (Koran and Hamburg 1975, p. 1681).

Menstrual-Cycle Distress. By far the most common disturbance of menstruation is the discomfort that precedes or accompanies menstrual bleeding. Discomfort ranges from minor inconvenience to acute disability, necessitating bed rest. The causes of these discomforts are not precisely known, but there is strong evidence that both physiological and psychological factors play important roles.

The symptoms of premenstrual tension are usually manifest during the few days preceding menstruation. They include pain in the lower back; a feeling of heaviness in the pelvic region, with or without an actual gain in weight due to fluid retention; headache; and a feeling of fatigue. Women, at this time, feel tense and are irritable and easily upset. They may be somewhat moody or even depressed.

Table 5.5.   Groups of premenstrual, menstrual, and intermenstrual symptoms.

Group 1: Pain
  Muscle stiffness
  Headache
  Cramps
  Backache
  Fatigue
  General aches and pains
	Group 5: Water retention
	  Weight gain
	  Skin disorders
	  Painful breasts
	  Swelling

Group 2: Concentration
  Insomnia
  Forgetfulness
  Confusion
  Lowered judgment
  Lowered ability to concentrate
  Distractible
  Accident-prone
  Lowered motor coordination
	Group 6: Negative effects
	  Crying
	  Loneliness
	  Anxiety
	  Restlessness
	  Irritability
	  Changes in mood
	  Depression
	  Tension

Group 3: Behavioral changes
  Lowered school or work performance
  Take naps; stay in bed
  Stay home
  Avoidance of social activities
  Lowered efficiency
	Group 7: Arousal
	  Feelings of affection
	  Orderliness
	  Excitement
	  Feelings of well-being
	  Bursts of energy; activity

Group 4: Autonomic reactions
  Dizziness; faintness
  Cold sweats
  Nausea; vomiting
  Hot flashes
	Group 8: Control
	  Feeling of suffocation
	  Chest pains
	  Ringing in the ears
	  Pounding of the heart
	  Numbness; tingling
	  Blind spots; fuzzy vision

Source: R. H. Moos, Typology of Menstrual Cycle Symptoms, *Am. J. Obstet. Gynecol.* 103(1969):390–402.

The symptoms of premenstrual tension may disappear as soon as bleeding starts, or they may merge with the symptoms of painful menstruation (dysmenorrhea). Dysmenorrhea can occur without being preceded by premenstrual tension. The discomforts at this stage consist of pain or cramps in the pelvic region, frequently accompanied by backache, headache, and nausea.

The foregoing symptoms are some of the more common ones, but more than 150 symptoms linked to the menstrual cycle have been identified (Moos 1969). Such symptoms do not occur randomly but are intercorrelated and can be grouped into several clusters (Table 5.5). The pain symptoms (Group 1) are usually associated with dysmenorrhea; the negative affects (Group 6) are more characteristic of premenstrual tension. The groups can be positively correlated (especially pain, concentration, behavior change, and negative affect): a woman who has some of the symptoms of one group will be likely to have some of the symptoms of the others.

About one out of three young women in the United States is bothered to some extent by menstrual-cycle distress, and it is severe enough to interfere with the daily activities of one out of ten women.

Menstrual disorders begin at an early age, but usually not right after menarche. They seem to be more characteristic of ovulatory periods. At any rate, if a woman has not begun to experience such discomfort by age 20 or so, she is unlikely to do so later on. Furthermore, in many cases, menstrual disorders tend to disappear after childbirth.

Additional circumstantial evidence for the stress that many women experience in connection with the menstrual cycle shows that premenstrual and menstrual periods coincide with a significant increase in the number of women admitted to hospitals for emergency treatment, absent from work because of illness, in accidents, admitted to psychiatric hospitals, attempting suicide, and engaging in disorderly conduct in prisons (O'Connor, Shelley, and Stern 1974).[9]

Such evidence is presented not to substantiate the traditional claim that menstruation is a "curse"; rather, the intent is to emphasize the fact that, at puberty, girls can be greatly affected by hormonal changes. Not only does the concentration of gonadal hormones increase, but a girl at puberty will have from 300 to 500 menstrual cycles in the next 30 to 40 years of her life (Tepperman 1973).

The behavioral implications of these biological events are not clearly understood. Knowing the pattern of menstrual distress that a woman experiences is useful in taking measures to cope with the discomforts. Medication to allay anxiety or depression can be used judiciously. Diuretics relieve water retention. If there are significant psychological conflicts over menstruation, their exploration may also be beneficial. The biological importance of these events need not detract from their psychological and social significance.

This discussion of menstrual distress is not intended to convey the erroneous idea that menstruation is an illness. It is a normal physiological function, and countless women experience no discomfort or interference with their occupational, recreational, or sexual activities. Some of the problems associated with menstruation are socially generated, and the fact that women have monthly periods is used, often covertly, to discriminate against them.

Vaginal Infections

Vaginal discharges (leukorrhea) and inflammation of the vagina and adjoining parts (vulvovaginitis) are fairly prevalent among young women.

---

[9]See also Dalton (1960, 1964a and b); Wetzel, Reich, and McClure (1971); and Janowsky et al. (1969).

There are numerous causes for these disorders, some of which are worth brief consideration (Orley et al. 1969).

For several months before menarche, there may be a whitish discharge from the vagina. This discharge is normal and, unlike pathological discharges, it is not irritating to tissues or malodorous, and disappears with the onset of menstruation (Altchek 1972*a*).

A common cause of vulvovaginitis is an infection by the fungus *Candida albicans.* Candidiasis is manifested by intense itching of the genitalia, which are red, swollen, and sensitive to physical contact. *C. albicans* can infect other parts of the body as well (Wittner 1972). The protozoan *Trichomonas vaginalis* is a common cause of leukorrhea, producing a profuse, yellowish, malodorous discharge accompanied by itching, a burning sensation, and pain of varying severity. Males may also harbor this organism, but usually without symptoms. Infections caused by both organisms can be readily treated medically, although they do tend to recur. Even though these conditions produce vaginal discharges and are transmitted by close contact, they should not be confused with gonorrhea, which also often produces a vaginal discharge.

Inflammation of the pubic region may be caused by the bite of crab lice (*Phthirus pubis*). Like venereal disease, infestation of pubic hair by lice is prevalent among youth, particularly if hygienic standards are lowered, sexual relations are indiscriminate, living quarters are crowded, and bedding and clothing are shared with others. The main symptom is itching. Crab lice can be effectively eliminated by appropriate chemical treatment.

Other causes of vaginal infections will be mentioned only briefly. Urethral inflammation may result from long bicycle rides, especially on racing-style seats. A forgotton or "lost" tampon in the vagina will produce a foul discharge, as can masturbatory objects. More commonly, deodorant sprays and other unnecessary "hygienic" preparations can elicit allergic reations. General cleanliness with the use of ordinary soap and water is often all that is required. Vaginal douches that are commercially prepared can also be harmful. Plain tap water that has been slightly acidified (two tablespoons of vinegar to a quart of water) is perfectly adequate and safe for douching.

Disorders in Pregnancy

An adolescent girl who becomes pregnant before she is 17 years of age is more susceptible to toxemias such as preeclampsia than an older woman; the younger the woman, the greater the risk (Battaglia, Frazier, and Hellegers 1963). Preeclampsia is characterized by hypertension, edema, and loss of proteins in the urine (which is why pregnant women must have their urine examined periodically). If the illness is not checked, it can progress to convulsions and coma (Israel and Wouteraz 1963). The risk of delivering a premature baby (whose weight is less than 2,500 grams) is twice as high in young women. Neonatal and infant mortality rates are also higher. Delivery itself presents no unusual problems for those above age 15, but younger women, not having completed their bone growth, may require delivery through Caesarian section because of a small pelvic outlet (Grant and Heald 1972).

Many of the disorders of pregnancy in a teen-age girl are the result of negligence and inadequate prenatal care. Adolescents who undergo abortions are also more likely to have problems because they wait too long before seeking medical care and they may be unsure of the length of the pregnancy, the sequence of their cycles, and so on (Hausknecht 1972).

VENEREAL DISEASES

The venereal diseases have been ungallantly named after Venus, the goddess of love, because their primary mode of transmission is through sexual activity. An alternative designation, sexually transmitted diseases (STD) has now been adopted by the World Health Organization (World Health Organization 1975b). There are a number of ailments included in this category, the two most important of which are syphilis, which is the most serious, and gonorrhea, which is the most common (see Box 5.1 on pages 146 and 147).[10]

Venereal diseases are a major public-health problem, particularly among youth. About half of the cases reported in the United States occur among persons who are younger than 25 (Johns, Sutton, and Webster 1975). About one in ten persons in this age group contract venereal diseases in a given year. An estimated two million people including 200,000 teen-agers, contract venereal diseases (usually gonorrhea) each year, making these infections only less common than the common cold. The highest rates of gonorrhea among women are at age 18. Because many cases of venereal diseases are not reported, the official figures do not indicate the actual number.

From a medical perspective, the epidemic proportions of venereal diseases are unwarranted, because there are very effective measures for its prevention and cure. Following the introduction of penicillin after the second world war, the occurrence of venereal disease steadily declined, especially syphilis: there were 100,000 reported cases in 1947, but only 6,250 in 1957 (Finberg 1972, p. 652). Unfortunately, as shown in Figures 5.7 and 5.8, this trend

---

[10]There is extensive literature on venereal diseases. All standard texts in internal medicine (Wintrobe et al. 1974), pediatrics (Vaughan and McKay 1975), dermatology (Stewart, Danto, and Stuart 1974), and communicable diseases (Hoeprich 1972) deal with them, as have numerous conferences and popular books (Keyl 1972; Brooks 1971). For a list of references on the behavioral aspects of venereal-disease control, see Darrow (1971).

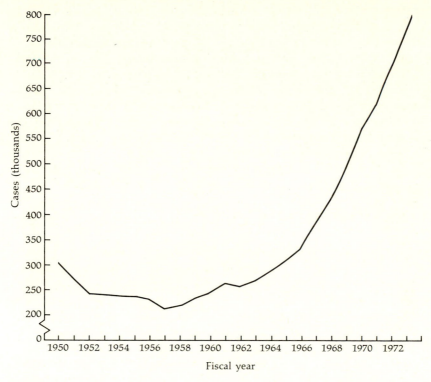

FIGURE 5.7
Cases of gonorrhea reported in the United States, 1950–1973. [Redrawn from American Social Health Association, *Today's VD Control Problem*, 1974.]

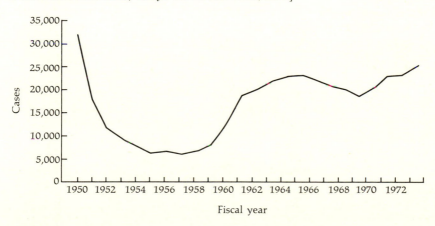

FIGURE 5.8
Cases of primary and secondary syphilis, reported in the United States, 1950–1973. [Redrawn from American Social Health Association, *Today's VD Control Problem*, 1974.]

BOX 5.1
Major sexually transmitted diseases (World Health Organization 1975a).

SYMPTOMS	DISEASE	PERIOD OF INCUBATION
Urogenital inflammation **In men** Urethritis (inflammation and purulent discharge from genital organ, pain on urinating, urine sometimes turbid). **In women** There is sometimes vaginitis (inflammation of the vaginal mucous membrane); however, urethritis may be present, contagious, and liable to complications without presenting any particular symptoms.	Gonococcal urethritis (gonorrhea): the throat, anus, and skin may be affected.	From 2 to 6 days.
	Nongonococcal urethritis due to *Mycoplasma*.	Uncertain (from 4 days to several months).
	Urethritis due to *Trichomonas vaginalis*.	From 3 days to 1 month.
	Urethritis due to *Chlamydia*.	Several days (often not known).
	Urethritis due to *Candida*. Balanitis (inflammation of the glans penis). Vaginitis.	From 3 days to 1 month.
Chancre Ulceration at the site of entry of the infection, usually in the genital region.	Syphilitic chancre with a hard base but painless, may occur in the anus, on the lips, tongue, or tonsils. It is followed by adenopathy (ganglions in the groin) if the chancre is genital.	**Chancre:** from 2 to 4 weeks, or more. **Secondary syphilis** (second stage if the primary stage was not treated): from 3 to 14 weeks. **Late syphilis:** from 5 years.
	Chancroid, painful with soft base, deep localized ulceration on genital organs, accompanied after several days by adenopathy of the groin, which may become ulcerated.	From 2 to 5 days.
Genital ulcerative lesions	Genital herpes.	From 2 to 7 days, sometimes more.
Adenopathy Growths in the lymphatic ganglions of the groin, with or without genital ulceration.	Lymphogranuloma venereum (Nicolas-Favre). Genital ulcerations. Adenopathy.	From 5 to 25 days, sometimes more.
	Granuloma inguinale (Donovan). A small, round-shaped tumor in the groin.	From a few days to several months.
	Adenopathy and enlargement of the spleen with fever.	

PATHOGENIC AGENT	COMMONEST COMPLICATIONS
A bacterium called gonococcus, or *Neisseria gonorrhoeae.*	**In men** Prostatitis. Epididymitis. Stricture. Sterility. **In women** Metritis of the cervix. Annexitis. Sterility. **In men and women** Arthritis. Dermatitis. Conjunctivitis of the newborn.
Bacteria known as *Myco-plasma* (strain T and *M. hominis*). A protozoan (unicellular parasite) *Trichomonas vaginalis.*	**In women** Salpingitis. Miscarriage. Puerperal infections (affecting women in childbirth). **In men and women** Salpingitis, Epididymitis.
Chlamydia (micro-organism similar to the rickettsia, responsible for urogenital and ocular infections).	Reiter's syndrome (conjunctive-urethrosynovial). Arthritis. Uveitis (eye inflammation). Valvular lesions of the heart and cardiac insufficiency.
A yeast (unicellular fungus) called *Candida albicans.*	Cystitis (inflammation of the bladder). Endometritis (inflammation of the internal mucosa of the uterus).
Treponema pallidum (treponeme), a micro-organism of the spiro-chete family (long, flexible, and undulating.	Skin and mucous, nervous, or abdominal complaints. Death of fetus. Congenital syphilis.
A bacterium, *Hemophilus ducreyi* (Ducrey's bacillus).	Destruction of tissue. Suppurative disorders and lesions of the lymphatic ganglions (adenopathies).
Herpes virus type II.	Meningo-encephalitis (infection of newborn). Cancer of the cervix.
Chlamydia.	Ulcerative lesions of the genital organs. Adenopathies. Strictures.
A bacterium, *Calymma-tobacterium granulomatis* (Donovania granulomatis).	Ulcerations in the genital region and groin. Lesions of the bone.
Cytomegalovirus of the herpes virus group.	Transmission to the child through the placenta. Nervous disorders.

has been reversed, and the incidence of both syphilis and gonorrhea has sharply increased.

The increase is attributed to a number of causes, including promiscuity, a decrease in the use of condoms (owing to an increase in the use of oral contraceptives), and the appearance of penicillin-resistant strains (some of them brought back by Vietnam veterans). The incidence of venereal diseases among homosexuals has increased to an even greater extent, particularly among males, who tend to have more frequent contacts.

Gonorrhea

Gonorrhea is an illness known to have existed for a long time. It was named by the second-century Greek physician Galen, who used the term to mean "flow of semen" because he confused the gonorrheal discharge with involuntary loss of seminal fluid. The colloquial term for it is "clap" (from the French word *clapier* for brothel) (Johnson 1972).

Gonorrhea is caused by a coffee-bean-shaped bacterium (*Neisseria gonorrhoeae*), named after A. L. S. Neisser who discovered the organism in 1879. This organism can survive and multiply only in the human body, so that transmission requires contact with infected mucous membranes, usually those of the genital tract. The infection cannot be transmitted by toilet seats.

The symptoms of gonorrhea usually appear from several days to a week or so after exposure. But they may also appear as early as one day and as late as three weeks after infection. The first and most common symptom in males is a yellowish purulent discharge from the urethra, which is the primary site of infection. An infected person may note the pus coming out of his penis or note its staining. This discharge is sometimes confused with nocturnal emissions, but burning, stinging, and itching sensations at the time of urination are indications that something is wrong. This is further substantiated by general symptoms of discomfort, fever, and fatigue (Holmen and Beaty 1974).

With treatment, almost all cases of gonorrhea can be cured promptly. If the disease is not treated, the acute symptoms continue for a month or so and then either subside or persist in chronic form. The infection may spread to the rest of the genital tract, to the joints, and in some cases to the valves of the heart. The resultant scarring in the reproductive system often leads to sterility. Even though chronic symptoms are not particularly bothersome and an infected person feels well, he may go on infecting others as long as he remains untreated.

In females, the uterine cervix is usually the first site of gonorrheal infection. Early symptoms tend to be milder than those in males, consisting of only a thin vaginal discharge, or there may be no symptoms at all. Because of this, and because there are other common forms of vaginal discharge, women are less likely to become aware of being infected and may remain an unwitting source of transmission to others. Meanwhile, in untreated cases, gonorrhea is likely to spread throughout the reproductive organs—accompanied by acute symptoms of pelvic pain, fever, and vomiting—and eventually cause scarring of the fallopian tubes, which results in sterility. Women are also subject to the same joint and heart complications as men.

Kissing does not entail risk of infection, but pharyngeal and rectal gonorrhea occur among male homosexuals. The former is manifested by symptoms of sore throat with fever and enlarged cervical lymph nodes (Fiumara 1971). Rectal gonorrhea results in itching and anal discharge, but may be quite mild (Schrocter 1972).

Gonorrhea can usually be prevented by the use of condoms (but not cervical diaphragms) and by careful washing of the genitals with bactericidal soap or solutions after coitus. Prophylactic use of appropriate antibiotics within several hours of exposure is also effective. Unlike syphilis, gonorrhea cannot be detected by a simple blood test.

In giving birth, an infected mother may transmit gonorrhea to the baby's eyes, resulting in a serious condition called gonorrheal ophthalmia neonatorum. This used to be a common cause of blindness, but, currently, penicillin ointment or silver nitrate drops effectively prevent such infection (Apt and Breinin 1972).

Syphilis

Syphilis is one of the most interesting diseases in the annals of medicine. The fact that syphilitic lesions have been found in the bones of pre-Columbian Indians but not in the ancient skeletons from other continents has suggested that the disease was brought into the Old World from the West Indies. This is further substantiated by the outbreak of a highly virulent epidemic in Europe shortly after the return of Columbus from Haiti in 1493. The epidemic coincided with the invasion of Italy by the French army in 1494 (Holmes 1974).

The microorganism causing syphilis was not identified until 1905, and its treatment was tedious and painful until the discovery of penicillin several decades ago.

Syphilis is relatively less common but far more serious than gonorrhea. It is caused by a corkscrew-shaped microorganism (*Treponema pallidum*). Its first manifestation is usually a hard, round ulcer with raised edges, which appears from two to four weeks after contact and at the site of contact, most often somewhere in the genital area (Figures 5.9 and 5.10). This *chancre* is usually painless and tends to disappear in a few weeks, even without treatment, before any significant damage has occurred or before infecting others in turn.

If the disease is not treated in its primary stage, the secondary stage of syphilis becomes apparent after a few weeks, most often in the form of a gen-

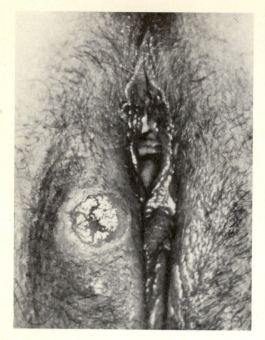

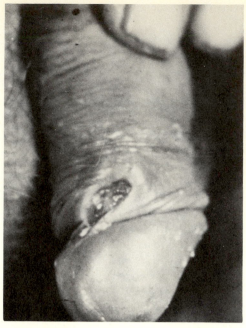

FIGURE 5.9
Chancre on female external genitalia. [From
R. S. Weiss and H. L. Joseph, *Syphilis.* © 1951
The Williams and Wilkins Company.]

FIGURE 5.10
Chancre on the penis. [From A. I. Dodson and
J. E. Hill, *Synopsis of Genitourinary disease,* 7th ed.,
Mosby, 1962.]

eralized skin rash, which also is transient. There may be additional symptoms, such as headache, fever, sore throat, and aches and pains.

If the condition is not treated in its secondary stage, it becomes latent and may remain so for many years, while causing extensive damage to many vital organs (Holmes 1974). So pervasive are the effects of syphilis when they become manifest again in the tertiary stage that syphilis has been called the "great imitator" for the way in which it mimics many other illnesses.

About half of all untreated syphilitics suffer the ravages of tertiary syphilis, which often affects the cardiovascular and central nervous systems, resulting in neurological, mental, and other disorders. Treatment can be effective even at this stage, although the damage done to the brain or the vascular system may be irreversible.

Syphilis is also transmittable to fetuses. During the early stages of syphilis, an untreated mother runs a 95-percent risk of infecting her unborn child with serious consequences, including death of the infant (Finberg 1972, pp. 652–658).

From a public-health perspective, syphilis has the advantage of being detectable by means of simple blood tests. But condoms are not as effective in preventing syphilis as they are in gonorrhea because syphilitic lesions may be on sites other than the penis.

Because of the social stigma, many infected people do not seek treatment; if they do, their cases may not be reported to public-health authorities, which is necessary if their sexual contacts are to be located and treated. Figure 5.11 summarizes an analysis of an outbreak of syphilis in a southwestern urban area.

Moral considerations have sometimes complicated the control of venereal disease. To some people, it seems like well-deserved punishment for promiscuity. Moral considerations may be central to sexual activity, but to use venereal

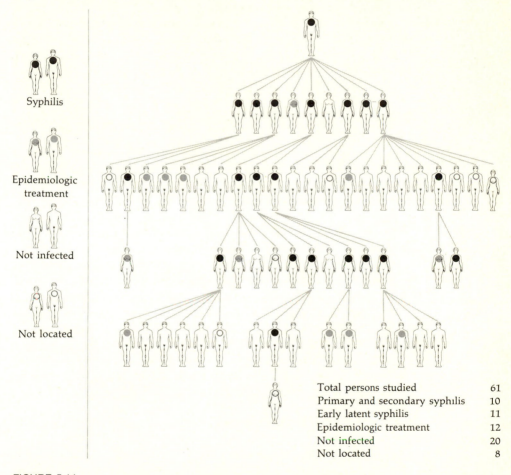

Total persons studied	61
Primary and secondary syphilis	10
Early latent syphilis	11
Epidemiologic treatment	12
Not infected	20
Not located	8

FIGURE 5.11

An analysis of an outbreak of syphilis. The disease was introduced into a southwestern urban area by one person and 33 people were known to be subsequently infected; the spread of the disease was brought under control through treatment by health officials. [Adapted from American Social Health Association, *Today's VD Control Program*, 1972.] In another study, 1,639 people were found to have become infected from just one source (*World Health Organization* 1975b).

disease as a moral club is neither effective nor ethical. People forget that countless innocent spouses and children also get penalized as long as the disease is around. Besides, it is usually the poor, the ignorant, and the young who are less likely to seek treatment.

Attitudes toward venereal disease range from one extreme to the other. Some people are both careless and callous. The decision to engage in sexual activity should be based on more than just health considerations, but the threat of illness should also be taken into account, especially by those having numerous sexual partners. At the other extreme, it is possible to develop a morbid fear of venereal disease. Not every itch and discharge are indications of gonorrhea, nor do every sore and pimple signify syphilis. When in doubt, medical advice should be sought. Venereal disease is an illness like any other illness, and in almost all communities there are physicians and agencies that are willing and able to treat it discreetly and effectively.

EATING DISORDERS

Puberty is normally accompanied by increased nutritional needs, as discussed in Chapter 2 and illustrated in Figure 3.15. But, apart from the obvious fact that adolescents eat more in response to higher caloric requirements, psychological and social factors also exert significant influences on adolescent eating patterns. The consumption of food may be linked to emotional needs and conflicts. Eating certain foods may become part of the routine of spending time at the local ''hangout,'' often a hamburger ''joint'' or ice cream parlor.[11]

Many adolescents consume large quantities of high-caloric foods in addition to what they eat at home, thus becoming prone to gain excessive weight. Or, they may subsist on select foods to the relative exclusion of more balanced diets, becoming subject to deficiency in proteins or vitamins.

Most adolescents develop into adults without serious eating disturbances; that is, they conform to national adult norms in this regard, even though these norms may not be optimal from a health perspective. A significant number, however, suffer from eating disorders, usually producing obesity.

Obesity

Obesity is a complex and poorly understood problem that is difficult to remedy (Stunkard 1975). It has well-established patterns linked to biological, psychological, and social factors. The two major epidemiological variables

---

[11]In one study, the ten most-liked foods were found to be: carbonated soft drinks, milk, steak, hamburgers, pizza, chicken, french-fried potatoes, ice cream, spaghetti, and orange juice. The foods most disliked were: liver, fish, squash, clams, coffee, spinach, cabbage, and beets.

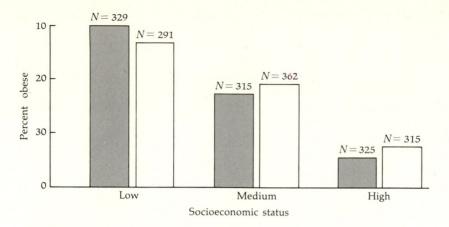

FIGURE 5.12
The prevalence of obesity among women in a large American city decreases as
socioeconomic status increases. The socioeconomic status of origin (solid bars) is
almost as strongly linked to obesity as is a person's own socioeconomic status
(shaded bars). [Redrawn from P. B. Goldblatt, M. E. Moore, and A. J. Stunkard,
Social Factors in Obesity, *J. Am. Med. Assoc.* 192(1965):1039. Copyright 1965, American
Medical Association.]

associated with it are social class and age. Obesity is six times as common
among women of low socioeconomic status than among those of high status.
A similar rate applies to men (Goldblatt, Moore, and Stunkard 1965). As shown
in Figure 5.12, the social class of origin is almost as closely linked to obesity
as is a subject's own social class. Between childhood and middle-age, there
is a steady, general increase in the prevalence of obesity; between the ages
of 20 and 50, the increase is threefold (Moore, Stunkard, and Srole 1962).

Criteria for obesity vary and are culturally determined. For clinical purposes,
those who are 10 percent above the mean weight for their height are considered
overweight; those 20 percent above the mean are *obese.* By these criteria,
obesity is the most prevalent eating disorder at all ages, including puberty.
About 10 percent of grade-school children and from 10 to 15 percent (or by
some estimates as many as 30 percent) of high-school students are obese
(Paulsen 1972, p. 215).

At birth, the weights of future obese and nonobese children do not differ. But,
at 1 year of age, such differences become discernable (Heald and Hollander
1965). This first childhood obesity continues to age 4 and is followed by a
second between ages 7 and 11 (Mossberg 1948). The pattern is thus set quite
early: 80 percent of overweight children remain so in adult life and comprise
50 percent of the markedly obese adult population (Paulsen 1972, p. 215).

There are numerous unanswered questions about the mechanisms controlling appetite and the causes of obesity. Caloric intake and expenditure

are highly relevant, but simple balance sheets relating these factors do not provide sufficient explanation. Genetic factors affect the efficiency of energy utilization and the regulation of appetite and metabolic processes. Even the number of fat cells varies and is established in childhood (Hirsch and Knittle 1970). In short, no one grows obese on thin air, but not all who eat a lot become overweight (Sims et al. 1968).

The psychological and social factors that promote and complicate obesity are just as complex. Western society is generally disapproving and contemptuous of obesity. Aesthetic norms, especially for middle-class women favor the slender person. These social norms and departures from them become especially significant for the adolescent's self-esteem. The psychological tasks of adolescence may thus become hampered by obesity and, in turn, interfere with efforts to control it.

It is necessary, furthermore, to differentiate psychological factors that lead to overeating from the psychological effects of being overweight and the additional impact of attempts at dieting. Because the causes of obesity are many and unclear, the control of the problem is unusually difficult. Overweight persons are thus in a position to refuse to accept responsibility for their actions on one hand, or to feel unnecessarily guilty on the other. The agonies that some adolescents experience in this regard may make conflicts over sexuality seem frivolous by comparison. What is frequently not fully realized is that the problem of overweight has ramifications that go far beyond the simple balance sheets of caloric intake and expenditure. Eventually, it has to be resolved in the context of an adolescent's overall relationship to himself and to others in his world. Eating should be integrated into an overall scheme that includes what a person derives satisfaction from, how much his health matters to him, and how important his physical appearance is to others.[12]

Undernutrition

Although obesity is, by far, the more frequent problem, its opposite, malnutrition, is also encountered in adolescence. A serious problem is malnutrition due to poverty. In addition to the traditional poor, youth among the "street people" may also suffer from malnutrition as a result of poverty, being distracted by drugs, self-neglect, and so on.

Selective nutritional deficiencies may arise from poorly balanced diets determined by a narrow range of food preferences, aversions to a large class of nutritious foods, or austere diets based on religious fasting or crash programs

---

[12]For further sources on adolescent obesity, see Bruch (1971) and Hammar et al. (1972). For general sources on obesity, see Bruch (1973) and Stunkard (1975).

to lose weight. As a result of recent interest in Eastern religions, "organic" foods, and the food habits of less-industrialized cultures, some adolescents have taken to devising their own food regimens. Some of these regimens are as good, if not better, than what they would ordinarily eat. But others are inadequate because more attention has been paid to the trappings than to the substance of these alternative diets (Frankle and Heussenstamm 1974).

Some exotic diets may actually be harmful. Serious medical warnings have been issued, for example, against Zen macrobiotic diets. Originated by Georges Ohsawa, this dietary regimen comprises a series of diets, the "highest" level of which consists only of cereals and purportedly not only leads to the best of health, but also cures cancer, mental disease, heart trouble, and so on. Instead, the result seems to be scruvy, anemia, hypoproteinemia, hypocalcemia, emaciation, and other forms of malnutrition. Because fluids are also restricted, there have been cases of loss of kidney function leading to death (Council on Foods and Nutrition 1971).

Appetite is subject to mood as well as to physiological hunger. Mood changes in response to external events or intrapsychic states often influence eating habits. There are no fixed associations, however, and apparently the same state of mind will lead one adolescent to raid the refrigerator and another to skip his dinner.

Such minor fluctuations are a part of normal life. But, in some cases, emotional problems lead to a serious and sustained loss of appetite or refusal to eat. Although this may occur in many psychiatric states, it is most severe in a condition known as anorexia nervosa, which is characterized by extreme loss of weight (as much as 50 percent of normal body weight). It is accompanied by a number of other symptoms, including amenorrhea. Paradoxically, instead of feeling weak, the patients tend to be hyperactive.

Anorexia nervosa was first described in the second half of the sixteenth century; yet its precise course remains obscure. It is generally assumed to be of psychogenic origin, but some claim that it is somatogenic as well (Ushakov 1971, p. 289). There is no doubt about its profound somatic effects and its 10-to-15-percent mortality rate.

Anorexia nervosa is predominantly an illness of adolescent girls. Typically, a girl begins to lose weight with a self-imposed diet obstensibly for aesthetic reasons, even though she does not seem to be overweight to others. This leads to a progressive restriction of food, followed by a fear of eating and preoccupation with food, diet, and related functions. Such patients tend to deny any awareness of their emaciated state, and the associated psychological symptoms vary widely from relatively mild neurotic symptoms to severe psychotic reactions.[13]

---

[13]For further sources, see Langford (1972); Bruch (1973); and Bliss (1975).

OTHER DISORDERS COMMON TO ADOLESCENCE

A number of other disorders are worth brief consideration. They do not complete the list of illnesses suffered during puberty, but rather are representative of the kind of medical problems adolescents have to contend with.

Acne

The most common disorder of medical significance in puberty is acne (acne vulgaris), or "pimples" (Arundel 1971) (Figure 5.13). Because many teen-agers are affected by it to some extent (Figure 5.14), this condition seems

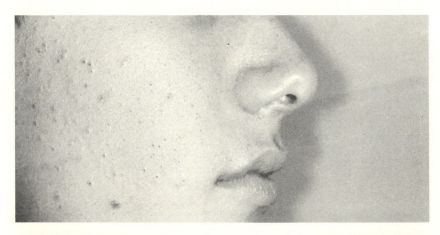

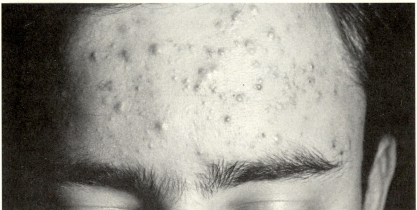

FIGURE 5.13
Acne: papular pustules and comedones. [From W. D. Stewart, J. L. Danto, and S. Maddin, *Dermatology,* 3d ed., St. Louis, 1974, The C. V. Mosby Co.]

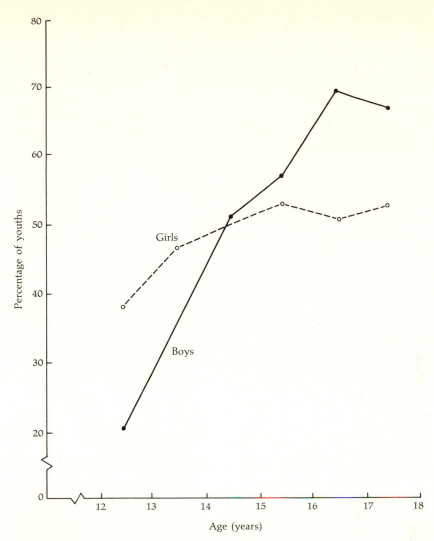

FIGURE 5.14
Percentage of U.S. youths reporting acne, pimples, or blackheads, by age and sex. [Redrawn from U.S. National Center for Health Statistics, *Vital Health Stat.* ser. 11, no. 147, 1975.]

like a normal event of puberty. Nevertheless, it is a source of considerable concern and may be mildly disfiguring. The earlier the onset, the more severe acne is likely to be. The worst age for acne is between 14 and 17 for girls and 16 and 19 for boys (Burgoon 1975).

Comedones (blackheads), papules (which are inflamed), pustules (which contain pus), and cysts exist in various numbers and combinations in a given case of acne (McGuire 1972, p. 1814).

The predisposition to acne is enhanced by androgens (Stewart, Danto, and Stuart 1971). This is why it is more common among boys, rare among children, and nonexistent among eunuchs. Androgens cause hypertrophy and hyper-secretion of the sebaceous glands in the skin. When a plug of sebum and keratin block the opening of the hair follicle, a comedo is formed. The surrounding tissue reacts to the comedo or to the products that have accumulated behind the blockage, and the result is an inflammatory papule, which may subside or progress to a pustule. Two microorganisms *(Corynebacterium acnes* and *Staphylococcus albus)* probably participate in this process (Shehadeh and Kligman 1963).

The lesions of acne are usually on the face, upper chest, back, and shoulders or they may be restricted to one site, such as the forehead. Acne usually clears with the termination of puberty, which suggests that perhaps hormonal changes and imbalance rather than simply an increase in androgens are responsible. Acne is also noted to be more severe among girls with highly irregular menstrual cycles.

Adolescents spend more than $40 million a year for "over the counter" acne preparations (Arundel 1971). Yet, there is no convincing evidence that even medical treatment shortens its course or cures it. What a teen-ager should do is keep his skin clean with soap and water, avoid using creams and oily preparations, and promptly seek medical treatment if acne develops.

The purpose of treatment is to attenuate the process and prevent scarring caused by the large pustules and cysts that erode the skin. To this end, various chemical agents and antibiotics have been used internally or applied to the skin. Sunlight can benefit acne, but the humidity and heat of summer tend to worsen it. Ultraviolet light used with precaution can be useful.

It often takes superhuman effort not to squeeze and handle pimples, but the extrusion of comedones or aspiration of pustules is better done either by a physician or under medical guidance. Dietary restrictions may be helpful if individualized. The person affected is often the best judge of what seems to exacerbate the condition. Foods that are usually bad for acne are those with a high fat content, such as pork, french-fried potatoes, potato chips, chocolate, nuts, and milk. Sometimes the simple expedient of brushing hair away from the forehead may be helpful. Scarring can be remedied by various plastic procedures.

Infectious Mononucleosis

Infectious mononucleosis is neither as grave as it may sound, nor is it particularly infectious. It is probably caused by a virus. The disease is most often contracted by older children, adolescents, and young adults. It usually occurs sporadically, although epidemics have been known in orphanages and schools. Peak incidence is in the spring and autumn.

Following an incubation period ranging from four to fourteen days, the disease may start in acute form with loss of appetite, malaise, fever, sore throat, and enlargement of lymph nodes, especially in the neck. Or, the onset may be more insidious, with feeling tired and listless. Other signs include enlargement of the spleen, characteristic changes in certain cells of the blood, and a positive response to special laboratory tests. Additional symptoms may arise if the liver, skin, and the central nervous system are affected.

The illness usually lasts several weeks and the prognosis is generally excellent, although occasional fatalities have been known. Therapy is symptomatic (Krugman 1972; Blattner 1975).

Epilepsy

Seizure disorders have been known since antiquity. The Greeks and Romans considered epilepsy a sacred disease, even though Hippocrates disputed its divine orgins. Certain forms of seizure are so dramatic that they continue to awe people. There is also an unwarranted stigma attached to the illness.

Epilepsy (from the Greek word for "to seize"; hence, "seizure," "fit," "spell") has many forms. A seizure, as such, is not a disease, but a symptom caused by an abnormal neuronal discharge in the brain. The resultant manifestations depend on the location of the discharge and its pattern of spread. They may consist of motor activities (tonic and clonic contractions), abnormal sensory experiences, a change in the state of consciousness, and a wide variety of other abnormal manifestations (Baird 1975). The term epilepsy is used if seizures are chronically recurrent. Frequently, no specific structural lesion can be demonstrated in the brain, despite the dysrhythmia evident on electroencephalograms (EEG).

The actual prevalence of epilepsy has not been definitively established, but it certainly ranks high among chronic disorders with an estimated 17 million cases in the United States (about 1 in 100 persons or 5 in 100 children) (Chao 1972).

Most epileptics have their first seizure before age 20. Certain forms of epilepsy (*petit mal* seizures) tend to disappear with the approach of puberty so that the most common type in adolescents is the *grand mal* form, characterized by major, generalized convulsions.

Currently, between 50 and 60 percent of the cases of epilepsy can be controlled with drugs. However, control is more difficult at the time of puberty. Adolescent girls may experience more seizures before their menstrual periods. The hormonal imbalance, physiological adjustments, the stress of psychological conflicts, family problems, and other factors may also contribute to the intensification of seizure activity.

Epilepsy, as such, is neither a crippling nor a debilitating illness. But, it can be hard on adolescents because of the restrictions it imposes. Thus, along with the proper medical treatment, it is necessary to help an afflicted young person make the psychological adjustments entailed.

The restrictions arise from the risk of seizures, which would be dangerous under certain circumstances. An epileptic may have to forego driving cars or motorcycles, along with sports like mountain climbing. Other activities, like swimming, may be undertaken in responsible company and with due precautions. Certain occupations requiring the operation of machinery may have to be ruled out. In short, the fact that an epileptic may unexpectedly lose consciousness must be taken into account in work and in play. Yet, such limitations notwithstanding, an active and full life is not outside the realm of possibility.

Girls who are epileptic may worry about pregnancy, which, in fact, may increase seizures, but it is possible to adjust the administration of anticonvulsant drugs to counter this possibility. Although certain convulsive disorders have some genetic basis, the added risk is not sufficient to bar epileptics from parenthood.

Diabetes

Diabetes (diabetes mellitus) is another disease that has been known since classical times. It is a chronic illness that involves a complex disturbance of carbohydrate metabolism. In many cases, it eventually damages the circulatory system, which results in a wide variety of symptoms, depending on the sites and the severity.

Most probably a genetic abnormality underlies this illness (Drash 1975). The disease manifests itself in childhood or adult life. Until 1914, the life expectancy of a child diabetic was only one year after the onset of the illness. With the development of dietary programs and the discovery of insulin in 1921, and subsequent refinements in treatment, juvenile diabetics now have a far better chance of surviving and leading reasonably normal lives.

Currently, the prevalence of juvenile diabetes in the United States is estimated at 40 cases per 100,000 persons 15 years of age and younger. About 10,000 new cases appear each year. Among juvenile diabetics, 40 percent develop their symptoms between the ages of 10 and 15. The ages at which the onset of illness is most likely to occur are 6 (starting school) and 12 (entering puberty) (Weil and Kohrman 1972).

Juvenile diabetes has an acute onset and the most common symptoms are excessive urination (polyuria), excessive thirst (polydipsia), and excessive appetite (polyphagia). Despite overeating, a diabetic loses weight, tires easily, and becomes lethargic. If the disturbed metabolic processes are not brought under control progressively, rather serious complications arise.

Once the acute phase has been brought under control, a young diabetic faces a lifelong process of keeping the illness under control, for there is no cure as yet. Such control is aimed at keeping the blood sugar at normal levels by dietary regulation and the injection of insulin. The blood sugar is monitored by testing the urine for carbohydrates. All of these control measures can eventually be taken over by the young diabetic under medical supervision.

Food intake, physical activity, and emotional states affect the level of blood sugar. With the onset of puberty, there is a marked increase in insulin requirements, which eventually taper off and become stabilized. From then on, the body should have neither too little or too much insulin; otherwise, the amount of sugar in the blood will increase (hyperglycemia) or decrease (hypoglycemia) with numerous consequences.

Although treatment is rigorous, many juvenile diabetics learn to manage very well with competent guidance. But problems often arise if an adolescent rebels against the regimentation, the food restrictions, or the routine of urine tests. The presence of a chronic illness thus leads to psychological problems and the temptation to use it as a weapon against others or as a means of punishing oneself (Bennett and Johanssen 1954).

ALLERGIES

The term *allergy* was coined by a pediatrician named C. von Pirquet to designate the changed reactivity that develops in an animal following contact with chemical substances foreign to the body. Pirquet noted that, once the allergic state had developed, subsequent contact with the foreign substance led either to a state of immunity, which is a condition favorable to the host, or to a state of hypersensitivity, which is harmful (Ellis 1972*a*). Currently, the term is used in a more restrictive sense for reactions of clinical hypersensitivity that result in illness.

The chemical substances that are responsible for allergic reactions are called allergens. Both the nature and the severity of the allergic reactions they produce cover a broad range. Some types of reactions amount to no more than a mild itch or a short bout of sneezing; others are severe and may result in death.

Potential allergens include countless substances in foods, in the air (such as pollens), or associated with pets. Some, like poison ivy or poison oak, affect large numbers of people; others are far more specific and trouble only a few.

There are many conditions that are thought to be produced by allergies, but some of the more common illnesses known to have an allergic basis are

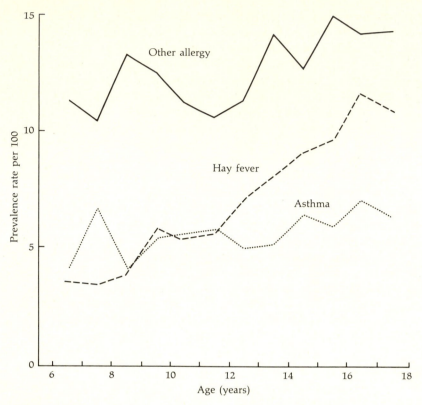

FIGURE 5.15
Prevalence rates for reported symptoms of hay fever, asthma, or other allergies for
U.S. children from 1963 to 1965 and for youths from 1966 to 1970. [Redrawn from
U.S. National Center for Health Statistics, *Vital Health Stat.* ser. 11, no. 129, 1975.]

hay fever, asthma, and atopic dermatitis. Figure 5.15 shows the prevalence
of these conditions between the ages of 6 and 18. Many factors, including a
very strong emotional component, contribute to allergic ailments, making them
complicated and not fully understood. Psychological factors alone can pre-
cipitate an attack in a predisposed person with no demonstrable contact
with the allergen.

Hay Fever

Hay fever (seasonal allergic rhinitis) is the most common allergic disorder. It becomes increasingly prevalent in late childhood and adolescence.
Its prominent symptoms are paroxysmal sneezing, a watery nasal discharge

that causes sniffling, and nasal obstruction. There may also be itching of the eyes, lacrimation, and other symptoms in the pharynx, ears, and so on (Go and Pearlman 1962; Ellis 1975).

Asthma

Asthma is a less common but more serious condition. It is the leading cause of chronic illness in people under 17 years of age and is responsible for 25 percent of the time lost from school because of chronic illness (Ellis 1972).

The symptoms of asthma result from the obstruction of lung airways. Its primary sign is wheezing while breathing, especially in exhaling. There is a feeling of tightness, difficulty in breathing (dyspnea), and rapid breathing (tachypnea). In severe cases, the person's posture and behavior are dominated by his attempts to breath.

Atopic Dermatitis

Also known as atopic eczema, atopic dermatitis is an inflammatory skin disease characterized by redness, swelling, exudation, and crusting. It is usually found on the face, neck, wrists, hands, elbows, and the back of the knees.

The condition typically starts in infancy with intense itching. It tends to improve at about 3 years of age, but is exacerbated at puberty. It usually clears up with adulthood (Goltz and Ellis 1972; Ellis 1975).

All of these allergic conditions place considerable burdens on those afflicted. Normal activities may be markedly curtailed, particularly in severe cases of asthma. As with other chronic ailments, an adolescent may develop adverse psychological reactions, which can cause further complications. Fortunately, there are increasingly effective therapeutic means to alleviate allergic conditions.

MISCELLANEOUS AILMENTS

Other ailments that occasionally or chronically affect youth include cardiovascular and respiratory diseases, neuromuscular and joint disorders, teeth ailments, injuries and broken bones, kidney conditions, problems with the sense organs—particularly the ears—and so on.

Infectious diseases have come under better control, but other conditions, like cancer, that are far more difficult to deal with have become relatively more prominent. Malignant neoplasms now constitute the second leading cause of death between the ages of 10 and 14 and the third leading cause between 15 and 19 (refer to Table 5.7 on page 172). Cancer is even more frequent among younger children, so that it is the leading cause of death of children in the United States between 1 and 15 years of age (Fernbach and Starling 1975).

Acute leukemia, which is a cancer of white blood cells, is the most common childhood malignancy (4 cases per 100,000 children). The peak incidence of acute myeloid leukemia is during puberty, as is that of bone cancers. Definitive causes of cancer have not yet been established, but it is possible that the increased incidence of both leukemia and bone cancer is somehow related to rapid bone growth during puberty (Puberty and Cancer 1970). The frequency of other cancers affecting other tissues in the body varies in adolescence (Arey 1975). Although cancer is a very serious disease, it is by no means necessarily fatal if discovered and treated early.

THE PREVALENCE
OF ILLNESS AND MORTALITY

To place the foregoing discussion of common ailments in broader perspective, brief consideration will be given here to the relative prevalence of some of these conditions in the population of youth at large, before turning to the more frequent causes of mortality.

GENERAL HEALTH STATUS

Most of our information on illness comes from patients who consult doctors. But, this gives us an incomplete view of the health of the general population because, for a variety of reasons, many others who are ill may never seek medical care. By surveying appropriate samples of the general population, we obtain a far more realistic view of the nature and distribution of diseases that are prevalent. The information to be presented comes from such a survey, carried out nationwide by the National Center for Health Statistics of the U. S. Public Health Service (U. S. National Center for Health Statistics 1975a and b). Its conclusions are applicable to 23 million noninstitutionalized youth between 12 and 17 years of age.

When asked to describe their current health, American youth (between the ages of 12 and 17) tend to perceive themselves as quite healthy. As shown in

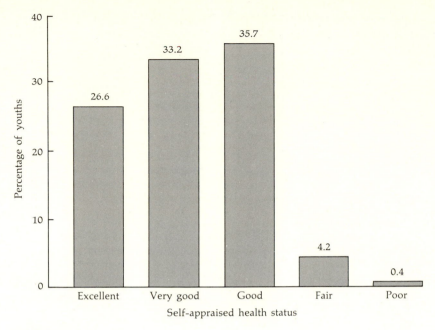

FIGURE 5.16
Self-appraised health status of U.S. youths between 12 and 17 years of age. [Redrawn from U.S. National Center for Health Statistics, *Vital Health Stat.* ser. 11, no. 147, 1975.]

Figure 5.16, about 60 percent rate their health as being excellent or very good, 36 percent describe it as good, and less than 5 percent as fair or poor. This view is consistent with the opinions of parents about the health of their children between the ages of 6 and 17: only about 5 percent rate it as fair or poor (bottom line in Figure 5.17). A greater proportion of parents, nevertheless, worry about the health of their offspring.

Findings in physical examinations show that the optimistic view held by adolescents and their parents is somewhat contradictory to the actual abnormalities that are manifested by children and more so by youth (Figure 5.17). An estimated 4.9 million youths between 12 and 17 years of age have some such abnormality. The types found are shown in Figure 5.18. Their increased frequency, relative to that in childhood is due primarily to conditions like acne, which are commonly associated with puberty. The higher rates of pathology in puberty are also due to a tripling of the rate of serious accidents affecting children between 6 and 17 years of age and a doubling of the rate of hay fever and heart conditions. The proportion of children with convulsions remains at about 3 percent, with hearing difficulties at 4 percent, and with eye trouble at 7 percent.

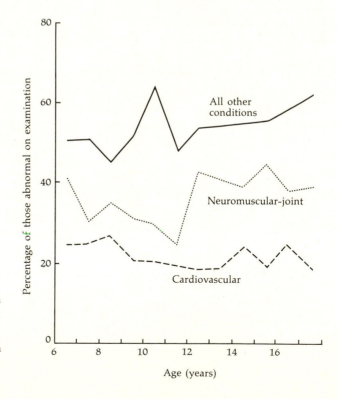

FIGURE 5.17
Results of survey examination of U.S. children (1963–1965) and youths (1966–1970) showing percentage who have significant abnormalities and percentage of parents who rate the health of their children as fair or poor or who consider the health of their children a worry. [Redrawn from U.S. National Center for Health Statistics, *Vital Health Stat.* ser. 11, no. 129, 1975.]

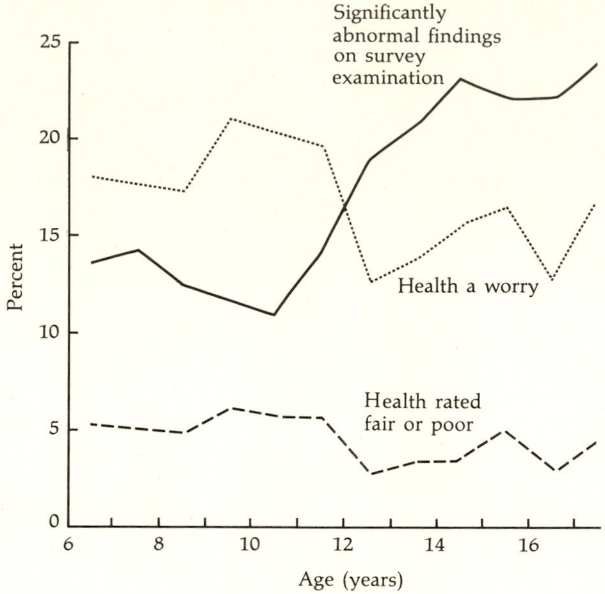

FIGURE 5.18
Results of survey examination of U.S. children (1963–1965) and youths (1966–1970) showing the percentage who have significant abnormalities, by type of condition. [Redrawn from U.S. National Center for Health Statistics, *Vital Health Stat.* ser. 11, no. 129, 1975.]

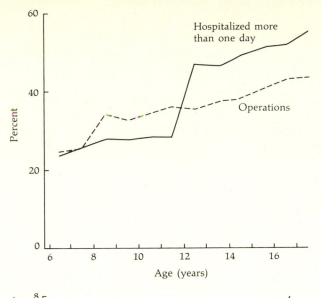

FIGURE 5.19
The percentage of U.S. children (1963–1965) and youths (1966–1970) with a history of operations or hospitalizations. [Redrawn from U.S. National Center for Health Statistics, *Vital Health Stat.* ser. 11, no. 129, 1975.]

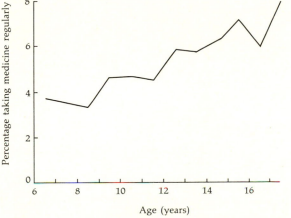

FIGURE 5.20
The percentage of U.S. children (1962–1965) and youths (1966–1970) taking medicine regularly. [Redrawn from U.S. National Center for Health Statistics, *Vital Health Stat.* ser. 11, no. 129, 1975.]

The proportion of those who have had at least one operation increases steadily from age 6 (24 percent) to age 16 or 17 (43 percent) (Figure 5.19). Most of the operations consist of tonsillectomies or adenoidectomies. The proportion taking medicine (more than 90 percent under doctors' orders) also increases: from 3 to 5 percent of children are on medication and from 6 to 8 percent of youths are (Figure 5.20).

Significant abnormalities are found more frequently among black children than white. A similar difference in frequency exists between black and white youth, but the difference in rates is not statistically significant. Children in the Western United States are least likely and youth in the South are most likely to have abnormalities. There is also a significant inverse association between family income and the health of children and youth: the proportion of abnormalities decreases with increasing family income (U. S. Center for Health Statistics 1975a).

Health-Related Attitudes and Behaviors

Most youth find their physical appearance acceptable and satisfactory. About two-thirds claim that their height and weight are about what they prefer (Figure 5.21). But only slightly more than half are satisfied with their body builds. Girls are generally somewhat less content with their height and weight than boys. Furthermore, there are differences between the sexes with regard to perceived and preferred body build or weight. For example, many girls who perceive themselves to be thin prefer to remain thin or even get thinner, whereas most boys who think they are thin would like to be heavier. Almost 80 percent of boys and 70 percent of girls think that the amount of food they

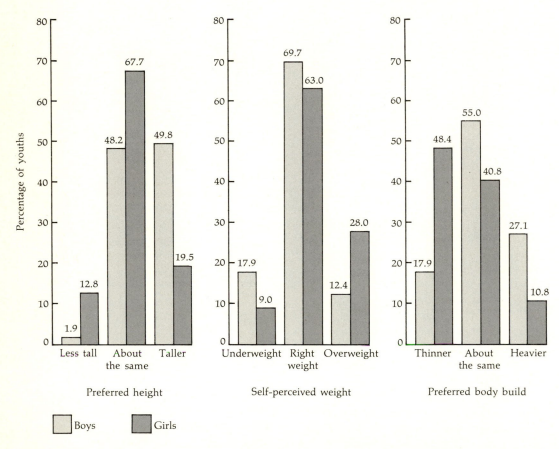

FIGURE 5.21
Distribution of U.S. youths between 12 and 17 years of age by preferred height, self-perceived weight, and preferred body build, according to sex. [Redrawn from U.S. National Center for Health Statistics, *Vital Health Stat.* ser. 11, no. 129, 1975.]

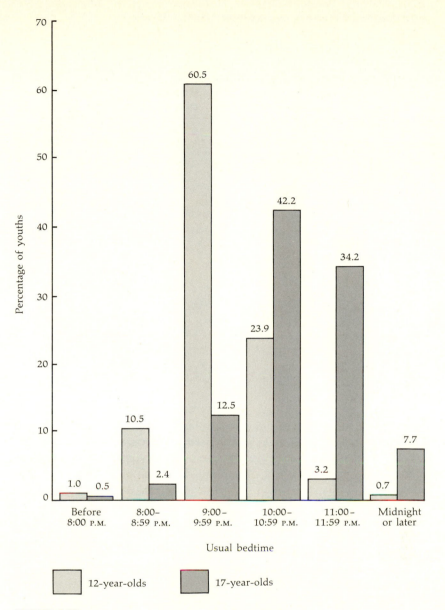

FIGURE 5.22
Usual bedtime on weeknights for U.S. youths between 12 and 17 years of age.
[Redrawn from U.S. National Center for Health Statistics, *Vital Health Stat.* ser. 11, no. 129, 1975.]

eat is about right. About 23 percent of girls and 14 percent of boys think they eat too much. About 7 percent of both sexes think they eat too little.

Figure 5.22 shows when adolescents generally go to bed. About 7 percent report that they very often have trouble getting to sleep or staying asleep. Another 44 percent have such difficulty from time-to-time. About half never have insomnia. Girls generally have more difficulty sleeping than boys. Among

Table 5.6.   Need for a doctor for selected medical symptoms as perceived by adolescents from 12 to 17 years of age in the United States, 1966–1970. Distribution given in percentages.

Condition or symptom	Definitely want to see doctor	Probably want to see doctor	Do not want to see doctor
Blood in urine or feces	74.5	19.6	5.9
Lump in stomach or abdomen	71.7	22.9	5.4
Pain in chest	50.1	39.3	10.6
Hurt all over	44.6	39.4	15.9
Stiff neck or back	23.8	37.8	38.4
Loss of appetite	19.4	39.9	30.7
Overtiredness	14.8	35.8	49.4
Nervousness	13.7	43.3	42.9
Vomiting	11.9	34.3	53.8
Sore throat	8.1	36.5	55.4
Stomach ache	4.3	19.6	76.1
Headache	2.8	14.0	83.2

Source: U. S. National Center for Health Statistics 1975b.

adults, women also experience more insomnia (National Center for Health Statistics 1970).

Frequent nightmares are experienced by 3 percent of both boys and girls. About 39 percent of boys and 47 percent of girls have bad dreams from time to time. Somewhat larger proportions of boys (59 percent) than girls (50 percent) never have disturbing dreams. Sleepwalking is reported by 6 percent of boys and 4 percent of girls. The experience tends to decrease with age among boys.

About half of the subjects in this study sleep in their own rooms. The percentage varies with age: 36 percent of boys and girls at age 12, as against 62 percent of 17-year-old boys and 55 percent of 15-year-old girls. More 17-year-old boys than girls have their own rooms.[14]

Finally, Table 5.6 shows how adolescents perceive the need for medical care in response to a number of symptoms. The seriousness of the conditions are perceived somewhat differently by the two sexes. More girls than boys would definitely want to see a doctor if they had a lump in the stomach (76 against 68 percent); a pain the the chest (56 against 45 percent); "hurt all over" (47 percent against 42 percent); and stiff neck or back (26 percent against 21 percent). Both sexes considered dental care to be necessary for a cavity in a tooth (more so than for crooked teeth, a toothache, sore mouth and gums, or bad breath).

[14]For information on the use of leisure time, school, work, and other aspects of social behavior, see U. S. National Center for Health Statistics (1975b).

CAUSES OF DEATH

It has been said that fortunate are those who die young, since they shall always be so remembered. Far more prevalent is the sentiment that death before old age is premature and particularly sad at the time of the flowering of adulthood (Figures 5.23 and 5.24).

FIGURE 5.23
Handle of a cista: two youths carrying the dead body of a companion. Etruscan, fourth to third century B.C. [The Metropolitan Museum of Art, Rogers Fund, 1913.]

FIGURE 5.24
Girodet: *The Entombment of Atala.*
[National Museums, Paris.]

Table 5.7. Mortality from five leading causes of death in the United
           States in 1970.

Cause	Number	Percentage	Rate/100,000
AGES 10 TO 14			
Accidents	4,218	49.9	20.3
Malignant neoplasms	1,078	12.8	5.2
Congenital anomalies	352	4.2	1.7
Influenza and pneumonia	307	3.6	1.5
Homicide	244	2.9	1.2
Other causes	2,247	26.6	10.8
Totals	8,446	100.0	40.6
AGES 15 TO 19			
Accidents	12,188	58.0	63.9
Homicide	1,536	7.3	8.1
Malignant neoplasms	1,389	6.6	7.3
Suicide	1,123	5.3	5.9
Influenza and pneumonia	406	1.9	2.1
Other causes	4,387	20.9	23.0
Totals	21,029	100.0	110.3
ALL AGES			
Major cardiovascular diseases	1,007,984	52.5	496.0
Malignant neoplasms	330,730	17.2	162.8
Cerebrovascular diseases	207,166	10.8	101.9
Accidents	114,638	6.0	56.4
Influenza and pneumonia	62,739	3.2	30.9
Other causes	197,774	10.3	97.4
Totals	1,921,031	100.0	945.3

Source: U.S. Public Health Service, National Center for Health Statistics 1974.

Table 5.7 shows the five leading causes of death between the ages of 10 and 14 and the ages of 15 and 19. The five leading causes of death at all ages are given for the purpose of comparison. Suicide ranks eleventh and homicide twelfth in this group and, therefore, do not appear in the table.

Figures 5.25 and 5.26 show how the more common causes of death change in importance during the first two-and-one-half decades of life.

The superior ability of females to survive was mentioned in an earlier chapter. In the general population of the United States, females have, in fact, lower mortality rates than do males throughout the life cycle. From birth to old age, women have shown this advantage in every decade since 1900 and the differential has been widening (Table 5.8). Table 5.9 shows sex differentials in death rates for different age groups from the leading causes of death for the U. S. population in 1970.

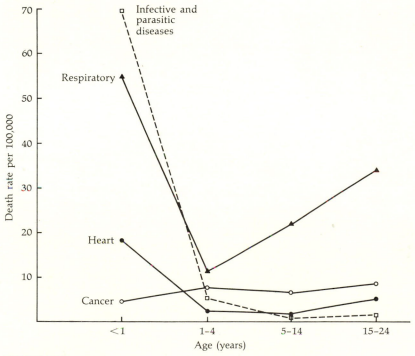

FIGURE 5.25
Death rates from major illnesses from birth to young adulthood. The figures plotted for each age group are the average number of deaths per year in each 100,000 persons of a given age in the total population. For example, the average number of deaths from respiratory disease is 11.4 per 100,000 children between the years of 1 and 4. [Redrawn from M. Marshall, in *The Seven Ages of Man*, ed. R. R. Sears and S. S. Feldman. Copyright © 1973 by William Kaufman, Inc., Los Altos, California. All rights reserved. (The data are from U.S. Department of Health, Education, and Welfare, 1968 Mortality Statistics, Monthly Vital Statistics Report, vol. 19, no. 12, 1971.)]

174

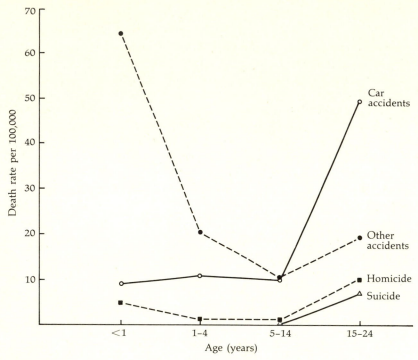

FIGURE 5.26
Death rates from major external causes from birth to young adulthood. As in Figure
5.25, the plotted figures are averages for different age groups. [Redrawn from
M. Marshall, in *The Seven Ages of Man,* ed. R. R. Sears and S. S. Feldman. Copyright
© 1973 by William Kaufman, Inc., Los Altos, California. All rights reserved.]

Table 5.8. Sex ratio of mortality by age, United States, from 1900 to 1970.

Year	All ages*	Under 1	1–4	5–14	15–24	25–34	35–44	45–54	55–64	65–74	75–84	85 and over
					Number of female deaths per 100 male deaths by age groups							
1970	57	77	81	63	36	47	57	54	48	53	67	87
1960	62	76	82	67	40	57	62	53	52	58	75	90
1950	69	77	84	69	53	66	68	60	59	68	81	89
1940	77	77	86	76	79	81	77	69	69	77	86	92
1930†	84	79	87	81	91	91	82	78	80	84	90	94
1920†	93	78	92	88	104	111	97	93	91	93	95	97
1910†	86	81	92	94	88	88	79	79	83	89	92	96
1900†	91	81	93	101	97	99	91	90	90	90	93	95

Source: Metropolitan Life Insurance Company, *Stat. Bull.,* August 1974.

*Adjusted on basis of age distribution of the United States total population, 1940.

†Includes only those states in which deaths were registered.

Table 5.9. Sex ratio of mortality from leading causes of death, by age, United States, 1970.

Cause of death	All ages*	Number of female deaths per 100 male deaths by age groups										
		Under 1	1–4	5–14	15–24	25–34	35–44	45–54	55–64	65–74	75–84	85 and over
All causes	57	77	81	63	36	47	57	54	48	53	67	87
Diseases of heart	50	72	87	92	63	51	31	29	36	50	69	90
Malignant neoplasms	69	115	81	78	60	103	124	99	67	55	56	64
Cerebrovascular diseases	83	69	57	76	78	109	99	88	69	74	87	106
Accidents	35	87	70	46	25	24	29	34	35	46	65	88
Influenza and pneumonia	58	77	76	103	73	72	63	54	47	46	54	76
Bronchitis, emphysema, and asthma	24	73	64	†	†	148	83	51	26	16	14	23
Cirrhosis of the liver	49	70	†	†	†	58	59	52	43	36	45	47
Suicide	39	†	†	†	31	43	54	45	35	25	16	14
Diabetes mellitus	107	†	†	†	116	88	64	93	108	115	117	107
Arteriosclerosis	79	†	†	†	†	†	†	44	49	68	79	102
Homicide	25	91	102	70	24	22	26	21	21	25	44	34

Source: Metropolitan Life Insurance Company, *Stat. Bull.,* August 1974.

*Adjusted on basis of age distribution of the United States total population, 1940.

†Mortality rates less than 0.5 per 100,000 population; ratio not computed.

Chapter 6   Health Hazards

There are no formal medical definitions of what constitutes a health hazard. Presumably, anything that increases the likelihood of illness or disability would qualify. But the term is usually used in a more restrictive sense. An environmental factor such as fire, smog, or radiation, for example, can constitute a health hazard only if there is a chance of someone's becoming exposed to it. Important as they may be, hazards that affect the health of the population at large will not be discussed here. Rather, this chapter will treat of specific threats to those in the second decade of life. Furthermore, it will deal mostly with hazardous activities in which participation is largely elective and volitional.

Accidents and drugs are responsible for many casualties among youth, and participation in hazardous activities or the use of drugs is largely a matter of personal choice. It is not the purpose here, however, to be categorically judgmental of these activities. Driving a car or motorcycle is clearly hazardous, but that is not to say that these vehicles should therefore not be used. It is impossible to live in an industrialized society without mechanical transportation. Even without mechanical transportation, there is a risk of injury in getting from one place to another by horse or by foot. An equally compelling argument could be made against activities undertaken for pleasure. Yet, surely, there are differences between going for a leisurely drive in a properly equipped car on well-maintained roads and speeding on a serpentine road when half drunk. There is no need to multiply the number of examples to demonstrate the fact that the sane approach to these problems requires choices between the hoped-for benefits of an activity and its potential hazards. Common sense also indicates that the inevitable aspects of a danger be distinguished from other elements that can be mitigated if not eliminated.

Whereas most people would concede the necessity of risk-taking in an activity like driving, they may think (either out of conviction or to comply with convention) that the use of drugs does not deserve a similar concession. This position, admirable as it may be in principle, seems highly dubious in practice. One hardly can or needs to quarrel with those who claim that the world would be better off if people would forego entirely the use of chemicals for non-medicinal needs. Historical and cross-cultural evidence shows, however, that people have generally found this ideal unrealizable if not undesirable. The use of chemicals for psychological and social purposes, whether productive or destructive, is very much a part of contemporary reality. In that sense, for significant numbers of people, tobacco, alcohol, and other drugs seem almost as necessary as the automobile, and not more risky. This justifies, at least on statistical grounds, the classification of drug use as a health hazard rather than an ailment. However, the risks entailed vary widely: a glass of beer among friends is surely not the same as a shot of heroin in a dark alley.

Some people concede the seeming inevitability of tobacco and alcohol use, but object to the legitimization and social acceptance of other drugs. After all, the argument goes, having one "monkey" on our backs does not justify adding another. There is some logic to this, but not enough to uphold the argument. In a pluralistic society, people may want to choose their "monkey." If a new practice is not demonstrably more hazardous than those already in existence, on what grounds can one discriminate against it? A more legitimate distinction is between drug use and drug abuse or misuse, by which the relatively innocuous practices are separated from the more dangerous. But, as in driving a car, there is always a risk: no drug, under any circumstance, is totally and unequivocally safe.

The issue is complicated by social and psychological considerations. It entails problems of individual freedom and social control, psychological motivations, psychopathological concerns, and so on. But these considerations are beyond the scope of this book. What will be discussed here instead are the activities that commonly cause accidents and the nature of the drugs that are in current use, the underlying assumption being that whatever one is going to do, and for whatever reasons, it is better to know what one is dealing with.

ACCIDENTS

Accidents are a very serious health hazard and constitute the fourth most frequent cause of death for all ages. More than 100,000 people are killed accidentally and about 10 million are injured each year in the United States. In 1970, accidents were the cause of the deaths of 114,638 people (79,756 males and 34,882 females), resulting in a fatality rate of 56.4 per 100,000 (U.S. Public Health Service 1974). The annual casualties are more than double the 56,743 Americans killed in the Vietnam war (*World Almanac and Book of Facts* 1976, p. 364).

Accidents seem to affect youth in particular; they are by far the leading cause of death during the second decade of life (refer to Table 5.7). In 1970, 4,218 persons between the ages of 10 and 14 and 12,188 persons between the ages of 15 and 19 died in accidents in the United States (20.3 and 63.9 per 100,000, respectively). As shown in Table 5.7, accidental fatalities account for more than half of all deaths from all causes between the ages of 10 and 19 (total deaths 8,496 + 21,029 = 29,475; accidental deaths 4,218 + 12,188 = 16,406).

Despite these staggering figures, accidental deaths seem to be of little concern to many young people and adults. They tend to be thought of as the sort of thing that happens to other people or as a totally unexpected stroke of bad luck. It is also common to think that accidents happen only to those engaged in foolhardy activities or in "dangerous" places. In fact, most accidents happen at home: in the United States, 80,000 people are injured in their homes per week; 4 million suffer disability and about 30,000 die yearly (Johns, Sutton, and Webster 1975). Accidents also occur, of course, on the road, in school, in industry, on farms, and so on. For example, about 170,000 accidental injuries occur yearly among farmers and ranchers (Berry et al. 1975). In short, accidents can happen almost anywhere and anytime.

Accidents are not exclusively the bane of industrialized countries. There are more than 13,000 accidents a year in the tiny Persian Gulf state of Kuwait, and the fatality rate per 10,000 vehicles in Indian cities is 10 to 15 times that of the United States. An estimated quarter of a million persons die accidentally each year and 7 million are injured throughout the world (Kaprio 1975). The scene shown in Figure 6.1 is from an African highway.

Mortality figures represent only part of the toll and do not take into account the much larger group of accidentally injured, some of whom are maimed or disfigured for life. It is estimated that nonfatal injuries outnumber fatalities by a ratio greater than 200 to 1 (Einhorn 1972, p. 517). Figure 6.2 presents the distribution of three major types of accidental injuries incurred between the ages of 6 and 17. Note that, by age 15 to 17, almost one out of five adolescents has had a broken bone.

FIGURE 6.1
Road accident on an African highway.
[From World Health Organization,
Road Accidents, *World Health*,
October 1975]

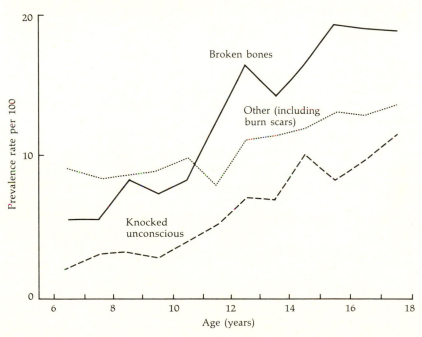

FIGURE 6.2
Prevalence rates for major types of serious accidental injuries among U.S. children
(1963–1965) and youths (1966–1970). [Redrawn from U.S. National Center for Health
Statistics, *Vital Health Stat.* ser. 11, no. 129, 1975.]

Table 6.1. Mortality from leading types of accidents, by sex and age, United States, 1968.

	Accidental death rates per 100,000 population										
Type of accident	All ages*	1–4	5–14	15–19	20–24	25–29	30–34	35–44	45–54	55–64	65 and older
MALES											
Accidents—all types	81.4	35.9	27.8	100.5	129.2	94.1	78.5	74.7	82.1	98.5	180.7
Motor vehicle	40.8	12.2	12.9	66.5	95.0	59.9	44.1	37.7	38.3	41.9	58.9
Traffic	40.0	10.6	12.6	65.7	94.2	58.8	43.1	36.8	37.4	40.8	57.9
Pedestrian	6.4	5.9	5.4	4.3	4.4	3.7	4.0	4.2	6.0	9.2	19.5
Nontraffic	0.8	1.6	0.3	0.8	0.8	1.1	1.0	0.9	0.9	1.1	1.0
Falls	9.5	1.7	0.7	2.1	2.3	2.6	3.4	4.9	8.2	15.1	67.2
Accidents mainly of industrial type	5.5	2.0	1.6	4.3	5.5	7.3	7.0	7.5	9.0	9.3	6.6
Drowning†	5.1	6.8	5.8	12.2	6.9	3.8	3.5	3.1	2.9	2.9	3.0
Fires and flames	4.4	6.4	1.7	1.0	1.7	2.5	2.7	3.7	5.1	7.8	14.3
Firearms	2.1	0.7	1.7	4.9	3.2	2.4	2.2	1.9	1.9	1.9	1.3
Accidental deaths as a percentage of all deaths	7	38	54	64	59	47	34	18	8	4	2
Deaths due to motor-vehicle accidents as a percentage of all accidental deaths	50	34	46	66	74	64	56	50	47	43	33
FEMALES											
Accidents—all types	34.6	26.9	12.6	28.9	24.9	20.3	18.8	22.2	26.3	35.4	125.7
Motor vehicle	14.7	9.9	6.9	23.8	19.3	14.5	12.2	12.9	13.8	17.0	25.1
Traffic	14.5	8.6	6.8	23.7	19.2	14.4	12.1	12.8	13.7	16.8	24.7
Pedestrian	2.6	3.7	2.9	1.6	0.7	0.8	0.9	1.5	1.6	2.9	7.7
Nontraffic	0.2	1.3	0.1	0.1	0.1	0.1	0.1	0.1	0.1	0.2	0.4
Falls	9.1	1.3	0.3	0.3	0.3	0.4	0.5	1.4	2.3	5.7	73.7
Fires and flames	3.0	5.5	1.6	0.7	0.8	1.0	1.3	1.8	2.8	4.0	9.3
Inhalation and ingestion of food or other object	1.3	1.5	0.3	0.2	0.3	0.2	0.6	0.7	0.9	1.6	3.1
Drowning†	1.0	3.1	1.4	1.0	0.6	0.4	0.3	0.5	0.4	0.5	0.8
Poisoning by solids and liquids	0.9	1.6	0.1	0.4	0.6	0.7	1.3	1.5	1.7	1.4	1.0
Accidental deaths as a percentage of all deaths	4	34	38	48	34	23	15	9	5	3	2
Deaths due to motor-vehicle accidents as a percentage of all accidental deaths	43	37	55	82	78	72	65	58	53	48	20

Source: Metropolitan Life Insurance Company, *Stat. Bull.*, May 1971.
*Includes less than 1 year.   †Exclusive of deaths in water transportation.

Table 6.1 presents a distribution of various causes of fatal accidents by age and sex. The rate for males is consistently much higher than that for females in every age group but particularly during the years of adolescence and young adulthood. The rate for both sexes is higher during adolescence and young adulthood than during any other period except that after 65 years of age. In the 15-to-19-year-old group, accidental deaths comprise 64 percent of all deaths for males and 48 percent of all deaths for females.

Motor-vehicle fatalities account for about half the total accidental deaths of males and about two-fifths of the total deaths of females. The number of accidents that are not caused by motor vehicles increases in later years. The hazard of pedestrian death is greatest for children under 5 years of age, for men 45 and older, and for women 65 and older.

Falls constitute the second greatest cause of accidental fatality, for both sexes of all ages. Rates are higher for males than for females in every age group, except age 65 and older. However, in the 15-to-19-year-old group, drowning ranks second for both sexes (12.2 for males and 1.0 for females per 100,000). The third greatest cause is firearms for males (4.9 per 100,000 and fires and flames for females (0.7 per 100,000).

Although homes are the most frequent sites of accidental injury, the most serious accidents occur more often in public places, such as public buildings, parks, and streets. Men become disabled as a result of public accidents at a rate of more than 6 per 1,000 per year; work accidents account for about 5 per 1,000 and home accidents for 4 per 1,000. Women suffer disabling injuries at the rate of 11 per 1,000 in public places, 6 per 1,000 at home, and 3 per 1,000 at work (Metropolitan Life 1970).

Twenty-two colleges and universities enrolling 207,000 full-time students report that almost 15,000 injuries come to the attention of student health services per year. Because there are more than 8 million college students in the United States, the total number of injuries can be extrapolated to be about 600,000. This does not take into consideration the fact that an undetermined number of injuries go unreported and that there are fewer students in school during the summer, which is the peak accident season.

These same data also reveal that male students sustain nearly three-quarters of the injuries, even though they comprise less than two-thirds of the total enrollment. More than one-third of the reported injuries occur off-campus. Of the on-campus accidents, about 52 percent are in athletic or recreational facilities, 20 percent in residence halls, 15 percent in academic buildings, and 11 percent on the campus grounds. Only 2 percent of the injuries occurring on campus are caused by motor vehicles (Johns, Sutton, and Webster 1975).

MOTOR-VEHICLE ACCIDENTS

In 1899, a Mr. Bliss was struck by a car and became the first known automobile casualty in this country (Alsever 1968a). Little was it known then that motor-vehicles would become the leading cause of accidental deaths, claiming both the famous (Figure 6.3) and, just as tragically, the nonfamous. Motor-vehicle

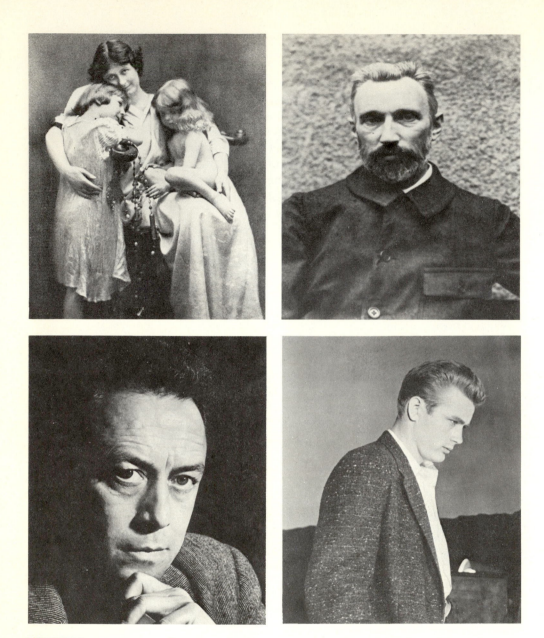

FIGURE 6.3
Some famous accident casualties: Isadora Duncan (upper left), the legendary American dancer (1877–1927), was strangled to death by a long scarf that caught in a wheel of a roofless car on the French Riviera. She is pictured here with her two children, Patrick and Deirdre. Not long after this photograph was taken, the two children and their governess drowned in the Seine, near Paris, when their car plunged off the road. Pierre Curie (upper right), French Nobel Prize winner in physics in 1903, was run down and killed by a truck in Paris in 1906, when he was 47 years old. Albert Camus (lower left), French author who received a Nobel Prize in literature, was 47 when he died in a car crash in the south of France in 1960. James Dean (lower right), American film star, was 24 years of age when he died in a car crash near Salinas, California, in 1955. [From World Health Organization, Road Accidents, *World Health*, October 1975. Photographs by Len Sirman Press, Geneva.]

accidents account for 50 percent of such deaths among males and 43 percent among females (Table 6.1). Note that the percentages are even higher for the 15-to-19-year-old group: 88 percent of accidental deaths of females and 66 percent of males are due to vehicular accidents. Figure 6.4 illustrates mortality rates from motor-vehicle and other accidents for males and females of various age groups.

Figure 6.5 shows the distribution of different kinds of motor-vehicle fatalities. Note the increase in the number of drivers killed in motor vehicles in the 15-to-

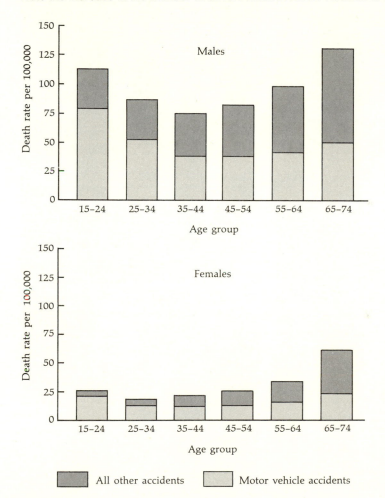

FIGURE 6.4
Mortality from motor-vehicle and all other accidents, by sex and age, in the United States, 1968. [Redrawn from Metropolitan Life Insurance Company, *Stat. Bull.*, May 1971.]

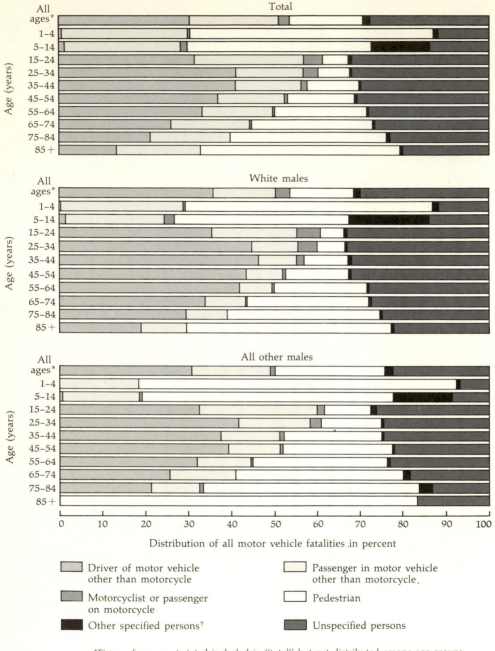

Distribution of all motor vehicle fatalities in percent

Driver of motor vehicle other than motorcycle

Passenger in motor vehicle other than motorcycle.

Motorcyclist or passenger on motorcycle

Pedestrian

Other specified persons†

Unspecified persons

*Figures for age not stated included in "total" but not distributed among age groups.
†Other specified person includes "occupant of streetcar," "rider of animal-drawn vehicle," "pedal cyclist," and "other." Pedal cyclists comprise more than 94 percent of this category.

FIGURE 6.5
Distribution of all motor vehicle fatalities in the United States, 1969. [Redrawn from U.S. National Center for Health Statistics, *Vital Health Stat.* ser. 20, no. 16, 1974.]

BOX 6.1
Facts about accidents (World Health Organization 1975b).

• Nearly 10 percent of beds in the large hospitals of some countries are occupied by road-accident victims.

• For every person killed in a road accident, between 10 and 15 persons are seriously injured, and 30 or 40 receive minor injuries.

• It was estimated 10 years ago in the United Kingdom that more than half the children born will sooner or later be injured in road accidents, and that one in 50 will lose his or her life on the roads. The situation is little better today.

• Accident surveys have shown that accident involvement per mile driven is highest in youth, falls steadily until late middle-age and rises only slightly thereafter. In the USA, drivers over 60 have an accident ratio below the average for all ages.

• Road accidents are responsible for over 30 percent of all deaths in the 15–25 age group, although this is the minimum-risk age group for pedestrians. Males between 15 and 25 are many times more likely to be killed than females.

• Serious traffic infringement or careless driving was the cause of 77 percent of a series of 92,000 accidents resulting in injuries, according to French police statistics. Of these, 20 percent were due to excessive speed, 17 percent to refusal of priority, 11 percent to driving on the wrong side of the road, 10 percent to careless driving, and 7 percent to faults in overtaking.

• In all countries, deaths from road accidents are higher in males than in females.

24-year-old group, as well as the marked increase in motorcycle fatalities. Note also that more than 94 percent of the group designated as "other specified persons" consists of "pedal cyclists," or bicycle riders. The accidental deaths in this group are caused by motor vehicles. Pedestrian deaths in the 15-to-24-year-old group comprise the lowest percentage among all age groups.[1] Further information on road accidents is presented in Box 6.1.

Other interesting facts about accidents on the road are the time and the place of their occurrence. For example, a study of motor-vehicle deaths in 1967 showed that, of 53,100 deaths, more than half (28,100) occurred at night. About seven out of ten deaths were at places classified as rural: 1,750 people lost their lives while walking on a rural road at night (Johns, Sutton, and Webster 1975).

The causes of this modern epidemic—and accidents deserve to be called just that—are complex but not beyond comprehension. The manner in which cars

---

[1]For further details, see U. S. National Center for Health Statistics (1974).

and roads are constructed and maintained is important. But, a major share of the responsibility rests with the driver.

As early as 1926, attention was called to the presence of an "accident habit," which referred to the fact that people who have had accidents are more likely to repeat them. Such observations led to the notion of accident proneness. What constitutes an accident-prone person and how to account for it are subject to various interpretations. The classical psychoanalytic view is that an unconscious impulse toward self-punishment and self-destruction underlies such cases (Freud 1901). Attempts have been made to draw personality profiles of accident-prone persons. Perhaps not surprisingly, those who are in accidents repeatedly emerged as people who tend to be aggressive, impulsive, thoughtless, and disrespectful of authority (Tillman and Hobbs 1949) and who seem to have less control over hostility (Conger et al. 1959; Joseph and Schwartz 1975).

Given the complexity of human motivation, it is difficult to reach general agreement about accident proneness. Yet it seems almost self-evident that cars often become an extension of personality, and the manner in which a person drives expresses his mood of the moment. For some people fleetingly and for

FIGURE 6.6
The car as a roaring monster. [From World Health Organization, Road Accidents, *World Health*. October 1975.]

others habitually, cars take on the attributes of powerful raging monsters that perform on command (Figure 6.6). Car manufacturers blatantly exploit this image by designing and naming their products accordingly.

Far less mysterious is the role of psychophysiological states in accidents. The most important factors in this regard are fatigue and drugs, especially alcohol. About half of all automobile accidents involve some drinking on the part of the driver. Barbiturates, marijuana, and other drugs, like antihistamines, are also serious hazards. There are differences in how these substances affect people, but one thing is clear: everyone's capacity to drive safely is impaired by the intake of such chemicals.

The danger of driving under the influence of alcohol is recognized throughout the world. In the United States, the drinking driver is a significant factor in 50 to 60 percent of all fatalities, as is the drinking pedestrian in a comparable percentage of adult pedestrian fatalities (Campbell 1964). But the problem exists elsewhere as well. For example, a police spot-check in India revealed one out of four truck drivers entering Delhi to be drunk (World Health Organization 1975). Educational efforts (Figures 6.7 and 6.8) and attempts at law enforcement have had limited success so far.

FIGURE 6.7
Chilean poster. [From World Health Organization, Road Accidents, *World Health*, October 1975.]

FIGURE 6.8
Kenyan poster. The message in Swahili is "If you drink pombe [a local beer], do not drive your car." [From World Health Organization, Road Accidents, *World Health*, October 1975.]

The capacity to drive safely can also be reduced markedly by fatigue and sleepiness, without the effects of alcohol or other drugs. Prolonged driving, especially at night, increases the risk of accidents. It has been shown that, after only three hours of driving, the likelihood of errors in performance increases. After seven hours of driving, the frequency of accidents increases disproportionately. Resting after three hours of driving is significantly helpful, but a second break after six hours does much less good. After nine hours, rest periods further deteriorate rather than help arousal and fitness to drive. The worst time to drive from a psychological point of view is in the very early morning hours, when many biological processes slow down (Levi 1975).

The risk of accidental fatality and injury is particularly high during adolescence. The mere awareness of the fact may have a sobering effect. Most adolescents know how to operate an automobile safely, but it is this awareness that persuades them to implement such knowledge.

Motorcycle Accidents

Motorcycles are fun to ride, cheaper than cars, and economical to run. Consequently, they appeal to many segments of the population, especially younger people. In 1950, there were 453,874 registered motorcycles in the United States. In the next two decades, this number increased by 454 percent to 2,514,450. In 1971, motorcycle registrations exceeded 3.3 million. In the same period, the number of motorcycles in California increased by 922 percent —from 54,948 to 561,621 (Kraus, Riggins, and Franti 1975*a*), (Figure 6.9). Although there is currently about one motorcycle for every 60 persons, cars still outnumber them: motorcycles comprise only about 3 percent of the motor vehicles on the road (Metropolitan Life 1973).

The greater use of motorcycles has coincided with a marked increase in motorcycle-accident deaths: the rate has more than tripled in ten years, from 697 deaths in 1961 to 2,410 in 1971. However, the rate of increase in fatalities is less than that in motorcycle registration. Thus, although the fatality rate has gone up in absolute terms, it has actually declined in relation to the number of registered vehicles (Figure 6.10).

The risk of fatality is higher for motorcycles than automobiles: the rate for motorcycle drivers is twice that for the drivers and occupants of other types of motor vehicles. If fatalities are computed on the basis of the number of miles driven, motorcycles emerge as the most hazardous of all motor vehicles. The risk is about four times higher (Metropolitan Life 1973).

Collision with other moving motor vehicles, particularly automobiles, is the predominant type of fatal accident for motorcyclists, whereas running into fixed obstacles, such as walls or abutments, accounts for only 5 percent of deaths. More than 90 percent of fatalities are males, and two-thirds of motorcycle deaths occur in the 15-to-24-year-old group.

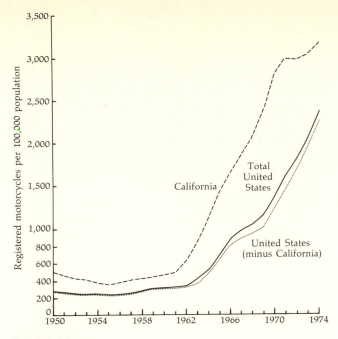

FIGURE 6.9
Registered motorcycles per 100,000 population for the United States, California, and the United States minus California, 1950–1970. [Redrawn from J. F. Kraus, R. S. Riggins, and C. E. Franti, *Am. J. Epidemiol.* 102(1975):74–98.]

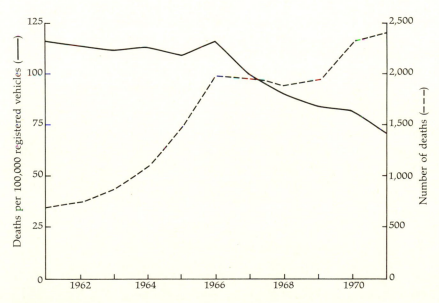

FIGURE 6.10
Deaths due to motorcycle accidents in the United States, 1961–1971. [Redrawn from Metropolitan Life Insurance Company, *Stat. Bull.* August 1973.]

Exclusive of fatalities, motorcycles are also more dangerous than cars. Accidents are more likely to result in injury, and the injuries are likely to be more severe. In a study conducted at the University of California, it was found that 55 percent of the students drove cars and only 6.5 percent rode motorcycles, but injuries from the latter were twice as frequent. The nature of the injuries led the investigators to conclude that there is probably no such thing as a minor motorcycle accident (Cracchiolo, Blazina, and MacKinnon 1968). On the more encouraging side, there was a 40 percent reduction in motorcycle fatalities and a 34 percent reduction in serious head injuries (which account for 2 out of 3 of such fatalities) in New York State after it had become mandatory to wear protective helmets there (New York State Department of Motor Vehicles 1969).

Recently, studies have been undertaken to examine the nature of motorcycle accidents more closely. One study shows that the incidence of injury is highest for 18-year-old drivers, that short persons run a higher risk than tall ones, and that risk of injury is not related to make of motorcycle but to engine size. It also reveals that collisions occur most frequently in the afternoon and early evening hours and in the summer, peaking during weeks that include a holiday, and that two-thirds of the collisions are with a motor vehicle (Kraus, Riggins, and Franti 1975a).

It has further been shown that male drivers suffer more serious injuries than female drivers or passengers of either sex. Serious injury is related to collisions at speeds estimated at more than 48 kilometers per hour but not to engine size. Risk of serious injury is greater for older male drivers than for younger drivers, although young drivers have a high incidence of injury producing collisions. As in other studies, helmets have been found to significantly reduce the risk of fatality (Kraus, Riggins, and Franti 1975b).

Bicycle Accidents

The bicycle was invented in 1790 and has been used by young and old in many parts of the world for recreation and transportation. But, in the United States, its popularity with adults has grown markedly only in the past decade or so. From the mid-1950s to 1970 the number of bicycles doubled: by 1970, there were an estimated 43 million, one for every 2.4 motor vehicles on the road (Metropolitan Life 1970).

Bicycles are not harmless toys: injuries and fatalities have been climbing with their increased use. Ninety percent more cyclists were killed in 1967 (a total of 755 persons) than in 1955, and 90 percent of the fatalities were a result of collisions with motor vehicles. About 85 percent of bicycle fatalities are male, and 70 percent are students. The rate peaks (15.6 per million population) for the 10-to-14-year-old group but declines for the 15-to-19-year-old group (5.0 million).

DROWNING

Drowning rates vary greatly, depending on the availability and utilization of bodies of water, the climate, and the age and sex distribution of the population. The highest rates are in the mountain and southern states.

Drowning ranks second only to motor-vehicle accidents as a cause of accidental death for 5-to-24-year-olds. Figure 6.11 presents the rates by age and race for the state of Maryland.

About 6,500 people drown each year in the United States (Dietz and Baker 1974). More than four out of five victims lose their lives while swimming, wading, or playing in the water, or by falling into it. The rest die in water-transport accidents.

More than half of all water fatalities occur in June, July, and August. Three out of five males and two out of three females who have fatal accidents are under age 20. Most drowning victims are male, although this varies by age: there is little difference among infants; by age 15, the ratio is 4:1; and for 15-to-

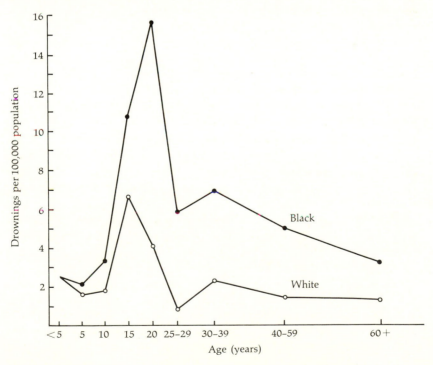

FIGURE 6.11
Drowning rates by age and race, based on Maryland population (1970 census). [Redrawn from P. E. Dietz and S. P. Baker, *Am. J. Public Health* 64(4), 1974.]

FIGURE 6.12
Electric lineman resuscitating co-worker.
[Photograph from the American Red Cross.]

24-year-olds, it is 12:1 (Metropolitan Life 1972). The peak rate for nontransport accidents is for males between the ages of 12 and 19 (12.2 per 100,000).

Most deaths in water-transport accidents are related to small craft and thus to recreational activities: 90 percent of the fatalities are male. The possibility of such accidents is enhanced by overloaded boats, disregard of bad weather, inexperience, and negligence. According to coast guard reports, seven out of ten drowning victims with lifesaving devices on board either had not used them or had used them improperly. The consumption of alcohol also plays a prominent part in deaths by drowning, usually by adults but not to the exclusion of adolescents (Dietz and Baker 1974).

Drowning also occurs in the bathtub, but such drownings are usually due to loss of consciousness. If a loss of consciousness can be expected—for example, in an epileptic—a preventive measure is to have only a small quantity of water in the tub.

Ignorance is also not to be discounted. Many adolescents may not realize, for example, that rapid or deep breathing before diving to increase the capacity to hold one's breath while diving is dangerous. This practice can lead to a loss of consciousness under water, because lower carbon dioxide pressure decreases arterial oxygen tension, which leads to cerebral ischemia (Einhorn 1972). In such situations, a diver's life can be saved by administering artificial respiration. The techniques of applying artificial respiration are easy to learn, but their usefulness depends on the ability to act promptly and calmly—if necessary, in the most unlikely situations (Figure 6.12).[2]

---

[2]For information on first aid, including mouth-to-mouth resuscitation, see American Red Cross (1957); U. S. Department of Health, Education, and Welfare (1964); Office of Civil Defense and Public Health Service (1965).

ACCIDENT PREVENTION

The expectation that all accidents should be prevented does not make sense and is not credible even as a pious hope. Numerous factors contribute to the probability of accidents, and at least some of them are beyond the control of the accident victim. We need to be active in order to live and enjoy life, and any activity carries a certain risk.

The purpose of accident prevention, therefore, is not to eliminate all risk, but to minimize whatever risks may be entailed in a given activity. A society has the responsibility of informing its members of these risks, but it is difficult to ascertain the extent to which society should interfere with rational human beings, who are willing to risk their own lives for thrills or gain. Lives have been lost and injuries sustained scaling heights and plumbing depths, racing against time, trading punches, and winning or losing games.[3] More exotic activities include crossing a chasm on a tightrope, being shot out of a cannon, going over Niagara Falls in a barrel, and so on. Most of us have neither the need nor the skills for such adventures, and others are protected by a keen sense of self-preservation and a healthy touch of cowardice. The risks we run are much more mundane, but by no means trivial.

Box 6.2 gives some reasons for the occurrence of several common types of accidents, together with recommendations for means of preventing them. Such information is useful, unfortunately, only if it is heeded. Hardly anyone will deny that riding a bike at night without a light is risky, but the risk does not stop people from doing it. People drive cars when less than sober or they drive faster than is safe for a ''short while,'' and so on, even though they are aware of the dangers.

Although public measures can be taken to make vehicles as safe as feasible and to keep roads well maintained, there is not that much that a single person can do in this regard. But there are some things that each of the 100,000,000 or more drivers in the United States can do everytime he or she is in a car—for example, conscientiously and correctly use seat belts. By doing that alone, thousands of lives would be saved and major injuries could be reduced by 50 percent (Alsever 1968a).

John Stapp showed in a rocket-sled experiment two decades ago that the human body, if properly restrained by belt and harness, could survive without permanent disability the tremendous force imposed by decelerating from 646 to 0 miles per hour in 1.4 seconds. That decelerative force is nearly twice the force of 25G in car accidents (Stapp 1955). A person adequately restrained in a car that was equipped with the appropriate bumpers and was moving at 25 miles per hour when it crashed against a barrier (the most lethal form of accident) could walk away from the vehicle. By 1962, the highly effective

---

[3]For a collection of essays on the effects of sports on health, see World Health Organization (1968).

BOX 6.2
Accidents and the factors that lead to their occurrence or their prevention. [From E. B. Johns, W. B. Sutton, and L. E. Webster, *Health for Effective Living,* 5th ed., McGraw-Hill, 1970.]

KIND OF ACCIDENT	OCCURRENCE	PREVENTION
Occupational Mechanical (manual skills)	Occur most frequently when employee is handling objects, working with machinery, working with vehicles, or using hand tools or falls on slippery surfaces or from heights	Less likely to occur when employee is adequately trained and proficient in skills of his trade and is protected from dangers, including falls
Personal	Likely to occur when an employee is fatigued or ill, is upset emotionally, disobeys safety rules, has physical disabilities, is maladjusted socially, is ignorant of job to be done, or lacks recreational skills	Less likely to occur if employee has adequate psychological counseling and medical services, receives precise pre-employment screening by personnel office, practices sound discipline both on and off job, helps plan rules of safety, understands requirements of job, and has opportunity to engage in wholesome recreational programs
Traffic Mechanical (manual skills)	Occur most frequently when motor vehicles collide with pedestrians, with each other, or with trains, streetcars, animals, or fixed objects, or when they overturn or run off highway	Less likely to occur if operator of motor vehicle possesses up-to-date license to drive, understands driving techniques, knows and obeys traffic regulations, respects rights of others, and is skillful in operating vehicle
Personal	Likely to occur when pedestrian or operator of vehicle, or both, are under influence of alcohol, fatigued, sleepy, careless, discourteous, upset emotionally, or ignorant of traffic regulations or have serious physical disabilities	Less likely to occur if pedestrian and vehicle operator keep off highway when under influence of alcohol and when physically, mentally, or emotionally incapable of good judgment

KIND OF ACCIDENT	OCCURRENCE	PREVENTION
Aquatic Mechanical (manual skills)	Likely to occur when one falls out of boat or canoe and is unable to swim, collides with objects in water, dives or steps into unknown depths, lacks adequate training in water-rescue techniques, or lacks skill in handling boat	Less likely to occur if one is skilled in handling boats and canoes, knows skills of swimming and diving, knows where these skills can be practiced safely, and is trained in techniques of water rescue
Personal	Likely to occur when one is overfatigued or under influence of alcoholic beverages, becomes frightened while swimming, ignores safety rules, or has uncompensated physical disabilities	Less likely to occur if one stays out of water when overfatigued or when one has been drinking alcoholic beverages, obeys rules established for safety, recognizes physical strengths or handicaps, and stays within safe limits while swimming, diving, or boating
Home, firearms Mechanical (manual skills)	Most likely to occur when one lacks skill in handling a gun (cleaning, pointing, etc.) or knowledge of correct ways to handle a gun while hunting	Less likely to occur if one possesses skill in handling firearms (cleaning, shooting, etc.) and never points a gun at another person when on a hunting trip or elsewhere
Personal	Likely to occur when one leaves an unused gun loaded, is upset emotionally, is careless in handling a gun, is ignorant of or disregards state laws governing hunting, or uses firearms while under influence of beverage alcohol (or drugs)	Less likely to occur if one makes sure unused firearms are left unloaded, never looks down barrel of a gun, never lets snow get into muzzle of gun, never gets into an automobile with loaded gun, never moves about in boat with loaded gun, understands regulations governing hunting in his state, and avoids using gun when drinking beverage alcohol (or drugs)
Home, burns Mechanical (manual skills)	Likely to occur when one smokes in bed or while lying down, is careless or ignorant of safe manner of handling fireworks, or lacks skill and understanding of safe ways to handle flammables	Less likely to occur if one does not smoke in bed or while lying down, if only skilled operators are permitted to handle fireworks, and if there is skilled and safe use of flammables

KIND OF ACCIDENT	OCCURRENCE	PREVENTION
Home, burns Personal	Likely to occur when an individual working with fire or flammable chemicals is overfatigued, has been drinking beverage alcohol, is upset emotionally, or is careless about an open fire	Less likely to occur if smokers who are intoxicated are kept under supervision, if proper safeguards are used around open fires, and if there is constant protection of children against misuse of fire or flammable materials
Home, falls Mechanical (manual skills)	Most likely to occur when good housekeeping techniques are lacking, floors are slippery, passageways and stairs are poorly lighted, or an unstable support is used in reaching for high places	Less likely to occur if good housekeeping techniques are practiced, floors and stairs are not slippery, all passageways are kept free from articles, steps are in good repair, steady hand rails are available on stairways, ladders and other articles used for climbing to high places are made secure and are appropriate for bearing desired weight, and a white line is painted on top and bottom steps
Personal	Likely to occur when one is careless or lacks proper safety attitudes, is intoxicated, or is not alert to environmental hazards	Less likely to occur if one has proper safety attitudes, if intoxicated persons are kept under control, and if members of household receive sound instruction on home safety
Home, poisonous gases Mechanical (manual skills)	Likely to occur when gas appliances are defective, when gas heaters are burning with windows of room closed, when coal-burning furnace is defective, when carbon monoxide is not permitted safe escape, or when one searches for gas leaks with lighted match or candle	Less likely to occur if all heating and cooking appliances are correctly installed and inspected regularly, if room heated by gas has fresh supply of oxygen, and if flashlight is used when searching for gas leaks

KIND OF ACCIDENT	OCCURRENCE	PREVENTION
Home, poisonous gases Personal	Likely to occur when there is carelessness or ignorance about safe heating and cooking facilities in house, about importance of fresh air in room heated by gas, about importance of protecting against fatal monoxide gas, or about determination of source of gas leakage; also occurs if one is overfatigued or intoxicated and unable to use gas appliances properly	Less likely to occur if members of household receive adequate instruction on safe use of all gas appliances and individuals realize dangers of carbon monoxide (as in working on running motor with garage door closed)
School-campus Mechanical (manual skills)	May occur in physical educational program when pupils engaged in body-contact sports and games use improper and unsafe equipment or play on slippery surfaces or in unprotected and unsafe areas May occur in shops, laboratories, and classrooms when pupils are not properly instructed in use of hand tools, fast-moving machinery, explosives, and other dangerous chemicals	Less likely to occur if there is proper instruction in skills, if adequate and safe equipment is used, if playing areas are made safe, if there is intelligent supervision of all physical activities, if proper instruction and supervision in use of dangerous equipment is provided in all shops, laboratories, and classrooms, and if dangerous machinery and chemicals are properly safeguarded
Personal	May occur in physical education program when pupil lacks game and sport skills, is overtense, has uncompensated bodily disabilities, is overfatigued or careless, or uses inadequate or unsafe equipment May occur in shops, laboratories, and classrooms when pupil lacks skill and understanding about proper use of assigned materials and equipment, fails to exercise proper safeguards while working with dangerous materials, or is fatigued or sleepy	Less likely to occur if there is adequate medical examination and counseling of all students, if recreation program is provided for entire student body, and if pupils are properly instructed in the skills and safeguards necessary for safe use of dangerous equipment in shops, laboratories, and classrooms

protection afforded by the combined use of seat belt and shoulder harness had been amply demonstrated (Aldman 1962).

Seat belts afford protection by preventing ejection, which is the commonest cause of death in car accidents, and by reducing the risk of the body striking against the front or rear doors or side panel, which is the second most common cause. But they do not provide adequate protection against hitting the windshield, especially for tall persons or for persons in small cars. For this, the additional use of the shoulder harness is necessary (but the harness should never be used without a seat belt). For these devices to render full service, they ought to be used properly (Figure 6.13) and consistently. For many people, this seems to be very difficult to do. Surveys have shown that seat belts are used only one-third of the time (Alsever 1968a). Seat belts are not just for long trips: 75 percent of deaths occur within 25 miles of home and 50 percent within 10 miles. Nor are they only for high-speed driving or slippery roads: most fatalities occur at less than 40 miles per hour; 90 percent happen in clear weather with good driving conditions (Alsever 1968b). The risk of injury due to seat belts and shoulder harnesses is minimal compared with their potential benefits. The fear of being trapped in them in a fire or if submerged in water is unrealistic: fire or submersion comprise only a fraction of 1 percent of acci-

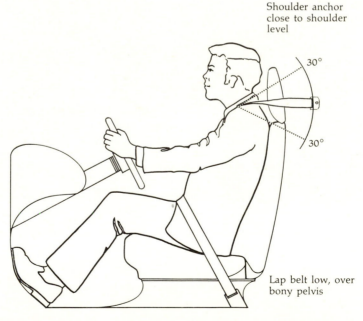

FIGURE 6.13
Recommended positioning of seat belt and shoulder harness to restrain upper part of body.

FIGURE 6.14
The sports car—highly valued by some youth. [From World Health Organization, Adolescence: The Quest, July–August 1969. Photograph by Jean Mohr.]

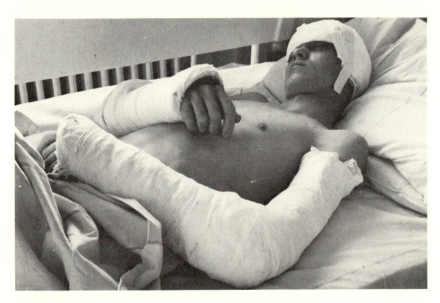

FIGURE 6.15
Victim of road accident. [From World Health Organization, Road Accidents, *World Health,* October 1975. Photograph by P. Almasy.]

dents. And, even then, an uninjured person has a better chance of extricating himself than otherwise (Seat belts: Helpful or harmful? 1962).

In the last analysis, perhaps the most significant factor is the perpetual realization—not morbid preoccupation but assuasive awareness—that it takes very little to move from the scene in Figure 6.14 to that in Figure 6.15.

DRUGS

One reason for the controversy over drug usage is that people have different notions of what constitutes a drug. Its traditional medical definition specifies it as "any substance, other than food, used in the prevention, diagnosis, alleviation, treatment, or cure of disease in man and animal" (*Stedman's Medical Dictionary* 1972). Currently, the term is used to designate substances other than chemical therapeutic agents and to include "any substance that, when taken into the living organism, may modify one or more of its functions" (World Health Organization 1974).[4]

This discussion treats of those drugs whose effects are primarily psychoactive; that is, they influence moods, thoughts, consciousness, and behavior. This means that tobacco, alcohol, and what are more commonly referred to as drugs will be considered together. In other words, the concern herein is with dependence-producing drugs. Such a drug has

> . . . the capacity to interact with a living organism to produce a state of psychic or physical dependence or both. Such a drug may be used medically or nonmedically without necessarily producing such a state. The characteristics of a state of drug dependence, once developed, will vary with the type of drug involved. Some types of drug, including those present in tea and coffee, are capable of producing drug dependence in a very broad sense. The existence of such a state is not necessarily harmful in itself. There are, however, several types of drug that, because they can produce substantial central nervous stimulation or depression, or disturbances in perception, mood, thinking, behavior, or motor function, are generally recognized as having the capacity, under certain circumstances of use, to produce individual and public health and social problems. [From WHO Expert Committee on Drug Dependence (1974).]

Drugs that commonly produce dependence have been categorized by the World Health Organization in the following way (WHO Expert Committee on Drug Dependence 1974):

> (1) alcohol-barbiturate type—e.g., ethanol, barbiturates, and certain other drugs with sedative effects, such as chloral hydrate, chlordiazepoxide, diazepam, meprobamate, and methaqualone;
> (2) amphetamine type—e.g., amphetamine, dexamphetamine, methamphetamine, methylphenidate, and phenmetrazine;

---

[4]Presumably, foods are excluded from this definition, otherwise anything edible would constitute a drug, which would make the term meaningless. On the other hand, the two classes of substances do overlap: alcohol, for example, readily fits most any definition of a drug, yet it also contains carbohydrates and is no less a food than candy.

(3) cannabis type—preparations of *Cannabis sativa* L., such as marijuana (bhang, dagga, kif, maconha), ganja, and hashish (charas);

(4) cocaine type—cocaine and coca leaves;

(5) hallucinogen type—e.g., lysergide (LSD), mescaline, and psilocybin;

(6) khat type—preparations of *Catha edulis* Forssk;

(7) opiate (morphine) type—e.g., opiates such as morphine, heroin, and codeine, and synthetics with morphinelike effects, such as methadone and pethidine; and

(8) volatile solvent (inhalent) type—e.g., toluene, acetone, and carbon tetrachloride.

Tobacco is not included in the preceding list, although it is clearly a dependence-producing substance and a serious health hazard.

The topic of drug use is vast. This discussion is necessarily limited to the nature of the substances, their effects on the body, and their potential as health hazards. Although a historical background of the use of psychoactive substances is included in this section, the prevalence of their use, their psychological motivations, and social repercussions will not be dealt with.

HISTORICAL BACKGROUND

The origins of drug use are lost in prehistory. Presumably, as early man foraged about for food, he discovered that certain plants produced mysterious effects on his perception and mood. Since then, in virtually all cultures, man has attempted to alter his mental states through the intake of substances containing active chemicals. But societies have varied a great deal in the emphasis they have placed on such practices, as well as the means they have used to carry them out (Shuster 1962).

American Indians used drugs extensively for ceremonial purposes, as well as for personal ones. Tobacco, a New World plant, is by far the most frequently used drug in the world. Yet, the early colonists did not adopt the use of other drugs known to the natives of the continent.

The use of alcohol dates back to ancient times. There are references to it in the Old Testament and in Egyptian documents of 4000 B.C. (Grinspoon 1969). The earlier alcoholic beverages were weak, fermented drinks, like beer and wine (Figure 6.16). The process of distillation, which produces stronger drinks, was introduced into Europe by Arabs in the Middle Ages. Distilled beverages acquired wide medical use as a panacea for all ills (the term *whiskey* is derived from the Gaelic *usquebaugh* and means "water of life") (Ritchie 1975).

FIGURE 6.16

Wall painting from the Tomb of Nakht: wine making—gathering and treading grapes (3,500 years ago). Thebes was a center of wine culture in ancient Egypt. The grapes were picked from the vines rather than cut with a knife, so as not to wound the spirit of the wine deity, and then trodden with bare feet; the new wine was stored in large jars to ferment and ripen. [The Metropolitan Museum of Art. Photograph by Egyptian Expedition.]

Marijuana, too, has been known for a long time. There is a description of it in the medical compendium of the Chinese Emperor Shen Nung, dated 2737 B.C. (some consider the date to be later). Its use spread in India and North Africa and, from there, it was introduced into Europe at the beginning of the nineteenth century, possibly brought there by the veterans of Napoleon's Egyptian campaign.

In the United States, the marijuana plant (Indian hemp) was first cultivated commercially for its fiber in Jamestown, Virginia, in 1611. But nothing was known of its intoxicating qualities until 1857, when Fitz Hugh Ludlow published a book on its euphoriant properties. Its use as a euphoriant attracted little attention for the next fifty years (Grinspoon 1975).

Marijuana has also been long used in medicine, especially in India. In the West, it was widely prescribed in the nineteenth century for such ailments as coughing, fatigue, rheumatism, asthma, delirium tremens, migrain, and painful menstruation. It remained in legitimate medical use in the United States until the 1930s, when the availability of more effective products eliminated it from medical use (Kaplan 1971).

The psychoactive effects of opium are thought to have been known to the Sumerians who referred to it as the "joy plant" as long ago as 4000 B.C. (Jaffe and Martin 1975). Derivatives of opium have been in medical use for many centuries. Their habit-forming characteristic was well known in the eighteenth century. Morphine was discovered in 1803 (named after Morpheus, the God of Sleep) and, with the introduction of the hypodermic syringe in the middle of the nineteenth century, its use became quite common in medicine, to the extent that patients were allowed to relieve their pain at their own discretion. The use of the drug increased during the Civil War, and addiction to morphine came to be known as the "army disease." Nevertheless, the use and abuse of morphine by the medical profession attracted no public attention.

After the Civil War, Chinese immigrants to the West coast introduced the practice of smoking opium, which was taken up by members of the underworld. Public reaction to such "street" use was quite different from the reaction to the medical use of what was fundamentally the same drug: in 1875, an ordinance was passed in San Francisco prohibiting the possession of opium or the paraphernalia for its smoking.

By the turn of the century, attempts at prohibition notwithstanding, there were more than 250,000 opiate-dependent individuals in the United States. This led to an intensification of attempts at control, and, in 1906, Congress passed the Pure Food and Drug Act. This was the first major federal drug law, and it required that all preparations containing "habit forming" drugs be so labeled.

Meanwhile, heroin had been introduced in 1898 and promoted as a substance with the virtues but not the shortcomings of its parent substance, morphine. But, within a decade, the medical profession became justifiably alarmed about the addictive nature of heroin. The concern was instrumental in the passage of the Harrison Narcotic Act in 1914. A national policy began to emerge concerning the nonmedical use of addictive substances. The term "narcotic," which originally referred to substances that produce sleep or narcosis (and would thus include alcohol), shifted in meaning to characterize any drug that found its way into groups who were already using opiates and cocaine. It is thus that peyote and marijuana became designated as narcotics in the laws of many states in the next several decades. Amphetamines and barbiturates were introduced into medical practice in the early 1930s, but similar laws were not enacted against them because their street use did not occur on a massive scale until the 1960s.

The use of hallucinogenic mushrooms and other substances also dates back many years in many cultures. Only lysergic acid diethylamide (LSD) is a recent discovery. It was first accidentally taken by a chemist, Albert Hofmann, in 1938, who was able to synthesize it (Hofmann 1970). Subsequently, Hofmann also discovered psilocybin in the Mexican magic mushroom and hallucinogenic compounds in ololiuqui, a tropical American morning glory (Cohen 1966).

Societal concern with the effects of drug use and abuse also date back to antiquity (Figure 6.17). But the "drug problem" as it is known today is a phenomenon of the last decade. During this period, a large variety of hallucinogens, stimulants, and sedatives found their way into the streets and would probably have gone unnoticed if the users had continued to be various social

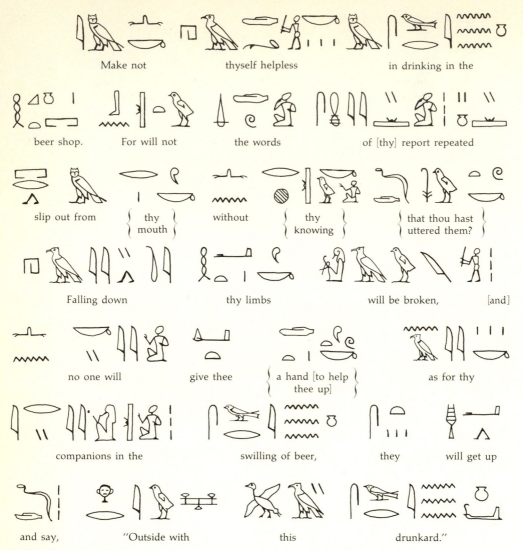

FIGURE 6.17
Cautionary remarks from an Egyptian book of etiquette, *The Percepts of Ani*, 1500 B.C. [From Sir E. A. Wallis Budge, *The Dwellers on the Nile*.]

outcasts. There has always been a fear that drug use would spread to the nation's youth, but, unlike the drug scares concerning cocaine at the turn of the century, heroin in the 1920s, marijuana in the 1930s, and heroin once again in the 1950s, what had been feared finally materialized in the 1960s.

Community and government reactions to the use of drugs by young people have been complicated by changes in their sexual behavior, political activities, and life styles, which conflict with established social norms. As stated in a report by the National Commission on Marijuana and Drug Abuse (1973):

The drug taking of this youth population coincides with pervasive social anxieties regarding social disorder in general and youthful behavior specifically. To many, youthful drug use offered a convenient explanation for these problems, and, as the Commission noted in its first Report, marijuana in particular came to symbolize the entire spectrum of social concern.

In 1965, the Drug Abuse Control Amendments designated as "dangerous" those drugs that are not narcotic, such as hallucinogens, amphetamines, and barbiturates. in 1968, federal bureaucracy was reorganized, and the drug agencies in the Department of the Treasury and the Department of Health, Education, and Welfare were merged into a new agency—the Bureau of Narcotics and Dangerous Drugs—in the Department of Justice. This agency now spends more than $1 billion annually. The extent to which Americans have come to rely on psychoactive or psychotropic drugs is very impressive. There are more than 1,500 compounds classified primarily as psychotropic agents (Usdin and Efron 1972). One out of every five prescriptions written in the United States is intended to mechanically influence mental processes and behavior (Byck 1975). The retail sales of medically prescribed psychoactive drugs (214 million prescriptions in 1970) amount to $1 billion, and the sale of psychoactive substances in the street amounts to an estimated $2 billion a year; yet, these figures are dwarfed in comparison with the revenue from the sale of alcohol, which amounts to $24 billion a year (National Commission on Marijuana and Drug Abuse 1973).

GENERAL CHARACTERISTICS
OF PSYCHOACTIVE DRUGS

All drugs have in common a number of general characteristics (Fingl and Woodbury 1975; Goldstein, Aronow, and Kalman 1974). For example, a drug does not produce a single effect but a range of effects, which is narrow in some cases and wide in others. The overall effect that a drug produces depends on dosage, among other factors. For each compound, there is an "effective dose"; that is, the amount required to produce the desired effect. A "toxic dose" (from the Greek word *toxikon* for poison) produces deleterious effects, and a "lethal dose" kills. Every drug is capable of producing toxic effects, though they range from mild to fatal. The potency and clinical margin of safety of drugs varies widely: the difference between an effective dose of some drugs and a toxic one is a few milligrams; of others, it is many grams. The "side effects" of a drug refer to the reactions that are extraneous to the desired effects. Side effects, too, can be mild or highly toxic.

Physicians are keenly aware that the use of any drug at any time constitutes a calculated risk. An ideal drug would have exclusively a specific and salutory effect, whereas the worst drug would have a generalized and deleterious effect: the first one doesn't exist, and the second we obviously have no use for. In practice, therefore, such substances can be both beneficial and harmful to varying degrees. Thus, the selection of a drug for therapeutic use depends on the circumstances. To alleviate a minor discomfort, only minimal risks are warranted; yet, in an effort to save a life, potent poisons or destructive physical forces (such as various forms of radiation to treat cancer) may be resorted to.

In addition to the chemical nature of a drug and the dosage, a host of other factors influence the end result. They include body weight, age, sex, the means and time of administration, the rate of inactivation and excretion, genetic factors, and other considerations related to the pathological condition and to the physiological variables operating within the person taking the drug.

In using psychoactive drugs, the circumstances under which they are taken are highly significant. The lower the dose or the less potent the drug, the more likely are these considerations to be significant. If, for example, someone is given large quantities of alcohol or barbiturates, he will inevitably go to sleep irrespective of all other considerations. Yet, how a person reacts to a few drinks or to smoking small amounts of marijuana very much depends on his psychological state, as well as on the circumstances under which the drugs are taken. Experiments have shown that situational determinants influence subjective sensations even to drugs (such as epinephrine) that ordinarily have well-defined physiological and psychological responses (Cantril and Hunt 1932; Schachter and Singer 1962).

The boundary between drug use and abuse is arbitrary. A strict definition would regard the use of all illegal drugs, as well as the nonmedical use of legal drugs, as constituting abuse. A more lenient criterion would consider a drug to be abused only if its use significantly interferes with physical well-being and psychosocial adjustment.

Dependence on drugs varies widely for different people and at different times. Some use drugs only on certain social occasions or under stressful conditions, whereas others use them most of the time. There is no difficulty in distinguishing between occasional use and addiction, but the wide range of use between the two extremes is more problematic.

An important distinction is between psychological and physiological dependence. Psychological dependence is like a habit: a person may have a strong emotional need for the effect of the drug because it is pleasurable or because it provides relief from psychological discomfort. Abstinence results in a craving for the drug, which may make the person feel anxious and miserable, but which produces no physiological effects when the substance ceases to be replenished in the body.

In physiological dependence, the body becomes dependent on the drug through prolonged use. Apart from psychological craving, there is a pathophysiological need for the chemical. When the amount circulating in the blood falls below a critical point, the person begins to experience distinct and predictable physical symptoms that are relieved by taking more of the drug. Such withdrawal symptoms constitute the "abstinence syndrome" for a given drug. It is as if the drug has acquired a self-sustaining life of its own, compelling the person to use it. In most cases, physical dependence is reinforced by psychological dependence, creating a formidable hold on the person.

A common feature of many psychoactive drugs is the development of *tolerance,* which means that to obtain the same effect a user must keep increasing the dosage. An addict is thus usually unable to maintain the intake of moderate doses. Long-term drug users may be able to tolerate doses that would kill a nonaddict. *Cross-tolerance* may develop between related drugs. For example, a heroin addict can also have a tolerance for morphine. After an addict has successfully withdrawn from the use of a drug, his tolerance is reduced to ordinary levels.

Some deleterious effects of drugs are a function of how they are administered or the presence of impurities. For example, heroin addicts often suffer ill effects from using contaminated needles or from impurities in the drugs they inject. In principle, such ill effects are not due to the drug itself, but an evaluation of the net effect of a drug must take into account all deleterious effects associated with its use, including those that are directly attributable to its chemical properties and those that are circumstantial.

Psychoactive drugs vary in behavioral effects, but, generally, in adequate doses they tend to produce a pattern of symptoms known in psychiatry as a *brain syndrome.* This syndrome may be acute and reversible or chronic and permanent. In either case, the syndrome has two sets of symptoms, which will be illustrated in the discussion of alcohol, which follows.

ALCOHOL

The intoxicating chemical in alcoholic beverages is ethanol, or ethyl alcohol, which is usually produced by the fermentation of grains and fruits.[5] Its concentration in nondistilled alcoholic beverages ranges from 3 to 8 percent in beers, is about 12 percent in table wines, is 20 percent in fortified or dessert wines (such as sherry, port, and vermouth), and ranges from 20 to 55 percent in liqueurs or cordials.

---

[5]Ethanol should not be confused with other alcohols commonly used in medicine and industry. The alcohol often used as a disinfectant is methyl alcohol, which is highly toxic if ingested. The term *alcohol* is derived from the Arabic *al-kuhl,* which is a cosmetic dye.

The alcohol content of distilled spirits is higher: brandy, 55 percent; whiskey, 40 percent; rum, 40 percent; gin, from 35 to 50 percent; vodka, from 40 to 50 percent.[6]

Ethanol is fully absorbed from the gastrointestinal tract within two to six hours of its ingestion: 20 percent through the stomach; 80 percent, the small intestine. Its effects depend in part on the concentration of alcohol in the beverage (up to 40 percent, the higher the concentration, the more rapidly it is absorbed) and on the presence of other chemicals (congeners), which give the beverage its flavor, odor, and color. Vodka, which is free of congeners, is the most rapidly absorbed; beers and wines, the most slowly.

The presence of food in the stomach slows the rate of absorption significantly. The time it takes the stomach to empty also affects the rate of absorption and is, in turn, influenced by anger, fear, stress, nausea, and so on. Rates of absorption also depend on the beverages themselves. Champagne and other carbonated wines are absorbed faster than ordinary wines, and their effects are felt more immediately. A given amount of alcohol in beer will produce an alcohol level in the blood that is about half as high as that produced by an equal amount of alcohol in whiskey. Generally, the effect of a 1-ounce drink of whiskey equals that of two 12-ounce cans of beer (American Medical Association 1967).

People differ in their basic rates of absorption, as does the same person at different times. Body weight is an important factor—a heavier person is affected relatively less. Finally, experienced drinkers can tolerate the effects of alcohol better than novices, but chronic alcoholics may eventually reach a point at which even a single drink has a marked effect on them.

Alcohol in the blood stream diffuses to all tissues (in pregnant women, it passes through the placenta to the fetus). Most of it is metabolized in the liver, and a small amount is excreted in the urine, exhaled in breathing, and lost in perspiration. Regardless of its rate of absorption, alcohol is metabolized (oxidized) at a constant rate of $\frac{3}{8}$ ounce per hour.[7] This means that it takes the body one hour to get rid of $\frac{2}{3}$ ounce of straight whiskey or 8 ounces of beer (Johns, Sutton, and Webster 1975). At the cellular level, alcohol acts as a stimulant at low concentrations and as a depressant at high concentrations. At extremely high concentrations, it causes cellular damage and death (Leake, Chauncey, and Silverman 1966).

Subject to the preceding variations, blood levels of alcohol and its effects conform to a general pattern. A 155-pound moderate drinker, on rapidly con-

---

[6]The alcoholic content of spirits is often expressed as "proof," which is double the percent of alcohol by volume. Thus, 80 proof whiskey is 40 percent alcohol. For further discussion of the nature of alcoholic beverages, see Leake and Silverman (1966).

[7]A gram of alcohol yields 7 calories. There are about 10 grams of alcohol in an ounce of whiskey, which makes a standard drink worth 70 calories.

suming 3 ounces of 90-proof whiskey on an empty stomach, will develop a peak alcohol blood level of 0.05 grams per 100 cubic centimeters of blood (50 mg/cm³).[8] This usually results in mild sedation, tranquility, and euphoria. Under similar conditions, 6 ounces will raise the alcohol blood level to 0.10 grams and will produce lack of coordination.[9] Six drinks (12 ounces) will produce a level of 0.20 grams and marked intoxication; 15 ounces and more will raise the blood level to 0.30 grams and higher, bringing about unconsciousness. Levels of 0.50 can be fatal (National Clearing House for Mental Health Information 1968).

The central nervous system is affected more markedly by alcohol than any other system of the body. Although alcohol seems to act as a "stimulant," it is primarily a depressant, the first effects of which are in those parts of the brain that participate in the most highly integrated functions (Ritchie 1975). It is the lifting of inhibitory controls that "releases" various forms of heightened activity.

A great deal of folklore surrounds the influence of alcohol on mood and behavior. Extreme claims are made both in its favor and against it; it has been said by some to be a source of artistic inspiration and by others to be an agent of the devil.

Much of the popular confusion about the effects of alcohol arises from the discrepancy between the perceptions of a person under its influence and performance: the person may feel boundless confidence; yet careful experiments have shown that alcohol does not enhance either mental or physical abilities. Efficiency, in fact, decreases as discrimination, memory, and concentration become gradually dulled. The ability to perform familiar tasks requiring low skills is less affected.

A person may perform better owing to moderate amounts of alcohol under circumstances in which psychological and social inhibitions would ordinarily hamper behavior. Thus, people who are anxious, shy, or fearful may be emboldened to act in ways that they would otherwise be unable to. Whether the outcome of such behavior is socially beneficial to the person depends on the circumstances.

A moderate amount of alcohol can enhance physiological activities as well; for example, it raises the threshold of pain. It can improve the ability to do physical work because the person becomes less conscious of fatigue (alcohol also supplies energy and improves blood circulation) (Ritchie 1975). In short, alcohol may help performance by temporarily removing mental handicaps,

---

[8]A standard drink of whiskey served at a bar consists of 1 ounce (a "shot"). What people call a "drink" varies widely in alcohol content.

[9]This is the legal limit for intoxication in a number of states, including California, and is the limit recommended by the American Medical Association. In most states, the limit is higher—0.15 grams per cubic centimeter. Actually, driving can be unsafe at the 0.04 level, which can be produced by a couple of drinks.

but it never improves on the basic performance one ought to be otherwise capable of.

The psychoactive effects of alcohol taken in excess constitute an *acute brain syndrome*. More commonly known as drunkenness, this condition has two components. One component comprises symptoms that are common to various states of inebriation and result from transient brain disorganization. They include states of mental disorientation, cognitive and perceptual difficulties, disturbances of gait and balance, slurred speech, and sleepiness, among others. The progressive effects of the depression of the central nervous system result in stupor, coma, and death.

The second component comprises manifestations that are more idiosyncratic. Most people feel euphoric, relaxed, and less inhibited, but others become depressed, withdrawn or belligerent. These symptoms are thought to result from the surfacing of the repressed aspects of the personality with the lifting of inhibitions. They may also be the result of direct brain stimulation.

The long-term effects of alcoholism result in a *chronic brain syndrome,* which, in some ways, parallels the acute form. One set of symptoms results from brain malfunction, including failure of memory and cognitive functions, a tendency to confabulate, and other neurological problems. Another set reflects deterioration of the personality, emergence of repressed traits, and so on. The excessive and prolonged use of alcohol produces a number of characteristic psychotic states (Chafetz 1975).

A third set of effects is physiological and includes the dilatation of blood vessels (which accounts for feeling flushed), hypothermia, or lowering of body temperature, (which makes alcohol a poor means of keeping warm), increased production of gastric acid (which is why it is bad for ulcers and causes gastritis), and increased urination. The excess alcohol consumed rapidly results in nausea, vomiting, and diarrhea. Chronic use disturbs liver metabolism and leads to permanent liver damage (compounded by malnutrition). The most common aftereffect of overindulgence is a "hangover," for which there is no "sure cure" despite claims to the contrary.

Alcohol is popularly thought of as an aphrodisiac. Many people do become sexually aroused under its influence and some act impulsively. This effect, however, is another manifestation of the lifting of inhibitions. A person may also get away with behavior that would otherwise be unacceptable, by virtue of being drunk or pretending to be so. In substantial doses, alcohol actually produces a lack of sexual responsiveness. Its effect in producing impotence has been immortalized by Shakespeare.[10]

People develop tolerance to alcohol and cross-tolerance to other central

---

[10]Macduff: What three things does drink especially provoke?

Porter: Marry, sir, nose-painting, sleep, and urine. Lechery, sir, it provokes, and unprovokes: it provokes the desire, but it takes away the performance. [*Macbeth,* act 2, scene 3.]

nervous depressants. Withdrawal symptoms (rarely seen in teen-age drinkers) range from slight tremulousness to delirium tremens (DT's) with hallucinations.

Chronic alcoholism with its mental and physical complications (such as cirrhosis of the liver) is not found among youth. Adolescent alcohol abuse is more likely to result in acute gastritis, pancreatitis, and severe depression of the central nervous system—all of which require the consumption of large amounts of alcohol. A far more frequent hazard of intoxication is reckless behavior, such as drunken driving, and the traumas that result from it.

The consumption of alcohol by youth is generally more a social than a medical problem. In large sections of society, attaining adulthood includes learning how to drink. Why some become discriminating wine connoisseurs and others "winos" cannot be entirely explained by the chemical properties of alcohol. There is no simple reason why people drink: for some, a drink is no more than a pleasant taste experience; for others, it is the glue that holds them psychologically together, in a fashion.

TOBACCO

Tobacco is prepared from the dried leaves of *Nicotiana tabacum,* a plant indigenous to America, but now cultivated in many parts of the world. The substance most commonly associated with tobacco is nicotine, but about five hundred compounds have been isolated from tobacco smoke (Volle and Koelle 1975). Nicotine is classified as a drug but not as a narcotic. It is the addictive substance that is responsible for the development of physiological dependence in heavy smokers. Although the pattern of habituation to smoking is similar to dependency on other drugs and potentially just as seriously harmful, smoking remains widespread and socially approved, despite medical warnings. Cigarette smoking, which is what will be discussed in this section, is the most hazardous to health of all forms of tobacco smoking. The habit is usually established during adolescence. Attempts to dissuade young people from smoking through public education (Figures 6.18 and 6.19) can barely compete with the massive advertising campaigns of the tobacco industry.

The harmfulness of cigarettes was established in the early 1960s and put forth in a major report by the Surgeon General of the Public Health Service (U. S. Public Health Service 1964). Subsequent research has confirmed earlier findings and identified further hazards (U. S. Public Health Service 1967, 1968, 1969; World Health Organization 1975). Some of the major conclusions of these extensive investigations are summarized in Box 6.3.

The statistics on the health hazards of smoking are devastating. An estimated 360,000 persons die annually in the United States because of tobacco use. It

"We'll miss ya, baby."

FEMME FATALE
Cigarettes are part of the costume. Next week she learns how to inhale.

MAN OF DESTINY
Smokes because he thinks it's good for his "image." Coughs a lot, too.

WISE GUY
Likes to keep a cigarette in his mouth when he talks. Very hard to understand.

ME-TOO
Smokes because his friends do. Doesn't know whether he likes it or not.

Cigarettes can kill you — keep smoking 'em and they may.

FIGURE 6.18
Youthful smokers. [American Cancer Society.]

FIGURE 6.19
Antismoking posters from the USSR and the United States. The child in the Soviet poster is saying, "We don't want to inhale nicotine." [From World Health Organization, *World Health*, February–March 1970. Photographs by Novosti (left) and American Cancer Society (right).]

has been calculated that, on the average, every cigarette shortens a smoker's life by 14 minutes, and about 800 billion cigarettes are smoked in the United States in a year (Volle and Koelle 1975). Evidence of pulmonary damage can be observed in high-school students who have smoked for one to five years. More serious consequences develop over longer periods (Figure 6.20).

Figure 6.21 (p. 216) shows the comparative death rates of smokers and non-smokers, by selected causes. There are other ailments, too many to enumerate here, that are demonstrably higher in cigarette smokers. Higher mortality rates for cigarette smokers are due to many ailments, but 80 percent of this excess is due to lung cancer, bronchitis, emphysema, and cardiovascular ailments (World Health Organization Expert Committee 1975). Smoking during pregnancy is associated with low birthweight and increased chances of prematurity, abortion, stillbirth and neonatal death (U. S. Public Health Service 1968).

There is no reasonable doubt anymore about the dangers of cigarette smoking, but what exactly makes it harmful remains unclear. About 60 percent of tobacco smoke consists of presumably harmless gases; 40 percent is composed of tar and nicotine, which purportedly account for its deleterious effects (Figure 6.22, p. 217). Damage to the cardiovascular system is caused by nicotine, whereas the carcinogenic agents are believed to be in tar.

BOX 6.3
Hazards of smoking (U.S. Public Health Service 1970).

• The risk of death is about 70 percent higher for men who smoke cigarettes than for men who do not. The risk is significantly higher for women who smoke cigarettes than for those who do not.

• The risk of death from chronic bronchitis and emphysema is from 3 to 20 times greater, depending upon age and total amount smoked.

• The risk of death from coronary artery disease—the major killer of smokers and nonsmokers alike—is 70 percent greater for smokers.

• The greater the number of cigarettes smoked daily, the higher the death rate; for men who smoke fewer than 10 cigarettes a day the rate is 40 percent higher than for nonsmokers, for those who smoke 10 to 19 cigarettes a day, 70 percent higher, and for those who smoke 40 or more a day, 120 percent higher.

• Life expectancy among young men is reduced by an average of eight years in heavy (over 2 packs a day) cigarette

smokers and an average of 4 years in light (less than $\frac{1}{2}$ pack a day) smokers.

• The risk is greater for those who start smoking at young ages.

• The risk is greater for those who inhale.

• Death rates for cigar and pipe smokers, who usually do not inhale the tobacco smoke, are not greatly higher than those of persons who do not smoke at all.

• A greater risk of unsuccessful pregnancy is experienced by women who smoke than by nonsmoking women.

• Workers who smoke as much as a pack of cigarettes a day spend a third more time away from their jobs because of illness as people who have never smoked.

• Men and women who smoke average 15 percent more days ill in bed than those who have never smoked. For heavy smokers (more than 2 packs a day) the rate is $1\frac{1}{2}$ times higher among males and $2\frac{1}{2}$ times higher for females.

FIGURE 6.20
Emphysema, for which smoking is a cause, has so reduced this man's lung capacity that he cannot blow out a match. [From World Health Organization, *World Health,* February–March 1970. Originally filmed by the American Cancer Society.]

The most obvious way to avoid the increased health risks associated with cigarette smoking is not to smoke. Nearly 60 percent of the nation's population over 17 years old (49 percent of the men and 66 percent of the women) are nonsmokers, either because they never started or because they have stopped smoking.

As more people become convinced of the health hazards associated with cigarette smoking, more people are giving up cigarettes. Even for persons who have smoked heavily and for very long periods of time, to stop is to reduce the risk, unless disease has already set in.

Per capita consumption of cigarettes in the United States dropped after publication of the Surgeon General's report in 1964; it recovered to some extent in the next few years, but has now fallen back to below the 1964 level.

The health hazards posed by cigarette smoking are of such gravity and affect such a vast segment of our population that continued remedial action is necessary.

● There must be a further reduction in the number of people now smoking—a number which amounts to 50 million adults or 42 percent of the adult population.

● Young people must be encouraged not to start smoking. At present as many as 36 percent of the boys and 22 percent of the girls in this country have become cigarette smokers by the time they are 18.

● Work must continue on developing less hazardous cigarettes and methods of smoking, and, concurrently, on developing a climate of opinion so that, if such cigarettes and methods are available, smokers will turn to them. There is no other known way to protect those millions of present smokers who may never be willing or able to give up smoking.

The health of 50 million present smokers is at risk, as is the health of today's generation of young persons who have not as yet taken up smoking.

The immediate effects of smoking on healthy young persons include an increase in heart rate and blood pressure. Other physiological measures show that smokers require more effort than nonsmokers to accomplish the same physical task (Fodor, Glass, and Weiner 1969). The chronic effects of smoking are insidious and take time, which is why smokers who are young can minimize future damage greatly by quitting or at least reducing the number of cigarettes, the number of draws, and the extent of inhaling or by switching to brands that contain less tar and nicotine and by smoking only the first part of a cigarette (the last third yields 50 percent of the harmful substances).[11]

---

[11]About 90 percent of the nicotine in inhaled smoke is absorbed, but if smoke is drawn into the mouth only, from 25 to 50 percent of the nicotine is absorbed into the body (Volle and Koelle 1975). The fact that mortality rates for pipe and cigar smokers generally are not substantially higher than those for nonsmokers is probably because most are moderate smokers who do not inhale. The mortality rates for those who smoke heavily or inhale are from 20 to 40 percent higher than those for nonsmokers (World Health Organization Expert Committee 1975).

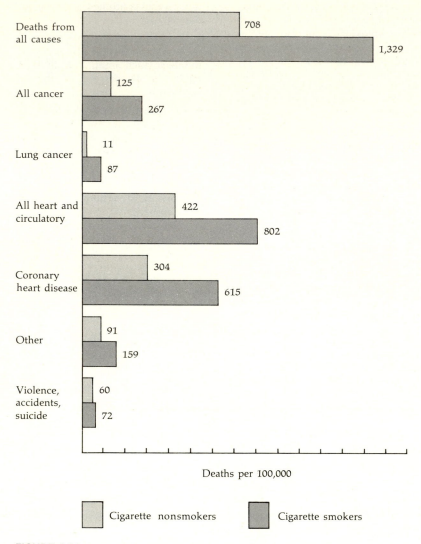

FIGURE 6.21
Death rates of cigarette smokers and nonsmokers among men aged 45 to 64, by selected diseases. [Redrawn from U.S. Public Health Service, *The facts about smoking and health,* pub. no. 1712, revised 1970.]

FIGURE 6.22
A smoking robot, an automatic device that puffs on cigarettes and traps tobacco tars. When painted on the backs of mice, these tars have produced cancer. [From World Health Organization, *World Health*, February–March 1970. American Cancer Society photograph.]

The physiological effects of smoking are not as dramatic as those of alcohol. Yet the psychological rewards to those dependent on it seem to be enormous. Attempts by heavy smokers to break the habit tend to be agonizing and often futile experiences. Young people may not be fully aware of this when they begin to smoke.

MARIJUANA

The Indian hemp *Cannabis sativa* is a common plant of temperate zones and hot, dry areas (Figure 6.23). The top leaves, flowers, and stems of the plant are dried, cleaned, and shredded for marijuana.[12] The active chemical substances are in the resin that permeates the plant, but whose concentration varies from one part of the plant to another, with the environmental conditions under which the plant is grown, and so on. The higher the resinous content, the more potent the drug.

---

[12]*Marijuana* is said to be derived from the Portuguese word *mariguango*, meaning intoxicant. For synonyms, see Box 6.4.

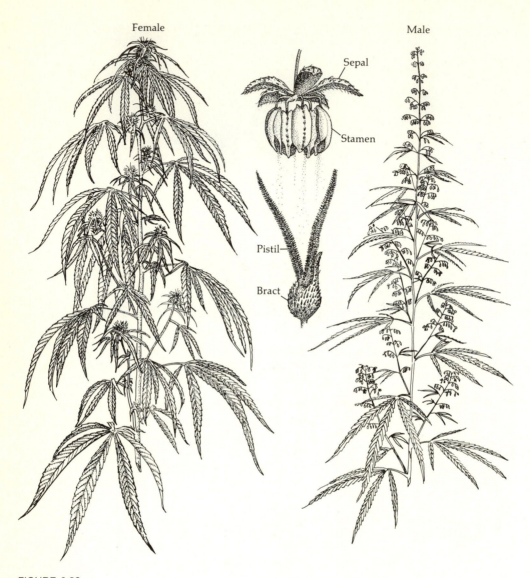

Female

Male

Sepal

Stamen

Pistil

Bract

FIGURE 6.23

Hemp plant (*Cannabis sativa*) is a common weed growing freely in many parts of the world, where it is used as a medicine, an intoxicant, and a source of fiber. It is classified as a dioecious plant; that is, the female reproductive parts are on one plant (left) and the male parts are on another (right). Details of the two types of flower are shown in the middle. The active substances in the drug are contained in a sticky yellow resin that covers the flower clusters and top leaves of the female plant when it is ripe. [Adapted from Marihuana by L. Grinspoon. Copyright © 1969 by Scientific American, Inc. All rights reserved.]

The least potent grade of marijuana is *bhang,* which is derived from the cut tops of uncultivated plants. Most of the marijuana smoked in the United States is of this quality. The next is *ganja,* obtained from selected and cultivated plants. The most potent grade is *charas,* made from the sticky yellow resin with a minty fragrance scraped from mature cultivated plants. *Hashish* properly refers to charas only and not to all forms of marijuana. It is five to eight times as strong as ordinary marijuana (Grinspoon 1969). (For other terms, see Box 6.4.)

Among the active compounds in the resin, the delta-9-tetrahydrocannabinol (Δ^9-THC) fraction has been synthesized and in pure synthetic form is a potent hallucinogen. Clandestine laboratories have recently developed a method of producing "hashish oil" or "liquid hashash," which may be more than 60 percent tetrahydracannabinol (Grinspoon 1975).

Marijuana can be smoked as a cigarette (Figure 6.24) and in pipes, brewed as a tea, or ingested (usually in sweets).

There are various accounts of the effects of marijuana dating back to the nineteenth century, but the pharmacologic actions of cannabis were systematically studied under laboratory conditions only in the 1960s. In man, the most prominent effects are on the central nervous and cardiovascular systems (Jaffe 1975).

FIGURE 6.24
Rolling a "joint" (a marijuana cigarette). [From World Health Organization, *World Health,* July–August 1969. Photograph by E. Mandelmann.]

Box 6.4
Lexicon of drug abuse terms (the words and phrases in capital letters are synonyms). [From H. L. Barnett and A. H. Einhorn, *Pediatrics*, 15th ed., 1972. Courtesy of Appleton-Century-Crofts, Publishing Division of Prentice-Hall, Inc.]

ACID	Hallucinogen (LSD, LSD-25, LYSERGIC ACID DIETHYLAMIDE, CUBE, BLACK TABS, PURPLE FLATS, SUGAR, ACID, INSTANT ZEN, BLUE ACID, THE CHIEF, THE HAWK, BLUE DOTS, OWSELYS, BIG D)
ACIDHEAD	Chronic LSD user (CUBEHEAD)
ADDICT	HOPHEAD, JUNKIE, DREAMER, SLEEPWALKER
ADDICTED	HOOKED, WIRED, VULTURE ON THE VEINS, MONKEY ON THE BACK
AMPHETAMINES	Stimulants (COPILOTS, BENNIES, CARTWHEELS, PEACHES, LID POPPERS, DEXIES, DOMINOES, FOOTBALLS, ROSES, ORANGES, HEARTS, JELLY BABIES, JOLLY BEANS, BROWNIES, BLACK BEAUTIES, DMA, DMDA, WHITES, WAKEUPS)
ARSENAL	Pusher's supply of drugs
ARTILLERY	Equipment employed in injecting drugs (WORKS, CANNON, FACTORY, G, GEAR, GUN, LAY-OUT, MACHINE, SPIKE)
BADHEAD	Emotionally confused from using drugs
BAG	Package of drugs (BUNDLE, FEED BAG)
BANG	To inject drugs
BARBITURATES	Depressants, sedatives (BARBS, GOOFBALLS, CANDY, DOUBLE TROUBLE, BLUEBIRDS, RED 88, NIMBY, PEANUTS, PINKS, RAINBOWS, RED DEVILS, YELLOW JACKETS, NEMMIES, BLUE DEVILS, BLUE HEAVENS, TOOIES, RED BIRDS, IDIOT PILLS, BLUE ANGELS, DOWNS)
BARBITURATE-AMPHETAMINE MIXTURE	GREENIES, FRENCH-BLUES, DOLLS
BLANK	Nonnarcotic or low grade narcotic (DUMMY, TURKEY, LEMONADE)
BLOW	Inhale
BLUE-VELVETS	Injectable mixture of paregoric and an antihistamine
BOMBITA	Amphetamine injection (occasionally with heroin)
BUMMER	Bad experience with psychedelics
BUTTON	Head of peyote cactus (mescal cactus—mescaline)
CAP	Gelatin capsule
CHIPPING	Using small quantities of drugs on an irregular basis (DABBLING)
CIBA	Glutethimide, Doriden
COCAINE	Stimulant (COKE, C, CANDY, DUST, GOLD DUST, SNOW, SPEEDBALL, CHOLLY, CHARLIE, BERNICE, GIRL, GIN)

CODEINE	POP, SCHOOLBOY
COLD TURKEY	Narcotic withdrawal without medication
COMBINATIONS	Mixtures of two or more drugs, one of which is usually LSD (L.B.J. STAY AWAY, PEARL PILL, WHITE LIGHTNING, QUINT)
CRASHING	To end an amphetamine binge
DEALER	A pusher, seller, or supplier of drugs
DMT	A synthetic hallucinogen, variants are DET, DPT
DOM	A potent synthetic hallucinogen (STP, "Serenity-Tranquility-Peace")
DOWNS	Sedatives
DROP	To ingest a drug
FIX	An injection of drugs (JOLT, SHOT, CHARGE, WAKEUP)
FLASH	The immediate effect of injecting a drug, a "rush"
GLUE SNIFFING	Inhalation of volatile solvents (GASSING, HUFFING, FLASHING)
HEAD	A chronic drug user
HEROIN	HARRY, ANTIFREEZE, BROWN, H, DOPE, BOY, HARD STUFF, DUGEE, WHITE STUFF, DOLLIES, HORSE, JUNK, SCAG, SMACK, SCAT
HOOKED	Addicted (STRUNG OUT)
KICK	To stop using drugs, to withdraw
MAINLINE	To inject drugs intravenously
MAO	Monoamine Oxidase Inhibitors
MARIHUANA	CONGO MATABY, DAGGA, DUBY, ACAPULCO GOLD, BOO, BU, GAGE, GAUGE, GANJA, GRASS, HASH, HASHISH, HEMP, HAY, MARYJANE, CANNABIS, KIEF, PANAMA RED, POT, ROPE, TEXAS TEA, WEED, MEZZ, MARY WARNER, MOTA, MUTA, MUD
MARIHUANA CIGARETTE	JOINT, STICK, REEFER, ROACH, ROCKET, PIN, TOKE
METHADONE	DOLLIES, DOLOPHINE
METHEDRINE	A potent amphetamine (MET, METH, METHAMPHETAMINE, SPEED, CRYSTALS, CHALK)
MORNING GLORY	A hallucinogen (WEDDING BELLS, HEAVENLY BLUE, FLYING SAUCERS, PEARLY GATES)
NOD	The stupor while on heroin
SCORE	To buy drugs
SHOOT UP	To inject drugs intravenously
SKIN POP	To inject drugs subcutaneously
SNIFFING	The inhalant route of drug abuse
SNORTING	The inhalant route for heroin abuse

The objective observable manifestations are quite modest. The effects of smoking are felt quite soon, which allows the user to modulate intake and thus control the intensity of the drug influence. They reach a peak in about 15 minutes and last from 2 to 4 hours. The action is slower if marijuana is ingested and lasts from 5 to 12 hours (Grinspoon 1971).

The main physical effects of the drug consist of increased heart rate, sometimes a short increase in blood pressure, reddening of the conjunctiva, dryness of the throat and mouth, and increased appetite. Contrary to popular belief, the size of the pupils remains substantially unchanged. There may be slight tremors and some loss of coordination.

The reason that people use marijuana obviously is not for the above effects, but to experience the "high," which consists of complex subjective sensations. They are highly variable, especially at low dosage levels: some people report very little change, others describe profound subjective experiences. The outcome is dependent on many factors: the dosage and the manner in which the drug is taken; the social setting in which it is used; the physical condition, mental state, and personality structure of the user; and the extent and nature of his past experiences with marijuana.

There are numerous descriptions of a marijuana "high" (see, for example, the accounts in Grinspoon [1971]; Nowlis [1969]; Goode [1970]; and Jones [1971]). A person's capacity to express himself is reduced when the experience is in progress, and, after the experience is over, the vividness of the sensations are lost. It is therefore difficult to understand another person's subjective experience in this regard. The effects can be grouped into several categories. Some are somatic, such as being suffused with a feeling of warmth and experiencing a feeling of lightness in the limbs and effortlessness of movements. Cognitive changes are experienced as a stream of disconnected ideas that flows rapidly and unhindered. Even ordinary statements tend to acquire new meanings and apparent profundity. Perceptions are altered as the senses become sharper: colors seem brighter, sounds clearer. Many report an enhanced appreciation of music. There may be a sensation of merging with the environment and a feeling of closeness to objects and people. The general mood is one of contentment, relaxation, contemplative peace, or carefree, childlike abandon.

There are numerous claims that marijuana acts as an aphrodisiac. It is difficult to determine if it enhances sexual performance. Subjectively, the experience may well be heightened or appear to have gained a new dimension (Goode 1969). These erotic properties of marijuana may be circumstantial and dependent on mood, setting, and so on. A decrease in testosterone has been reported for males who use marijuana frequently (Kolodny, Masters, Kilodner, and Toro 1974), but these findings have not been duplicated in other studies (Mendelson, Kuehnle, Ellingboe, and Babor 1974). Even if marijuana did lower testosterone levels, the effect on sexual function would remain to be shown.

The formal assessments of mental changes show that a person's sense of time is altered. Subjects report that an interval of 5 or 10 minutes seems to stretch out to an hour. In making time estimates, experienced users of marijuana can correct for this alteration to some extent. The ability to retain an objective consciousness of what is happening to oneself is characteristic of a marijuana high. Thus, unlike some heavy amphetamine users, who actually believe their paranoid thoughts, a person smoking marijuana who becomes suspicious usually remains aware of the irrationality of his paranoid thoughts and can discuss them and laugh at them. Because of the capacity to retain a hold on reality and because of the paucity of observable changes, experienced users of marijuana can manage to appear and act sober in public even when intoxicated.

Attempts at measuring cognitive and other psychological defects in subjects under the influence of ordinary marijuana have shown little pronounced impairment. In one study, eight tests of perception, coordination, and learning were used. Only two of the tests (those concerning reaction time and the learning of a digital code) indicated impairment in small samples of subjects (Clark and Nakashima 1968).

Other investigations also have failed to show significant deterioration of the ability to perform relatively simple mental tasks with low dosage (Jones and Stone 1969). However, the ability to perform complex tasks, such as driving, can be altered by smoking only one or two marijuana cigarettes (Rafaelsen et al. 1973), but not as much as by consuming alcohol (Figure 6.25). Nevertheless, persons who are "high" should not drive.

Marijuana impairs short-term memory. A subject can recall past events, but not what he was thinking or doing only a few seconds earlier. Curiously, it seems that this memory failure is cyclical because the ability to recall recent events waxes and wanes. The impairment of short-term memory leads to a reduced capacity to perform tasks that require multiple steps. The past, present, and future are often confused, and there is a sense of strangeness and unreality that characterizes a state of depersonalization (Melges et al. 1970).

Adverse physical reactions to marijuana include nausea, vomiting, and diarrhea, especially if the drug is ingested. Chronic marijuana smokers are more vulnerable to respiratory ailments such as bronchitis, sinusitis, and asthma. However, acute and chronic toxicity is low (American Academy of Pediatrics Committee on Drugs 1975).

Feelings of anxiety, which commonly herald the mental effects, are usually transient, but they may lead to intense apprehension and panic. Feelings of depression and paranoia may be quite marked. Perceptual distortions may eventuate in hallucinations. Among those who have used other hallucinogens,

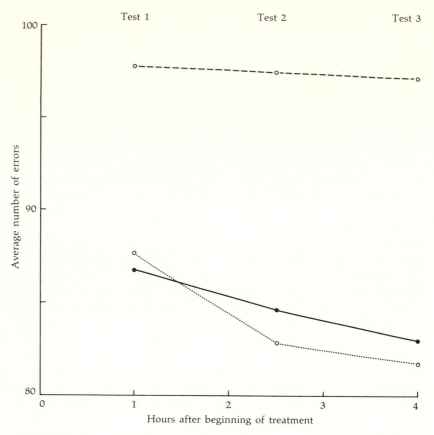

FIGURE 6.25
Comparative study of the effects of marihuana and alcohol on simulated driving
performance conducted by the Bureau of Motor Vehicles of the State of Washington.
The graph shows the average number of errors on tests administered at three stages
after treatment with alcohol (dashed line), marihuana (solid line), and a placebo
(dotted line). In general, it was found that marihuana causes significantly less
impairment of driving ability than alcohol does. [Redrawn from Marihuana by
L. Grinspoon. Copyright © 1969 by Scientific American, Inc. All rights reserved.]

the drug may cause "flashbacks" to past hallucinatory experiences. All of these
unpleasant and distressing emotional states are sometimes referred to as
"freakouts" and are reported by about 20 percent of experienced users (Tart
1970). These untoward reactions are commonly associated with high doses
(Jaffe 1975) and constitute a toxic psychosis (Chopra and Smith 1974).

The adverse reactions to marijuana do not commonly occur with ordinary
use, probably because those who have unpleasant experiences do not persist
in its use. Most habitual users rely on mild doses taken occasionally or in

moderation. Also important is the fact that the grade of marijuana presently used in the United States is a far weaker intoxicant than other hallucinogenic drugs, such as LSD.

Psychologically unstable persons may be upset by the psychoactive effects of marijuana, and borderline cases possibly tipped over into serious mental disturbances. In these cases, marijuana is more a trigger, as would be some other stress, than a cause of the mental disturbance itself.[13]

The potential deleterious effects of chronic use are more controversial. Marijuana has been thought to cause aggressive and criminal behavior and to lead to narcotic addition, sexual debauchery, social apathy *(amotivational syndrome),* personality deterioration, and so on. None of these effects have been adequately substantiated to the satisfaction of the scientific community (Grinspoon 1975).

Currently, there is considerable interest in reaching a conclusion about the possible deleterious effects of marijuana use: Is marijuana harmful? Unfortunately, a definitive answer does not yet seem possible. Certain facts are fairly well established. Marijuana users develop tolerance but do not become addicted to opiates. Habituation is no stronger than to tobacco and alcohol. Beyond that, present evidence does not show that moderate use of marijuana is a serious health risk for "normal" people. But scientific investigation of the effects of using marijuana has taken place for only a short time. When cigarettes came into use, they were considered harmless for many years and even advertised as being helpful to health. But now that we have the interest and means to investigate such matters, extensive research is in progress on the effects of marijuana (Tinklenberg 1975, Nahas 1976). Yet some aspects of the problem, such as possible genetic effects, defy quick resolution. Possible chromosomal damage will be discussed in the next section in connection with LSD.

Aside from these considerations, the wisdom of using marijuana must be evaluated in societal terms. The effects of chronic use are exceedingly difficult to evaluate. Fundamentally, the issues being dealt with are complex and involve many life circumstances. If people in abject poverty with no hope of ameliorating their lives use marijuana, is the drug aggravating their condition or relieving it? When "alienated" youths rely on its effects, does it further alienate them, is it just another facet of their alienation, or is it unrelated to their relationship to society?

In the past, societal reaction has tended to be alarmist. Sober views are becoming more prevalent, although the subject is still fraught with controversy (Kaplan 1971). Of particular interest are reports by commissions in the United

---

[13]For further consideration of the psychiatric consequences of marijuana use, see Meyer (ch. 16) and Jaffe (ch. 17) in Tinklenberg (1975).

States and Canada that call for the removal of criminal penalties for its use (National Commission on Marijuana and Drug Abuse 1973; Government of Canada 1973; Fourth Annual Report to the U. S. Congress from the Secretary of Health, Education, and Welfare 1974; American Academy of Pediatrics Committee on Drugs 1975).

PSYCHEDELICS

Low doses of the drugs included in this category produce various forms of euphoria, but higher doses inevitably lead to symptoms commonly associated with psychoses, such as hallucinations (hence, *hallucinogens*). Hallucinations are sensory experiences in the absense of the appropriate external objects or stimuli. They are to be differentiated from illusions, which are perceptual distortions and delusions that are pathologically generated false beliefs. For example, to imagine that a piece of thread is a snake is an illusion; to see a snake where there is nothing to suggest it is a hallucination; to believe that one is being pursued by snakes that do not exist is a delusion. Hallucinogens are capable of producing all three symptoms, as are a large variety of physical and mental ailments.

Psychedelics is an alternative term that lacks pejorative connotation. The term is also used to characterize objects and phenomena that suggest or evoke experiences produced by these drugs (for example, "psychedelic colors"). These compounds are also called *psychotomimetics* or *psychotogenics,* because they seem to mimic or produce "model" psychoses.

LSD

Lysergic acid diethylamide (LSD: the "S" stands for *Säure,* German for acid) is the best-known hallucinogen. It is rapidly absorbed from the gastro-intestinal tract and widely distributed in body tissues, concentrating in the lungs, kidneys, liver, and brain. It is excreted mainly in the feces. The exact mechanism of its action on the central nervous system is unclear (Byck 1975).

LSD is a highly potent chemical that was originally extracted from a fungus growing on wheat and rye but can now be synthesized in the laboratory. As little as 20 micrograms (two millionths of a gram) produces its effects, although regular users may ingest as much as 500 micrograms per dose. Tolerance to LSD and cross-tolerance to other hallucinogens, such as mescaline, develop with use (Jaffe 1975).

The objective effects of LSD include elevation of body temperature (hyperthermia), slight elevation of blood sugar (hyperglycemia), and increased heart rate (tachycardia). The pupils become dilated and there is piloerection (''goose pimples''). These physical signs are absent in hallucinatory states due to psychoses.

The subjective effects include mood changes, which are euphoric on a ''good trip'' and dysphoric on a ''bad trip'' (Figure 6.26). The perceptual distortions, hallucinations, cognitive malfunctions, and so on, are basically similar to the hallucinogenic experience, or the acute brain syndrome, produced by the high doses of marijuana described earlier (see also Box 6.5). ''Acid trips'' are notable for their vividness of visual hallucination, the brightness and range of colors, and feelings of merging with the environment. Occasionally, there is a crossing-over of sensory modalities (synesthesia), in which sounds are ''seen'' (flowing out like toothpaste from amplifiers, according to one observer) and colors are ''heard'' in various tones and intensities (Cohen 1966). Auditory hallucinations are rare, which provides another point of differ-

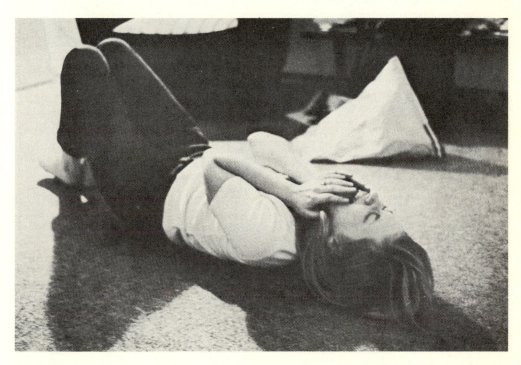

FIGURE 6.26
A "bad trip" on LSD. [From World Health Organization, *World Health*, July 1967. Photograph by Larry Schiller.]

BOX 6.5

The first "acid trip." [From W. A. Stoll, *Swiss Arch. Neurol.* 60(1947). Based on the notes of Albert Hofmann. English translation is from *The Beyond Within: The LSD Story* by S. Cohen, Atheneum, 1967.]

Last Friday, the 16th of April, I had to leave my work in the laboratory and go home because I felt strangely restless and dizzy. Once there, I lay down and sank into a not unpleasant delirium which was marked by an extreme degree of fantasy. In a sort of trance with closed eyes (I found the daylight unpleasantly glaring) fantastic visions of extraordinary vividness accompanied by a kaleidoscopic play of intense coloration continuously swirled around me. After two hours this condition subsided. . . .

On that Friday, however, the only unusual substances with which I had been in contact were d-lysergic acid and isolysergic acid diethylamide. I had been trying various methods of purifying these isomers by condensation, and also breaking them down into their components. In a preliminary experiment I had succeeded in producing a few milligrams of lysergic acid diethylamide (LSD) as an easily soluble crystal in the form of a neutral tartrate. It was inconceivable to me, however, that I could have absorbed enough of this material to produce the above described state. Furthermore, the symptoms themselves did not appear to be related to those of the Ergotamine-Ergonovine group. I was determined to probe the situation and I decided to experiment upon myself with the crystalline lysergic acid diethylamide. If this material were really the cause, it must be active in minute amounts, and I decided to begin with an extremely small quantity which would still produce some action in equivalent amounts of Ergotamine or Ergonovine. . . .

I asked my laboratory assistant to escort me home since I assumed that the situation would progress in a manner similar to last Friday. But on the way home (a four-mile trip by bicycle, no other vehicle being available because of the war), the symptoms developed with a much greater intensity than the first time. I had the greatest difficulty speaking coherently and my field of vision fluctuated and was distorted like the reflections in an amusement park mirror. I also had had the impression that I was hardly moving, yet later my assistant told me that I was pedaling at a fast pace. . . .

So far as I can recollect, the height of the crisis had passed by the time the doctor arrived; it was characterized by these symptoms: dizziness, visual distortions, the faces of those present appeared like grotesque colored masks, strong agitation alternating with paresis, the head, body and extremities sometimes cold and numb; a metallic taste on the tongue; throat dry and shriveled; a feeling of suffocation; confusion alternating with a clear appreciation of the situation; at times standing outside myself as a neutral observer and hearing myself muttering jargon or screaming half madly.

The doctor found a somewhat weak pulse, but in general a normal circulation. Six hours after taking the drug, my condition had improved definitely.

The perceptual distortions were still present. Everything seemed to undulate and their proportions were distorted like the reflections on a choppy water surface. Everything was changing with unpleasant, predominantly poisonous green and blue color tones. With closed eyes multihued, metamorphizing fantastic images overwhelmed me. Especially noteworthy was the fact that sounds were transposed into visual sensations so that from each tone or noise a comparable colored picture was evoked, changing in form and color kaleidoscopically.

entiation from functional psychoses, in which they are more common. Another characteristic of LSD use is the "flashback" phenomenon, by which aspects of the experience are spontaneously relived at a future time without subsequent ingestion of LSD. LSD can cause extremely unpleasant experiences that lead to severe anxiety and panic. More lasting personality disorganization may be attributed to underlying psychological instabilities; yet many of the persons suffering such breakdowns may not otherwise have done so.

Of great importance is the possibility of damage to the future offspring of a user. One form of damage may be chromosomal, or genetic, in which case the threat to the health of the offspring persists, even though the mother does not take LSD during pregnancy. At present, that such chromosomal damage can occur remains unresolved (Corey et al. 1970; Houston 1969; Gilmour et al. 1971; Jaffe 1975). Adverse effects inflicted during pregnancy require that LSD be used by the mother while pregnant (genetic defects can come from either parent): LSD has been shown to cross the placental barrier in mice, but, as yet, this has not been demonstrated in humans.

Experiments in which pregnant rats and other animals are given LSD show a high incidence of stunted and stillborn offspring (Alexander et al. 1967). Studies of humans suggest similar outcomes, but, because the pregnant women investigated have histories of poor nutrition, illness, and multiple drug use, it becomes difficult to attribute with certainty the higher rate of congenital abnormalities in their offspring to the use of LSD (McGlothlin, Sparkes, and Arnold 1970). Nevertheless, the possibility of the adverse effects of LSD on human offspring (whether they are transmitted during pregnancy or through breast feeding) can hardly be dismissed. There is experimental evidence indicating that marijuana also may cause chromosomal abnormalities (Tinklenberg 1975; Nahas 1976), but the evidence is not conclusive (American Academy of Pediatrics Committee on Drugs 1975). This area of research is fairly new and not yet fully developed. The first evidence that chemicals could produce chromosomal damage was established only three decades ago (Darlington and Kohler 1947).

Virtually all drugs that pass the placental barrier—and the great majority do—are potentially capable of inducing chromosomal mutations and damage causing abnormalities in fetal development. The risk is highest in early pregnancy when the embryo is most vulnerable and the woman may not yet know that she is pregnant.

Even when not pregnant, women run a higher risk than men because they are born with all the ova they are ever going to produce, and so the entire pool of ova is constantly at risk. In adult males, there is a turnover of stored sperm that takes about two months to accomplish, so that damage to one batch does not affect later sperm reserves. But should chromosomally abnormal sperm fertilize an egg, the result would be no less disastrous than if the egg were defective.

It is difficult to evaluate the various claims that have been advanced for the "mind expanding," "insight producing" properties of LSD and the conflicting reports about its effectiveness in the treatment of various emotional ailments. It is even more difficult to evaluate the purported philosophical and religious arguments in favor of its use (Solomon 1966). There are many unanswered questions about LSD, including its mechanism of action, although some theories have been proposed to explain it (Aghajanian and Haigler 1974). Other hallucinogens differ from LSD in potency and in certain aspects of subjective experience, but the mental states they induce are basically similar. Such compounds include substances that have been in use for a long time in various cultures, as well as newer chemical products.

Hallucinogenic Plants

Mescaline is derived from peyote, a cactus plant (*Lophophora williamsii*) that grows in certain regions of Texas and Mexico (Figure 6.27). So far, nine alkaloids have been isolated from peyote, of which only mescaline (which has also been synthesized) induces hallucinations.

The dried "buttons" of the cactus are chewed or brewed into tea. Ingestion is followed, after an hour or so, by dryness of the mouth and skin, which first becomes flushed and then pale. Heart rate slows down (bradycardia) and blood sugar drops (hypoglycemia). There is body odor, and there may be insomnia, chest pain, uterine contraction, headache, and numbness (Cohen and Litt 1972, p. 568).

FIGURE 6.27
Peyote cactus.

Mescaline is less potent than LSD. It produces similar hallucinatory experiences, but less detachment from reality, which makes the subject a more conscious spectator of the psychoactive effects (Coles, Brenner, and Meagher 1970). The generally pleasant mood may be replaced by terror, panic, and psychotic symptoms.

The active ingredient of the "sacred mushroom," (also called teonanacatl, or God's flesh) is psilocybin, which has only 1/200 of the hallucinogenic potency of LSD. Jimsonweed *(Datura stramonium)* has hallucinogenic properties that are marred by some of the side effects of the drug.

Morning glory seeds, which are soaked and chewed, contain an LSD derivative with 1/20 of its potency. Nutmeg is a spice from the seed of the apricot-like fruit of the tropical tree *Myristica fragrans.* A teaspoonful taken at one time produces visual hallucinations, temporal and spatial distortion, and feelings of detachment. These effects are accompanied by dryness of the mucous membranes, rapid heart rate, shortness of breath, nausea, dizziness, and headache.

Other Chemicals

STP (2,5-dimethoxy-4-methylamphetamine, or DOM) is a potent hallucinogen, and its effects may continue for as long as a week. DMT (dimethyltryptamine) is much shorter acting. THC (tetrahydrocannabinol) has already been discussed.

The management of a "bad trip" or "bummer" is not a task for amateurs. But, if professional help cannot be obtained, the approach to use in helping the subject should be calm, kind, and reassuring, but also firm and authoritative. The subject must be repeatedly and simply reoriented to reality. Quiet and calm surroundings are best. Tempering the effects of the drug with other drugs must be avoided (Taylor, Maurer, and Tinklenberg 1970).

STIMULANTS OF THE CENTRAL NERVOUS SYSTEM

Amphetamines

The most commonly used stimulants are the amphetamines. They are compounds whose effects simulate the stimulation of the sympathetic nervous system (hence, *sympathomimetic*) (Innes and Nickerson 1975). They are readily absorbed from the gastrointestinal tract, and the effects of intravenous injection are immediate.

A small initial dose of 10 milligrams results in wakefulness, cheerfulness, self-confidence, increased strength, better concentration, and loss of appetite.

However, this seemingly marvelous state does not last because tolerance develops quickly, and a chronic user must resort to larger doses, which produce hypertension, a decrease in cerebral blood flow, headache, depression, paranoia, and confusion. A person under the influence of the drug looks pale and may have dilated pupils and a rapid heart rate.

Amphetamines are usually taken orally—for example, as Benzedrine (amphetamine sulfate) or Dexedrine (dextroamphetamine sulfate). Methedrine (methamphetamine) is ''speed,'' which may be ''sniffed'' from a liquid or injected intravenously (''mainlining''). Injection immediately produces a chill, racing pulse, elevated blood pressure, dilated pupils, and blurred vision. After the initial ''rush,'' it is common for a user to attempt to maintain that state (''speed binge''), and enormous doses may be used (reportedly as much as 15,000 mg daily) (Cohen and Litt 1972, p. 565). If the drug levels are not maintained, extreme fatigue and depression follow (''crashing''), and the person may sleep for days. The paranoid reactions that occur both while taking the drug and afterward are frequent and severe, and they may lead to serious violence. The danger that methadrine poses to its user and others is widely recognized within the drug culture, as indicated by the warning ''speed kills.'' Acute toxic reactions are produced by large doses (in some cases, by as little as 30 mg), leading to profound physiological disturbances, coma, and death. A lethal dose for adults generally ranges from 20 to 25 milligrams per kilogram of body weight.

Complications incidental to injecting methadrine are infectious diseases such as hepatitis, from using contaminated needles, and lung lesions, from injecting dissolved tablets and capsules than contain talc or starch. There is no physiological addiction to amphetamines, but psychological dependence can be severe.

Cocaine

Cocaine is derived from the leaves of the Peruvian plant *Erythroxylon coca* (Figure 6.28) and causes euphoria and pleasurable hallucinations. It was once used as a local anesthetic but is no longer used as such.

The traditional method of use is to chew the leaves of the plant, but, currently, cocaine is usually taken by ingestion, injection, or sniffing (Grinspoon 1975).

Because the central nervous system is stimulated by cocaine, a user feels restless, active, and energetic and does not tire easily. After these effects wear off, he is fatigued and depressed. Like amphetamines, cocaine produces sympathomimetic effects. A cocaine ''high'' can be very intense, and the drug is sometimes used with heroin, the combination being known as a ''speedball.''

Chronic cocaine users may experience nausea, loss of appetite, severe weight loss, insomnia, tremors, and convulsions. Paranoid reactions are common. Inhalation or sniffing may eventually cause perforation of the nasal

FIGURE 6.28
Coca leaves.

septum. Subcutaneous injection frequently leads to abscess formation. Large doses injected intravenously can cause immediate death. Most of the drug is detoxified within an hour. Thus, if a patient who has overdosed can be kept alive for a while, he is likely to recover. There is no physiological addiction.

Caffeine

Caffeine is a mild stimulant in the amounts usually found in coffee and tea, whose extensive use as chemical "boosters" has become an integral part of our daily routines. Although they do not pose a serious threat to health, their overuse results in irritability, insomnia, loss of appetite, and other symptoms.

Glue and Other Solvents

The sniffing of cleaning solvents and glues is indulged in, mostly by younger teen-agers, to produce exhilaration. Plastic cement, or glue, used in making model airplanes was the first agent to be so used and remains the most popular. It is a mixture of toluene and ethyl acetate. The cleaning fluid most often used contains trichloroethylene and 1,1,1-trichloroethane. These substances may be inhaled from a saturated rag, a plastic or paper bag, or as fumes from a heated pan.

Volatile solvents are among the most dangerous substances abused by youth. Severe dependence is likely with risk of damage to the bone marrow, liver, brain, and kidneys (Grinspoon 1975).

Intoxication is characterized by euphoria, excitement, a floating sensation, dizziness, slurred speech, and motor incoordination. Inhibitions are broken down, resulting in reckless and aggressive behavior that is not remembered afterward. Large doses produce stupor and unconsciousness.

A syndrome of sniffing and sudden death (SSD) refers to sniffing followed by stress, exercise, and death. Autopsies on 110 adolescents who died in this way have failed to reveal the exact cause (Cohen and Litt 1972, p. 568). The use of a plastic bag has been known to result in death from suffocation. Some intoxicated young people have died by "flying" from apartment roofs, which are convenient sites for sniffing. In ghetto populations, glue sniffing is the first drug experience of most heroin addicts.

DEPRESSANTS OF THE CENTRAL NERVOUS SYSTEM

Depressants are usually used for their own effects, especially by youthful addicts, but they are often also relied on to counteract amphetamine overstimulation, to augment the effects of heroin, or to obtain relief from its withdrawal symptoms.

Barbiturates

The most common depressants are the barbiturates, which are classified as short-, intermediate-, or long-acting (Harvey 1975). They are used singly or in combination, as in Tuinal. (There are also many nonbarbiturate hypnotics, Doriden being one of the more common.)

Barbiturates have legitimate uses in medicine, such as in the control of seizures. They are also widely misused as sleeping pills. Ordinary doses for medicinal purposes are usually in the order of less than 10 milligrams per kilogram of body weight. An adolescent who has developed tolerance may consume as much as 3,500 milligrams a day. Because tolerance does not extend to the depressant effect on the respiratory system, such high doses can be lethal.

Barbiturates depress the central nervous system through their ability to raise the stimulation threshold of neurons (thus making them less responsive) and prolong their time of recovery. This is the basis for their medical use in controlling convulsions, inducing sleep, reducing pain, and producing anesthesia. Both the acute and chronic effects of mild intoxication with barbiturates resemble alcohol intoxication (Jaffe 1975).

Addiction sets in after a few months of daily use—in doses of 200 milligrams or more. Symptoms of withdrawal appear from 12 to 16 hours after the last dose and consist of anxiety and tremor, followed by nausea, vomiting, and abdominal cramps. If a short-acting barbiturate has been taken and treatment is not administered, a grand mal seizure may appear within 72 hours. But it may take as long as a week to appear if the barbiturate taken is of the long-acting variety. The treatment of acute overdose and detoxification are medical emergencies. Other complications result from the method of administration (hepatitis, abscesses, lung lesions, and so on).

OPIOIDS

The source of opium is a poppy (Papaver somniferum) principally grown in Asia Minor (Figure 6.29). Opium is smoked in its raw form, but, most often, it is the derivatives, especially heroin, that are abused. Compounds derived from opium are referred to as opiates. Because there also are synthetic chemicals with similar actions, the term opioids is more inclusive. It refers to a class of narcotic analgesics: agents that relieve pain but carry a risk of addiction (Jaffe and Martin 1975).

Opioids commonly used in medicine as analgesics, or pain killers, include morphine, codeine, and a number of other compounds, such as Demerol, which is a synthetic compound. Opioids depress the pain centers in the brain, the

FIGURE 6.29
Opium poppy.

FIGURE 6.30
"Shooting" heroin. [From World Health Organization, *World Health,* July–August 1969. Photograph by E. Mandelmann.]

respiratory center, and the cough center (hence, the use of codeine in cough medicines) and induce mental tranquility and euphoria.[14]

Heroin is derived from morphine and is a semisynthetic product that does not exist as such in nature. It is more potent than morphine but has no legitimate use in medicine. Its manufacture, possession, and use are illegal.

Pure heroin is a white crystalline powder that is bitter to the taste. It is rarely found in pure form on the streets: lactose, quinine, and various adulterants are added to dilute it or to disguise the dilutants.

An adolescent's first introduction is usually by "snorting" heroin through the nose. The effects follow in half an hour. The process cannot be repeated for 6 hours or so without causing nasal irritation. The next step is "skin popping," in which the drug is dissolved in warm water and injected subcutaneously with a syringe or jagged edged eyedropper (the "works"). Intravenous injection ("mainlining") is the most direct route, and its physical and psychoactive effects are immediate (Figure 6.30). To maintain blood levels, an addict must "shoot up" every 6 or 8 hours.

Heroin is physically addictive, and its abstinence syndrome is agonizing. Beginning with yawning, lacrimation, restlessness, and dilated pupils, an addict

---

[14]For more detailed accounts on the pharmacological effects of opiods, see Jaffe and Martin (1975); Kosterlitz, Collier, and Villarreal (1973); and Clouet (1971).

undergoing withdrawal will develop insomnia, "goose flesh," muscle cramps, diarrhea, hypertension, a rapid heart rate, and in some cases convulsions within 48 hours of the last dose. Not all of these symptoms are necessarily present in a given case, and their severity varies. Withdrawal is greatly eased by medical treatment to prevent seizures and cardiovascular collapse.

Heroin has numerous physiological effects. It produces drowsiness, nausea, and vomiting. Gastrointestinal effects include constipation (paregoric used by pediatricians to control diarrhea contains opiates). Other physiological effects include a lowering of the body temperature, excessive urination, and constriction of the pupils (miosis).

The single most common complication among adolescent heroin users is hepatitis. It is largely a result of using unsterilized needles for injection, although heroin may also have a direct toxic effect on the liver. Infections cause abscesses at the site of injections and are spread through the blood stream to the heart (bacterial endocarditis) and the brain. There is risk of tetanus with subcutaneous use. Duodenal ulcers are common among addicts.

The life styles of heroin addicts expose them to further hazards. Venereal disease is common because many rely on prostitution to support their habits, even though heroin depresses the sexual drive. The rate of teen-age pregnancies is no higher than among those who do not use heroin, probably because the drug interferes with ovulation, causing menstrual problems. Amenorrhea is especially common among young addicts. Heroin use by a pregnant woman causes addiction in the unborn child and other complications (Einhorn 1972, p. 573).

The addict lives in a violent world and sometimes resorts to extraordinary practices. For example, addicts have been known to stuff heroin in contraceptive condoms and swallow them for later recovery, but the result instead is intestinal obstruction and death. It is sobering to note that heroin was the leading cause of death among adolescents in New York City in 1969 and 1970 (Cohen and Litt 1972, p. 560).

Methadone is a synthetic opioid that came into clinical use after the second world war. Its pharmacological properties are similar to those of morphine, and its primary uses are to relieve pain, to treat patients undergoing narcotic abstinence syndromes, and to treat heroin users. Methadone retains a considerable degree of effectiveness if taken orally (Jaffe and Martin 1975) and is excreted slowly. It has been possible to treat heroin addicts by means of controlled doses of methadone without their experiencing withdrawal symptoms. Such treatment removes the need for injection several times a day, as well as the necessity to resort to criminal activity as a means of supporting the addiction. But this treatment perpetuates addiction rather than cures it.[15]

---

[15]Arguments for and against the use of methadone in treating heroin addiction may be found in Freedman (1975).

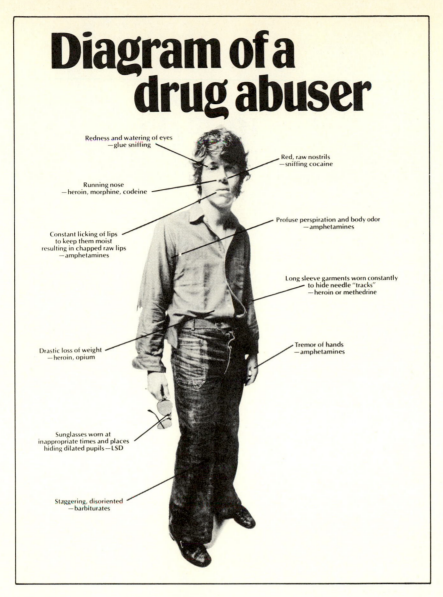

Diagram of a drug abuser

Redness and watering of eyes
—glue sniffing

Red, raw nostrils
—sniffing cocaine

Running nose
—heroin, morphine, codeine

Profuse perspiration and body odor
—amphetamines

Constant licking of lips
to keep them moist
resulting in chapped raw lips
—amphetamines

Long sleeve garments worn constantly
to hide needle "tracks"
—heroin or methedrine

Drastic loss of weight
—heroin, opium

Tremor of hands
—amphetamines

Sunglasses worn at
inappropriate times and places
hiding dilated pupils—LSD

Staggering, disoriented
—barbiturates

FIGURE 6.31
Signs of drug abuse. [Courtesy of the Advertising Council.]

The many overlapping effects of psychoactive drugs tend to obscure one another. Table 6.2 (on the next two pages) summarizes the characteristics of commonly abused drugs and their various reactions. Although tabulation helps to maintain important distinctions, it necessarily results in oversimplification. Figure 6.31 is another form of summary that gives clues to the types of drugs being taken by a hypothetical abuser.

Table 6.2. Characteristics of abused drugs and their acute reactions in adolescents.

Class	Example	Route	Behavioral signs	Physical signs	Medical complications
Opiates	Heroin, methadone, morphine	Subcutaneous, intranasal, intravenous	Euphoria, lethargy to coma	Constricted pupils, respiratory depression, cyanosis, rales	Injection-site infection, bacterial endocarditis, amenorrhea, peptic ulcer, pulmonary edema, tetanus
Hypnotic sedatives	Barbiturates, glutethimide	Oral, intravenous	Slurred speech, ataxia, short attention span, drowsiness, combative, violent	Constricted pupils (barbiturates), dilated pupils (glutethimide), needle marks	Injection-site infection, endocarditis
	Alcohol	Oral	As above		Gastritis, CNS depression
Stimulants	Amphetamines	Oral, subcutaneous, intravenous	Hyperactive, insomnia, anorexic paranoia, personality change, irritability	Hypertension, weight loss, dilated pupils	Injection-site infection, hepatitis, endocarditis, psychosis, depression
	Cocaine	Intravenous, intranasal	Restless, hyperactive, occasional depression or paranoia	Hypertension, tachycardia	Nausea, vomiting, inflammation or perforation of nasal septum

Class	Agent	Route	Acute Effects	Signs	Complications
Hallucinogens	LSD, THC, PCP, STP (DOM), mescaline, DMT	Oral	Euphoria, dysphoria, hallucinations, confusion, paranoia	Dilated pupils, occasional hypertension hyperthermia, piloerection	Primarily psychiatric with high risk to individuals with un-recognized or previous psychiatric disorder
Hydrocarbons, fluorocarbons	Glue (toluene)	Inhalant	Euphoria, confusion, general intoxication	Nonspecific	Secondary trauma, asphyxiation from plastic bag used to inhale fumes
	Cleaning fluid (trichloroethylene)	Inhalant	Euphoria, confusion, general intoxication, vomiting, abdominal pain	Oliguria, jaundice	Hepatitis, renal injury
	Aerosol sprays (freon)	Inhalant	Euphoria, dysphoria, slurred speech, hallucinations	Nonspecific	Psychiatric
Cannibis	Marihuana, hashish, THC	Smoke, oral	Mild intoxication and simple euphoria to hallucination (dose-related)	Occasional tachycardia, delayed response time, poor coordination	Occasional psychiatric, with de-pressive or anxiety reactions

Source: V. C. Vaughan and R. J. McKay, eds., *Nelson Textbook of Pediatrics*, 10th ed., Saunders, 1975.

Bibliography

Abraham, G. E., Odell, W. D., Swerdloff, R. S., and Hopper, K. 1972. Simultaneous radioimmunoassay of plasma FSH, LH, progesterone, 17-hydroxyprogesterone and estradiol-17β during the menstrual cycle. *J. Clin. Endocrinol. Metab.* 34:312–318.

Abraham, J. M., and Snodgrass, G. J. 1969. Soto's syndrome of cerebral gigantism. *Arch. Dis. Child.* 44:203–210.

Acheson, R. M. 1966. Maturation of the skeleton. In *Human development,* ed. F. Falkner. Saunders.

Adamopoulos, D. A. 1974. Pituitary-gonadal interrelationships in pubertal female subjects. *Acta Endocrinol.* 76:214–234.

Aldman, B. 1962. Biodynamic studies on impact protection. *Acta Physiol. Scand.* 56:suppl. 192.

Aghajanian, G. K., and Haigler, H. J. 1974. Mode of action of LSD on serotonergic neurons. In *Serotonin, new vistas.* Advances in Biochemical Psychopharmacology Series, vol. 10, ed. E. Costa, G. L. Gessa, and M. Sandler. Raven Press.

Alexander, J., Miles, B. E., Gold, G. M., and Alexander, R. B. 1967. LSD: Injection early in pregnancy produces abnormalities in offspring of rats. *Science* 157:459–460.

Alsever, W. D. 1968*a*. Student and faculty survival on the highway. *J. Am. Coll. Health Assoc.* 16:214–222.

Alsever, W. D. 1968*b*. The sequel to student and faculty survival on the highway. *J. Am. Coll. Health Assoc.* 16:411–412.

Altchek, A. 1972*a*. Adolescent vulvovaginitis. *Pediatr. Clin. N. Am.* 19:735–757.

Altchek, A. 1972*b*. Premature thelarche. *Pediatr. Clin. N. Am.* 19:543–545.

Altchek, A., ed. 1972*c*. Symposium on pediatric and adolescent gynecology. *Pediatr. Clin. N. Am.* 19:507–824.

American Academy of Pediatrics Committee on Drugs. 1975. Effect of marijuana on man. *Pediatrics* 56:134–143.

American Medical Association. 1967. *Handbook on alcohol and alcoholism.* American Medical Association.

American Red Cross. 1957. *First aid textbook.* Doubleday.

American Social Health Association. 1972. *Today's V. D. control problem.*

Apt, L., and Breinin, G. M. 1972. Gonococcal conjunctivitis. In *Pediatrics,* 15th ed., ed. H. L. Barnett and A. H. Einhorn. Appleton-Century-Crofts.

Arey, J. B. 1975. Neoplasms and neoplastic-like lesions. In *Nelson textbook of pediatrics,* 10th ed., ed. V. C. Vaughan and R. J. McKay. Saunders.

Arey, L. B. 1965. *Developmental anatomy,* 7th ed. Saunders.

Arundel, F. D. 1971. Acne vulgaris. *Pediatr. Clin. N. Am.* 18:853–874.

August, G. P., Grumbach, M. M., and Kaplan, S. L. 1972. Hormonal changes in puberty. 3. Correlation of plasma testosterone, LH, FSH, testicular size and bone age with male pubertal development. *J. Clin. Endocrinol. Metab.* 34:319–326.

Austin, C. R., and Short, R. V. 1972. *Reproduction in mammals,* 5 vols. London: Cambridge University Press.

Baird, H. W. 1975. Chronic or recurrent convulsions. In *Nelson textbook of pediatrics,* 10th ed., ed. V. C. Vaughan and R. J. McKay. Saunders.

Bakwin, H. 1964. The secular change in growth and development. *Acta Pediatr.* 53:79–89.

Bakwin, H., and McLaughlin, S. M. 1964. Secular increments in height: Is the end in sight? *Lancet* 2:1195–1196.

Barnett, H. L., and Einhorn, A. H., eds. 1972. *Pediatrics,* 15th ed. Appleton-Century-Crofts.

Battaglia, F. C., Frazier, T. M., and Hellegers, A. E. 1963. Obstetric and pediatric complications of juvenile pregnancy. *Pediatrics* 32:902.

Bayley, N. 1956. Growth curves of height and weight by age for boys and girls, scaled according to physical maturity. *J. Pediatr.* 48:187–194.

Beach, F. A. 1974. Human sexuality and evolution. In *Reproductive behavior,* ed. W. Montagna and W. A. Sadler. Plenum.

Beardwood, C. J., and Russell, G. F. M. 1970. Gonadotrophin excretion at puberty. *J. Endocrinol.* 48:469–470.

Behrens, L. H., and Barr, D. P. 1932. Hyperpituitarism beginning in infancy: The Alton giant. *Endocrinology* 16:120–128.

Benedek, T., and Rubinstein, B. 1939*a*. The correlations between ovarian activity and psychodynamic processes. 1. The ovulation phase. *Psychosom. Med.* 1:245–270.

Benedek, T., and Rubenstein, B. 1939*b*. The correlations between ovarian activity and psychodynamic processes. 2. The menstrual phase. *Psychosom. Med.* 1:461–485.

Bennett, E. M., and Johannsen, D. E. 1954. Psychodynamics of the diabetic child. *Psychol. Monogr.* 68:1.

Ber, A., and Brociner, C. 1964. Age of puberty in Israeli girls. *Fertil. Steril.* 15:640–647.

Bergersen, E. O. 1972. The male adolescent facial growth spurt: Its prediction and relation to skeletal maturation. *Angle Orthod.* 42:319–338.

Bermant, G., and Davidson, J. M. 1974. *Biological bases of sexual behavior.* Harper and Row.

Berry, C. M., Beard, R., Finklea, J., and Lloyd W., eds. 1975. *Conference on agricultural health and safety.* Society for Occupational and Environmental Health.

Billewicz, W. J. 1967. A note on body weight measurements and seasonal variation. *Hum. Biol.* 39:241–250.

Bishop, E., ed. 1957. *The diary of Helen Morley.* Farrar, Straus, and Giroux.

Blattner, R. J. 1975. Infectious mononucleosis. In *Nelson textbook of pediatrics,* 10th ed., ed. V. C. Vaughan and R. J. McKay. Saunders.

Bliss, E. L. 1975. Anorexia nervosa. In *Comprehensive textbook of psychiatry,* vol. 2, 2d ed., ed. A. M. Freedman, H. I. Kaplan, and B. J. Sadock. Williams and Wilkins.

Blizzard, R. M. 1972*a*. The anterior pituitary. In *Pediatrics,* 15th ed., ed. H. L. Barnett and A. H. Einhorn. Appleton-Century-Crofts.

Blizzard, R. M. 1972*b*. Psychologic dwarfism simulating idiopathic hypopituitarism. In *Pediatrics,* 15th ed., ed. H. L. Barnett and A. H. Einhorn. Appleton-Century-Crofts.

Blizzard, R. M., Johanson, A., Guyda, H., Baghdassarian, A., Raiti, S., and Migeon, C. 1970. Recent developments in the study of gonadotrophin secretion in adolescence. In *Adolescent endocrinology,* ed. F. P. Heald and W. Hung. Appleton-Century-Crofts.

Blizzard, R. M., Penny, R., Foley, T. P., Jr., Baghdassarian, A., Johanson, A., and Yen, S. S. C. 1972. Pituitary-gonadal interrelationships in relation to puberty. In *Gonadotropins,* ed. B. B. Saxena, C. G. Beling, and H. M. Gandy. Wiley-Interscience.

Blunck, W. 1975. Sexual precocity. In *Clinical review series: Pediatric medicine,* ed. M. I. Levine. Publishing Sciences Group.

Bongiovanni, A. M. 1972. Sexual precocity. In *Pediatrics,* 15th ed., ed. H. L. Barnett and A. H. Einhorn. Appleton-Century-Crofts.

Boyar, R., Finkelstein, J., Roffwarg, H., Kapen, S., Weitzman, E., and Hellman, L. 1972. Synchronization of augmented luteinizing hormone secretion with sleep during puberty. *N. Engl. J. Med.* 287:582–586.

Brazeau, P., Vale, W., Burgus, R., Ling, N., Butcher, M., Rivier, J., and Guille-min, R. 1973. Hypothalamic polypeptide that inhibits the secretion of immu-noreactive pituitary growth hormone. *Science* 179:77–79.

Bremer, J. 1959. *Asexualization.* Macmillan.

Bridgwater, W., and Kurtz, S., eds. 1963. *The Columbia encyclopedia.* Colum-bia University Press.

Brobeck, J. R., ed. 1973. *Best and Taylor's physiological basis of medical practice,* 9th ed. Williams and Wilkins.

Brooks, S. M. 1971. *The V. D. story.* Barnes.

Browne, Sir Thomas. 1876. *Christian morals,* part 3, section 8.

Bruch, H. 1971. Obesity in adolescence. In *Modern perspectives in adolescent psychiatry,* ed. J. G. Howells. Edinburgh: Oliver and Boyd.

Bruch, H. 1973. *Eating disorders: Obesity and anorexia nervosa and the person within.* Basic Books.

Brunswick, A. F., and Josephson, E. 1972. Adolescent health in Harlem. *Am. J. Public Health* 62(suppl. 2):1–62.

Burgoon, C. F., Jr. 1975. Acne vulgaris. In *Nelson textbook of pediatrics.* 10th ed., ed. V. C. Vaughan and R. J. McKay. Saunders.

Byck, R. 1975. Drugs and the treatment of psychiatric disorders. In *The phar-macological basis of therapeutics,* 5th ed., ed. L. S. Goodman and A. Gilman. Macmillan.

Campbell, H. 1964. Role of alcohol in fatal traffic accidents and measures needed to solve the problem. *Univ. Mich. Med. Bull.* 63:699–703.

Cantril, H., and Hunt, W. A. 1932. Emotional effects produced by the injection of adrenalin. *Am. J. Psychol.* 44:300–307.

Capraro, V. J., Bayonet-Rivera, N. P., Accto, T., Jr., and MacGillivray, M. 1971. Premature thelarche. *Obstet. Gynecol. Surv.* 26:2–7.

Chafetz, M. E. 1975. Alcoholism and alcoholic psychoses. In *Comprehensive textbook of psychiatry,* vol. 2, 2d ed., ed. A. M. Freedman, H. I. Kaplan, and B. J. Sadock. Williams and Wilkins.

Chao, D. 1972. Paroxysmal disorders. In *Pediatrics,* 15 ed., ed. H. L. Barnett and A. H. Einhorn. Appleton-Century-Crofts.

Cheek, D. B. 1967. *Growth and growth retardation with particular reference to the endocrine, cardiac and normal child.* Lea and Febiger.

Cheek, D. B. 1968. *Human growth, body composition, cell growth, energy and intelligence.* Lea and Febiger.

Cheek, D. B., Brasel, J. A., Ellicott, D., and Scott, R. 1966. Muscle cell size and number in normal children and in dwarfs (pituitary cretins and primor-dial): Before and after treatment. *Bull. Johns Hopkins Hosp.* 119:46.

Chopra, G. S., and Smith, J. W. 1974. Psychotic reactions following cannabis use in East Indians. *Arch. Gen. Psychiatry* 30:24–27.

Clark, L. D., and Nakashima, E. N. 1968. Experimental studies of marijuana. *Am. J. Psychiatry* 125:379–390.

Clouet, D. H., ed. 1971. *Narcotic drugs: Biochemical pharmacology.* Plenum.

Cloutier, M. D., and Hayles, A. B. 1970. Precocious puberty. *Adv. Pediatr.* 17:125–138.

Cohen, M., and Litt, I. 1972. Drug abuse. In *Pediatrics,* 15th ed., ed. H. L. Barnett and A. H. Einhorn. Appleton-Century-Crofts.

Cohen, S. 1966. *The beyond within.* Atheneum.

Coles, R., Brenner, J. H., and Meagher, D. 1970. *Drugs and youth: Medical, legal, and psychiatric facts.* Liveright.

Comenius, J. A. 1923. *The great didactic,* trans. M. W. Keating. London: A. and C. Black.

Conger, J., Gaskill, H., Glad, D., Hassell, L., Rainey, R., and Sawrez, W. 1959. Psychological and psychophysiological factors in motor vehicle accidents. *J. Am. Med. Assoc.* 169:1581–1587.

Corey, M. J., Andrews, J. C., McLeod, M. J., MacLean, J. R., and Wilby, W. E. 1970. Chromosome studies on patients (in vivo) and cells (in vitro) treated with lysergic acid diethylamide. *N. Engl. J. Med.* 282:939–943.

Corker, C. S., and Exley, D. 1968. Daily changes in urinary testosterone secretion in the male. *Clin. Endocrinol.* 2:552–568.

Council on Foods and Nutrition. 1971. Zen macrobiotic diets. *J. Am. Med. Assoc.* 218:397.

Cracchiolo, A., Blazina, M. E., and MacKinnon, D. S. 1968. Motorcycle injuries to university students. *J. Am. Med. Assoc.* 204:175–176.

Curtis, H. 1975. *Biology,* 2d ed. Worth.

Dalton, K. 1960. Menstruation and accidents. *Br. Med. J.* 2:1425–1426.

Dalton, K. 1964a. The influence of menstruation on health and disease. *Proc. R. Soc. Med.* 57:262–264.

Dalton, K. 1964b. *The premenstrual syndrome. Charles C Thomas.*

Daly, M. J. 1966. Physical and psychological development of the adolescent female. *Clin. Obstet. Gynecol.* 9:711–721.

Daniel, W. A., Jr. 1970. *The adolescent patient.* Mosby.

Darlington, C. D., and Kohler, P. C. 1947. The chemical breakage of chromosomes. *Heredity* 1:187.

Darrow, W. W., ed. 1971. *Selected references on the behavioral aspects of venereal disease control.* U. S. Public Health Service.

Davidson, J. M. 1974. Hypothalamic-pituitary regulation of puberty: Evidence from animal experimentation. In *Control of the onset of puberty,* ed. M. M. Grumbach, G. D. Grave, and F. E. Mayer. Wiley.

Daw, S. F. 1970. Age of boys' puberty in Leipzig, 1727–49, as indicated by voice breaking in J. S. Bach's choir members. *Hum. Biol.* 42:87–89.

De Beauvoir, S. 1959. *Memoirs of a dutiful daughter.* World.

de Majo, S. F., and Onativia, A. 1960. Acromegaly and gigantism in a boy: Comparison with three overgrown non-acromegalic children. *J. Pediatr.* 57:382–390.

Demos J., and Demos, V. 1969. Adolescence in historical perspective. In *Issues in adolescent psychology,* ed. D. Rogers. Appleton-Century-Crofts.

Dewhurst, C. J. 1969. Variations in physical signs in pubertal girls. *J. Obstet. Gynaecol. Br. Commonw.* 76:831–833.

Dickinson, R. L. 1949. *Atlas of human sex anatomy,* 2d ed. Williams and Wilkins.

Dietz, P. E., and Baker, S. P. 1974. Drowning: Epidemiology and prevention. *Am. J. Public Health* 64:303–312.

Di George, A. M. 1975. Precocious puberty. In *Nelson textbook of pediatrics,* 10th ed., ed. V. C. Vaughan and R. J. McKay. Saunders.

Donovan, B. T. 1972. Neural control of puberty. *J. Psychosom. Res.* 16: 267–270.

Donovan, B. T., and Van der Werff Ten Bosch, J. J. 1965. *Physiology of puberty.* Williams and Wilkins.

Dorfman, R. I., and Shipley, R. A. 1956. *The androgens: Biochemistry, physiology, and clinical significance.* Wiley.

Douglas, J. W. B., and Simpson, H. R. 1964. Height in relation to puberty, family size and social class. *Milbank Mem. Fund. Q.* 42:20–35.

Drash, A. 1975. Diabetes mellitus. In *Nelson textbook of pediatrics,* 10th ed., ed. V. C. Vaughan and R. J. McKay. Saunders.

Drucker, W. D., Blumberg, J. M., Gandy, H. M., David, R. R., and Verde, A. L. 1972. Biologic activity of dehydroepiandrosterone sulfate in man. *J. Clin. Endocrinol. Metab.* 35:48–54.

Duffy, R. J. 1970. Description and perception of frequency breaks (voice breaks) in adolescent female speakers. *Lang. Speech* 13:151–161.

Ehrhardt, A., and McCauley, E. 1975. Sexually precocious girls. *Med. Aspects Hum. Sexuality* 9:63–64.

Einhorn, A. H. 1972. Drowning. In *Pediatrics,* 15th ed., ed. H. L. Barnett and A. H. Einhorn. Appleton-Century-Crofts.

Ellis, E. F. 1972. Asthma. In *Pediatrics,* 15th ed., ed. H. L. Barnett and A. H. Einhorn. Appleton-Century-Crofts.

Ellis, E. F. 1975. Respiratory allergy. In *Nelson textbook of pediatrics,* 10th ed., ed. V. C. Vaughan and R. J. McKay. Saunders.

Engel, G. L. 1962. *Psychological development in health and disease.* Saunders.

Espenschade, A. 1940. Motor performance in adolescence. *Monogr. Soc. Res. Child Dev.* 5(no. 1).

Faiman, C., and Winter, J. S. D. 1974. Gonadotropins and sex hormone patterns in puberty: Clinical data. In *Control of the onset of puberty,* ed. M. M. Grumbach, G. D. Grave, and F. E. Mayer. Wiley.

Falkner, F. 1960. *Child development: An international method of study.* Basel: Karger.

Falkner, F. 1972. Physical growth. In *Pediatrics,* 15th ed., ed. H. L. Barnett and A. H. Einhorn. Appleton-Century-Crofts.

Federman, D. D. 1967. *Abnormal sexual development.* Saunders.

Fernbach, D. J., and Starling, K. A. 1975. Acute leukemia in children. In *Clinical review series: Pediatric medicine,* ed. M. I. Levine. Publishing Sciences Group.

Ferris, B. G., and Smith, C. W. 1953. Maximum breathing capacity and vital capacity of female children and adolescents. *Pediatrics* 12:341–353.

Ferris, B. G., Whittenberger, J. L,, and Gallagher, J. R. 1952. Maximum breathing capacity and vital capacity of male children and adolescents. *Pediatrics* 9:559–570.

Field, E. 1967. It. In *Variety photoplays*. Grove Press.

Fieser, L. F. 1955, Steroids. *Sci. Am.* 192(1):52–60.

Finberg, L. 1972. Syphilis. In *Pediatrics,* 15th ed., ed. H. L. Barnett and A. H. Einhorn. Appleton-Century-Crofts.

Fingl, E., and Woodbury, D. M. 1975. General principles. In *The pharmacological basis of therapeutics,* 5th ed., ed. L. S. Goodman and A. Gilman. Macmillan.

Fitschen, W., and Clayton, B. E. 1965. Urinary execretion of gonadotrophins with particular reference to children. *Arch. Dis. Child.* 40:16–26.

Fiumara, N. J. 1971. Gonococcal pharyngitis. *Med. Aspects Hum. Sexuality* 5:195–209.

Fodor, J. T., Glass, L., and Weiner, J. 1969. Immediate effects of smoking on young healthy males. *Public Health Rep.* 84:121–126.

Ford, C. S., and Beach, F. A. 1951. *Patterns of sexual behavior.* Harper and Row.

Ford, F. 1966. *Diseases of the nervous system in childhood and adolescence.* Charles C Thomas.

Forest, M. G., and Migeon, C. J. 1970. Percentage of testosterone, androstenedione, and dehydroisoandrosterone bound to plasma proteins in preadolescent children. *J. Pediatr.* 76:732–744.

Fourth Annual Report to the U. S. Congress from the Secretary of Health, Education, and Welfare. 1974. *Marijuana and health.* U. S. Government Printing Office.

Franchimont, P. 1971. The regulation of follicle stimulating hormone and luteinizing hormone secretion in humans. In *Frontiers in neuroendocrinology,* ed. L. Martini and W. F. Ganong. London: Oxford University Press.

Frank, A. 1952. *The diary of a young girl.* Doubleday.

Frankle, R. T., and Heussenstamm, F. K. 1974. Food zealotry and youth: New dilemmas for professionals. *Am. J. Public Health* 64:11–18.

Frasier, S. D., and Horton, R. 1966. Androgens in the peripheral plasma of prepubertal children and adults. *Steroids* 8:777–784.

Frasier, S. D., Gafford, F., and Horton, R. 1969. Plasma androgens in childhood and adolescence. *J. Clin. Endocrinol. Metab.* 29: 1404–1408.

Freedman, A. M. 1975. Drug dependence. In *Comprehensive textbook of psychiatry,* vol. 2, 2d ed., ed. A. M. Freedman, H. I. Kaplan, and B. J. Sadock. Williams and Wilkins.

Freedman, A. M., Kaplan, H. I., and Sadock, B. J., eds. 1975. *Comprehensive textbook of psychiatry,* vol. 2, 2d ed. Williams and Wilkins.

Freud, S. 1960. The psychopathology of everyday life (originally published in 1901). In *Standard edition of the complete psychological works of Sigmund Freud,* vol. 6. London: Hogarth.

Frisch, R. E. 1974. Critical weight at menarche, initiation of the adolescent growth spurt, and control of puberty. In *Control of the onset of puberty,* ed. M. M. Grumbach, G. D. Grave, and F. E. Mayer. Wiley.

Frisch, R. E., and Revelle, R. 1970. Height and weight at menarche and a hypothesis of critical body weights and adolescent events. *Science* 169: 397–399.

Frisch, R. E., and Revelle, R. 1971. Height and weight at menarche and a hypothesis of menarche. *Arch. Dis. Child.* 46:695–701.

Gallagher, J. R. 1960. *Medical care of the adolescent.* Appleton-Century-Crofts.

Gandy, H., and Peterson, R. 1968. Measurement of testosterone and 17-ketosteroids in plasma by the double isotope dilution derivative technique. *J. Clin. Endocrinol.* 28:949–977.

Garell, D. C., ed. 1973. Symposium on adolescent medicine. *Pediatr. Clin. N. Am.* 20(no. 4).

Gavan, J. A. 1953. Growth and development of the chimpanzee: A longitudinal and comparative study. *Hum. Biol.* 25:93–143.

Gemzell, C., and Roos, P. 1966. The physiology and chemistry of follicle-stimulating hormone. In *The Pituitary Gland,* vol. 1, ed. G. W. Harris and B. T. Donovan. University of California Press.

George, J. S. 1970. Constitutional precocious puberty in a girl aged four years and three months: Review of the literature. *Int. Surg.* 53:56–61.

Giedion, S. 1957. *The beginnings of art.* Pantheon.

Gilmour, D., Bloom, A. D., Lele, K. P., Robbins, E. S., and Maximilian, C. 1971. Chromosomal aberrations in the users of psychoactive drugs. *Arch. Gen. Psychiatry* 24:268–272.

Go, S., and Pearlman, D. S. 1972. Allergic rhinitis and serrus etitis media. In *Pediatrics,* 15th ed., ed. H. L. Barnett and A. H. Einhorn. Appleton-Century-Crofts.

Goldblatt, P. B., Moore, M. E., and Stunkard, A. J. 1965. Social factors in obesity. *J. Am. Med. Assoc.* 192:1039–1044.

Goldenberg, R. L., Vaitukaitis, J. L., and Ross, G. T. 1972. Estrogen and follicle stimulating hormone interactions on follicle growth in rats. *Endocrinology* 90:1492.

Goldstein, A., Aronow, L., and Kalman, S. M. 1974. *Principles of drug action: The basis of pharmacology,* 2d ed. Wiley.

Goltz, R. W., and Ellis, E. F. 1972. Atropic dermatitis. In *Pediatrics,* 15th ed., ed. H. L. Barnett and A. H. Einhorn. Appleton-Century-Crofts.

Goode, E., ed. 1969. *Marijuana.* Atherton.

Goode, E. 1970. *The marijuana smokers.* Basic Books.

Goodman, H. G., Grumbach, M. M., and Kaplan, S. L. 1968. Growth and growth hormone. 2. A comparison of isolated growth-hormone deficiency and multiple pituitary-hormone deficiencies in 35 patients with idiopathic hypopituitary dwarfism. *N. Engl. J. Med.* 278:57–68.

Goodman, L. S., and Gilman, A. 1975. *The pharmacological basis of therapeutics,* 5th ed. Macmillan.

Gorski, R. A. 1974. Extrahypothalamic influences on gonadotropin regulation. In *Control of the onset of puberty,* ed. M. M. Grumbach, G. D. Grave, and F. E. Mayer. Wiley.

Government of Canada. 1973. *Final report of the Commission of Inquiry into the Non-medical Use of Drugs.* Ottawa: Queen's Printer.

Grant, J. A., and Heald, F. P. 1972. Complications of adolescent pregnancy: Survey of the literature on fetal outcome in adolescence. *Clin. Pediatr.* 11:567–570.

Greenblatt, R. H., Jungck, E., and Blum, H. 1972. Endocrinology of sexual behavior. *Med. Aspects Hum. Sexuality* 6:110–131.

Grether, W. F., and Yerkes, R. M. 1940. Weight norms and relations for chimpanzee. *Am. J. Phys. Anthropol.* 28:181–197.

Greulich, W. W. 1957. A comparison of the physical growth and development of American-born and native Japanese children. *Am. J. Phys. Anthropol.* 15:489–515.

Greulich, W. W., and Pyle, S. I. 1959. *Radiographic atlas of skeletal development of the hand and wrist,* 2d ed. Stanford University Press.

Grinspoon, L. 1969. Marijuana. *Sci. Am.* 221(6):17–25.

Grinspoon, L. 1971. *Marijuana reconsidered.* Harvard University Press.

Grinspoon, L. 1975. Drug dependence: Non-narcotic agents. In *Comprehensive textbook of psychiatry,* vol. 1, 2d ed., ed. A. M. Freedman, H. I. Kaplan, and B. J. Sadock. Williams and Wilkins.

Grumbach, M. M., Grave, G. D., and Mayer, F. E., eds. 1974. *Control of the onset of puberty.* Wiley.

Guillemin, R., and Burgus, R. 1972. The hormones of the hypothalamus. *Sci. Am.* 227(5):24–33.

Gupta, D., McCafferty, E., and Rager, K. 1972. Plasma 5α-dihydrotestosterone (17β-hydroxy-5α-androstan-3-one) in adolescent males at different stages of sexual maturation. *Steroids* 19:411–431.

Hafez, E. S. E., and Evans, T. N., eds. 1973. *Human reproduction.* Harper and Row.

Halbrecht, I., Sklorowski, E., and Tsafriv, J. 1971. Menarche and menstruation in various ethnic groups in Israel. *Acta Genet. Med. Gemellol.* 20:384–391.

Hall, G. S. 1904. *Adolescence.* D. Appleton.

Hall, G. S. 1924. *Life and confessions of a psychologist.* D. Appleton.

Hambling, J., and Hopkins, P., eds. 1965. *Psychosomatic disorders in adolescents and young adults.* Pergamon.

Hamburg, B. A. 1974. Early adolescence: A specific and stressful stage of the life cycle. In *Coping and adaptation,* ed. G. V. Coelho, D. A. Hamburg, and J. E. Adams, Basic Books.

Hamburg, B. A., and Hamburg, D. A. 1975. Stressful transitions of adolescence: Endocrine and psychosocial aspects. In *Society, stress, and disease,* vol. 2, ed. L. Levi. London: Oxford University Press.

Hamburg, D. A. 1962. The relevance of recent evolutionary changes to human stress biology. In *Social life of early man,* ed. S. Washburn. Aldine.

Hamburg, D. A. 1971. Recent research on hormonal factors relevant to human aggressiveness. *Int. Soc. Sci. J.* 23:36.

Hammar, S. L., Campbell, M. M., Campbell, V. A., Moores, N. L., Sareen, C., Gareis, F. J., and Lucas, B. 1972. An interdisciplinary study of adolescent obesity. *J. Pediatr.* 80:373–383.

Harrison, G. A., Weiner, J. S., Tanner, J. M., and Barnicott, N. A., eds. 1964. *Human biology.* Oxford: Oxford University Press.

Harvey, S. C. 1975. Hypnotics and sedatives. In *The pharmacological basis of therapeutics,* 5th ed., ed. L. S. Goodman and A. Gilman. Macmillan.

Hasan, S. H., Jackson, C. M., Paterson, D. G., and Scammon, R. E. 1973. Plasma testosterone levels in childhood and puberty measured by radio-immunoassay. *Acta Endocrinol. Suppl.* 173:168.

Hausknecht, R. U. 1972. Termination of pregnancy in adolescent women. *Pediatr. Clin. N. Am.* 19:803–810.

Haymaker, W., Anderson, E., and Nauta, W. J. H. 1968. *The hypothalamus.* Charles C Thomas.

Heald, F., ed. 1969. *Adolescent nutrition and growth.* Appleton-Century-Crofts.

Heald, F. P., and Hung, W., eds. 1970. *Adolescent endocrinology.* Appleton-Century-Crofts.

Heald, F. P., and Hollander, R. J. 1965. The relationship between obesity in adolescence and early growth. *J. Pediatr.* 67:35.

Hellyer, C., Corning, B. A., and Corning, P. A. 1975. Biological aspects of aggressive behavior. In *Comprehensive textbook of psychiatry,* vol. 1, 2d ed., ed. A. M. Freedman, H. I. Kaplan, and B. J. Sadock. Williams and Wilkins.

Hertz, R. 1958. Accidental ingestion of estrogens by children. *Pediatrics* 21:203–206.

Hiernaux, J. 1965. La croissance des écoliers rwandais. *R. Acad. Sci.* (Outre-Mer, Brussels).

Hiernaux, J. 1968. Ethnic differences in growth and development. *Eugen. Q.* 15:12–21.

Hirsch, J., and Knittle, J. L. 1970. Cellularity of obese and nonobese human adipose tissue. *Fed. Proc.* 29:1516–1521.

Hoeprich, P. D., ed. 1972. *Infectious diseases.* Harper and Row.

Hofmann, A. 1970. The discovery of LSD and subsequent investigations on naturally occurring hallucinogens. In *Discoveries in biological psychiatry,* ed. F. R. Ayd, Jr., and B. Blackwell. Lippincott.

Holmes, K. K. 1974. Syphilis. In *Harrison's principles of internal medicine,* 7th ed., ed. M. M. Wintrobe, R. D. Adams, E. Braunwald, K. Isselbacher, R. Petersdorf, and G. W. Thorne. McGraw-Hill.

Holmes, K. K., and Beaty, H. N. 1974. Gonococcal infections. In *Harrison's principles of internal medicine,* 7th ed., ed. M. M. Wintrobe, R. D. Adams, E. Braunwald, K. Isselbacher, R. Petersdorf, and G. W. Thorne. McGraw-Hill.

Holt, E. L., Jr. 1972. Energy requirements. In *Pediatrics,* 15th ed., ed. H. L. Barnett and A. H. Einhorn. Appleton-Century-Crofts.

Houston, B. K. 1969. Review of the evidence and qualifications regarding the effects of hallucinogenic drugs on chromosomes and embryos. *Am. J. Psychiatry* 126:251–254.

Howe, P. E., and Schiller, M. 1952. Growth responses of the school child to changes in diet and environmental factors. *J. Appl. Physiol.* 5:51–61.

Hwang, P., Guyda, H., and Friesen, H. 1971. A radioimmunoassay for human prolactin. *Proc. Natl. Acad. Sci.* 68:1902–1906.

Iliff, A., and Lee, V. A. 1952. Pulse rate, respiratory rate, and body temperature of children between two months and eighteen years of age. *Child Dev.* 23: 237–245.

Illig, R. 1975. Delayed adolescence. In *Clinical review series: Pediatric Medicine,* ed. M. I. Levine. Publishing Sciences Group.

Innes, I. R., and Nickerson, M. 1975. Norepinephrine, epinephrine and the sympathomimetic amines. In *The pharmacological basis of therapeutics,* 5th ed., ed. L. S. Goodman and A. Gilman. Macmillan.

Israel, S. L., and Wouteraz, F. B. 1963. Teenage obstetrics. *Am. J. Obstet. Gynecol.* 85:659–688.

Israelsohn, W. J. 1960. Description and modes of analysis of human growth. In *Human growth,* ed. J. M. Tanner, Oxford: Pergamon. (*Symp. Soc. Hum. Biol.* 3:21–41.)

Jaffe, J. H. 1975. Drug addiction and drug abuse. In *The pharmacological basis of therapeutics,* 5th ed., ed. L. S. Goodman and A. Gilman. Macmillan.

Jaffe, J. H., and Martin, W. R. 1975. Narcotic analgesics and antagonists. In *The pharmacological basis of therapeutics,* 5th ed., ed. L. S. Goodman and A. Gilman. Macmillan.

Janowsky, R., Gorney, R., Castelnuovo-Tedesco, P., and Stone, C. B. 1969. Premenstrual-menstrual increases in psychiatric hospital admission rates. *Am. J. Obstet. Gynecol.* 103:189–191.

Jenner, M. R., Kelch, R. P., Kaplan, S. L., and Grumbach, M. M. 1972. Hormonal changes in puberty. 4. Plasma estradiol, LH, and FSH in prepubertal children, pubertal females, and in precocious puberty, premature thelarche, hypogonadism, and in a child with a feminizing ovarian tumor. *J. Clin. Endocrinol. Metab.* 34:521–530.

Johns, E. B., Sutton, W. C., and Webster, L. E. 1975. *Health for effective living,* 6th ed. McGraw-Hill.

Johnson, T. W. 1972. Gonorrhea. In *Infectious diseases,* ed. P. D. Hoefrich. Harper and Row.

Johnston, F. E., Malina, R. M., and Galbraith, M. A. 1971. Height, weight and age at menarche and the "critical weight" hypothesis. *Science* 174: 1148–1149.

Jolly, H. 1955. *Sexual precocity.* Charles C Thomas.

Jones, H. E. 1949. *Motor performance and growth: A developmental study of static dynamometric strength.* University of California Press.

Jones, R. T. 1971. Marijuana-induced "high": Influence of expectation, setting and previous experience. *Pharmacol. Rev.* 23:359–369.

Jones, R. T., and Stone, G. C. 1969. Psychological studies of marijuana and alcohol in man. Paper read at the 125th Meeting of the American Psychiatric Association, May 1969, Bal Harbour, Florida.

Joseph, E. D., and Schwartz, A. H. 1975. Accident proneness. In *Comprehensive textbook of psychiatry,* vol. 2, 2d ed., ed. A. M. Freedman, H. I. Kaplan, and B. J. Sadock. Williams and Wilkins.

Jowett, B., trans. 1921. *The Republic,* by Plato. Oxford: Clarendon Press.

Jowett, B., trans. 1953. *The Dialogues of Plato,* vol. 4, 4th ed. Oxford: Clarendon Press.

Kantero, R. L., and Widholm, O. 1971. The age of menarche in Finnish girls in 1969. *Acta Obstet. Gynecol. Scand.* 14:7–18.

Kaplan, J. 1971. *Marijuana: The new prohibition.* Pocket Books.

Kaprio, L. 1975. Death on the road. *World Health* (October):4–9.

Kase, N. G. 1969. The ovary. In *Duncan's diseases of metabolism,* 6th ed., ed. P. K. Bondy. Saunders.

Kastin, A. J., Schally, A. V., Schalch, D. S., Korenman, S. G., Miller, M. C., III, Gaul, C., and Perez-Pasten, E. 1972. Characterization of the hormonal responses in luteinizing hormone-releasing hormone (LH-RH) in prepubertal and adult subjects. *Pediatr. Res.* 6:481–486.

Katchadourian, H. A. 1972. The psychiatrist in the university at large. *J. Nerv. Ment. Dis.* 154:221–227.

Katchadourian, H. A. 1974. *Human sexuality: Sense and nonsense.* W. H. Freeman and Company.

Katchadourian, H. A., and Lunde, D. T. 1975. *Fundamentals of human sexuality,* 2d ed. Holt, Rinehart and Winston.

Keeton, W. T. 1972. *Biological science,* 2d ed. Norton.

Kelch, R. P., Grumbach, M. M., and Kaplan, S. L. 1972. Studies on the mechanism of puberty in man. In *Gonadotropins,* ed. B. B. Saxena, C. G. Beling, and H. M. Gandy. Wiley-Interscience.

Keniston, K. 1962. Social change and youth in America. *Daedalus* (winter): 145–171.

Keniston, K. 1970. Youth, a (new) stage of life. *American Scholar* 39:4.

Kenny, F. M., Gancayco, G. P., Heald, F. P., and Hung, W. 1966. Cortisol production rate in adolescent males in different stages of sexual maturation. *J. Clin. Endocrinol.* 26:1232–1236.

Kestenberg, J. S. 1967*a*. Phases of adolescence. 1. Antecedents of adolescent organization in childhood. *J. Am. Acad. Child Psychiatry* 6:426–463.

Kestenberg, J. S. 1967*b*. Phases of adolescence. 2. Prepuberty diffusion and reintegration. *J. Am. Acad. Child Psychiatry* 6:577–614.

Kestenberg, J. S. 1968. Phases of adolescence. 3. Puberty, growth, differentiation and consolidation. *J. Am. Acad. Child Psychiatry* 7:108–151.

Keyl, A. 1972. *V. D.: The people to people diseases.* Toronto: House of Anastasi Press.

Kinsey, A. C., Pomeroy, W. B., and Martin, C. E. 1948. *Sexual behavior in the human male.* Saunders.

Kinsey, A. C., Pomeroy, W. B., Martin, C. E., and Gebhard, P. H. 1953. *Sexual behavior in the human female.* Saunders.

Knorr, D., Bidlingmaier, F., Butenandt, O., Fendel, H., and Ehrt-Wehle, R. 1974. Plasma testosterone in male puberty. 1. Physiology of plasma testosterone. *Acta Endocrinol.* 75:181–194.

Kolodny, R. C., Masters, W. H., Kolodner, R. M., and Toro, G. 1974. Depression of plasma testosterone levels after chronic intensive marijuana use. *N. Engl. J. Med.* 290:872.

Koran, L. M., and Hamburg, D. A. 1975. Psychophysiological endocrine disorders. In *Comprehensive textbook of psychiatry,* vol. 2, 2d ed., ed. A. M. Freedman, H. I. Kaplan, and B. J. Sadock. Williams and Wilkins.

Kosterlitz, H. W., Collier, H. O. J., and Villarreal, J. E., eds. 1973. *Agonist and antagonist actions of narcotic analgesic drugs.* University Park Press.

Kramer, S. N. 1963. *The Sumerians.* The University of Chicago Press.

Kraus, J. F., Riggins, R. S., and Franti, C. E. 1975*a*. Some epidemiologic features of motorcycle collision injuries. 1. Introduction, methods, and factors associated with incidence. *Am. J. Epidemiol.* 102:79–98.

Kraus, J. F., Riggins, R. S., and Franti, C. E. 1975*b*. Some epidemiologic features of motorcycle collision injuries. 2. Factors associated with severity of injuries. *Am. J. Epidemiol.* 102:99–109.

Krugman, S. 1972. Infectious mononucleosis. In *Pediatrics,* 15th ed., ed. H. L. Barnett and A. H. Einhorn. Appleton-Century-Crofts.

Kulin, H. E. 1972. Endocrine changes at puberty. In *Pediatrics,* 15th ed., ed. H. B. Barnett and A. H. Einhorn. Appleton-Century-Crofts.

Kulin, H. E., Grumbach, M. M., and Kaplan, S. L. 1969. Changing sensitivity of the pubertal gonadal hypothalamic feedback mechanism in man. *Science* 166:1012–1013.

Kulin, H. E., Rifkind, A. B., Ross, G. T., and Odell, W. D. 1967. Total gonado-tropin activity in the urine of prepubertal children. *J. Clin. Endocrinol. Metab.* 27:1123–1128.

Langford, W. S. 1972. Anorexia nervosa. In *Pediatrics,* 15th ed., ed. H. L. Barnett and A. H. Einhorn. Appleton-Century-Crofts.

Leake, C. D., Chauncey, D., and Silverman, M. 1966. *Alcoholic beverages in clinical medicine.* Year Book Medical Publishers.

Lee, P. A. Midgley, A. R., Midgley, A. R., Jr., and Jaffe, R. B. 1970. Regulation of human gonadotropins. 6. Serum follicle stimulating and luteinizing hormone determinations in children. *J. Clin. Endocrinol. Metab.* 31:248–253.

Levi, L. 1975. Autosclerosis. *World Health* (October):1012.

Levine, M. I., ed. 1975. *Clinical review series: Pediatric medicine.* Publishing Sciences Group.

Lindner, H. R. 1961. Androgens and related compounds in the spermatic vein blood of domestic animals. 2. Species-linked differences in the metabolism of androstenedione in blood. *J. Endocrinol.* 23:139–159.

Liu, N., Grumbach, M. M., De Napoli, R. A., and Morishima, A. 1965. Prevalence of electroencephalographic abnormalities in idiopathic precocious puberty: Bearing on pathogenesis and neuroendocrine regulation of puberty. *J. Clin. Endocrinol.* 25:1296–1308.

McCann, S. M., and Porter, J. C. 1969. Hypothalamic pituitary stimulating and inhibiting hormones. *Physiol. Rev.* 49:240–284.

Maccoby, E. E., and Jacklin, C. M. 1974. *The psychology of sex differences.* Stanford University Press.

MacCurdy, H. L. 1953. *A test for measuring the physical capacity of secondary schoolboys.* Harcourt Brace Jovanovich.

McDonald, P. C. 1972. The ovaries. In *Pediatrics,* 15th ed., ed. H. L. Barnett and A. H. Einhorn. Appleton-Century-Crofts.

McDonough, P. G. 1971. Sexual precocity. *Clin. Obstet. Gynecol.* 14:1037–1056.

McGlothlin, W. H., Sparkes, R. S., and Arnold, D. U. 1970. Effect of LSD on human pregnancy. *J. Am. Med. Assoc.* 121:1483–1487.

McGuire, J. 1972. Acne. In *Pediatrics,* 15th ed., ed. H. L. Barnett and A. H. Einhorn. Appleton-Century-Crofts.

Magee, K., Basinska, J., Quarrington, B., and Stancer, H. C. 1970. Blindness and menarche. *Life Sci.* 9:7–12.

Maresh, M. M. 1948. Growth of the heart related to bodily growth during childhood and adolescence. *Pediatrics* 2:382–404.

Maresh, M. M. 1972. A forty-five year investigation for secular changes in physical maturation. *Am. J. Phys. Anthropol.* 36:103–110.

Marinoff, S. C., and Schonholz, D. H. 1972. Adolescent pregnancy. *Pediatr. Clin. N. Am.* 19:795–802.

Marshall, D. S., and Suggs, R. C. 1971. *Human sexual behavior.* Prentice-Hall.

Marshall, W. A. 1973. The body. In *The seven ages of man,* ed. R. S. Sears and S. S. Feldman. William Kaufman.

Marshall, W. A., and Tanner, J. M. 1969. Variations in the pattern of pubertal changes in girls. *Arch. Dis. Child.* 44:291–303.

Marshall, W. A., and Tanner, J. M. 1970. Variations in the pattern of pubertal changes in boys. *Arch. Dis. Child.* 45:13–23.

Marshall, W. A., and Tanner, J. M. 1974. Puberty. In *Scientific foundations of pediatrics,* ed. J. A. Douvis and J. Dobbing. London: William Heinemann Medical Books.

Martini, L., Motta, M., and Fraschini, F., eds. 1970. *The hypothalamus.* Academic Press.

Masters, W. H., and Johnson, V. E. 1970. *Human sexual inadequacy.* Little, Brown.

Mead, M. 1961. *Coming of age in Samoa.* Morrow.

Meiks, L. T., and Green, M., eds. 1960. Symposium on adolescence. *Pediatr. Clin. N. Am.* 7(no. 1).

Melges, F. T., Tinklenberg, J. R., Hollister, L. E., and Gillespie, H. K. 1970. Temporal disintegration and depersonalization during marijuana intoxication. *Arch. Gen. Psychiatry* 23:204–210.

Mendelson, J. H., Kuehnle, J., Ellingboe, J., and Babor, T. F. 1974. Plasma testosterone levels before, during and after chronic marijuana smoking. *N. Engl. J. Med.* 291:1051–1055.

Meredith, H. V., and Knott, V. B. 1962. Illness history and physical growth. 3. Comparative anatomic status and rate of change for school children in different long-term health categories. *Am. J. Dis. Child.* 103:146–151.

Metropolitan Life Insurance Company. 1970. *Stat. Bull.* (December):10.
Metropolitan Life Insurance Company. 1971. *Stat. Bull.* (May).
Metropolitan Life Insurance Company. 1972. *Stat. Bull.* (June):6–8.
Metropolitan Life Insurance Company. 1973. *Stat. Bull.* (August):9–11.
Metropolitan Life Insurance Company. 1974. *Stat. Bull.* (August):2–8.
Miller, N., Hubert, G., and Hamilton, J. B. 1938. Mental and behavioral changes following male hormone treatment of adult castration hypogonadism and psychic impotence. *Proc. Soc. Exp. Biol. Med.* 38:538–540.
Money, J. 1961. Sex hormones and other variables in human eroticism. In *Sex and internal secretions,* vol. 2, ed. W. Young. Williams and Wilkins.
Money, J. 1970. Hormonal and genetic extremes at puberty. *Proc. Am. Psychopathol. Assoc.* 59:138–158.
Money, J., and Alexander, D. 1969. Psychosexual development and absense of homosexuality in males with precocious puberty. *J. Nerv. Ment. Dis.* 148:111–123.
Money, J., and Ehrhardt, A. A. 1972. *Man and woman, boy and girl.* Johns Hopkins University Press.
Moore, M. E., Stunkard, A. J., and Srole, L. 1962. Obesity, social class and mental illness. *J. Am. Med. Assoc.* 181:962–966.
Moos, R. H. 1969. A typology of menstrual cycle symptoms. *Am. J. Obstet. Gynecol.* 103:390–402.
Moos, R. H., and Lunde, D. T. 1969. Fluctuations in symptoms and moods during the menstrual cycle. *J. Psychosom. Res.* 13:37–44.
Morley, C. 1939. *Kitty Foyle.* Lippincott.
Mossberg, H. D. 1948. Obesity in children. *Acta Paediatr. Scand. Suppl.* 2.
Motta, M., Fraschini, F., and Martini, L. 1969. "Short" feedback mechanisms in the control of anterior pituitary function. In *Frontiers in neuroendocrinology,* ed. W. F. Ganong and L. Martini. London: Oxford University Press.
Mussen, P. H., ed. 1970. *Carmichael's manual of child psychology,* vol. 1, 3d ed. Wiley.
Muuss, R. E. 1968. *Theories of adolescence.* Random House.

Nahas, G. G., Paton, W. D. M., and Idänpään-Heikkilä, J. E. 1976. *Marijuana: Chemistry, biochemistry, and cellular effects.* Springer-Verlag.
National Clearinghouse for Mental Health Information. 1968. *Alcohol and alcoholism.* U. S. Public Health Service (pub. no. 1640).
National Commission on Marijuana and Drug Abuse. 1973. *Drug use in America: Problems in perspective.* U. S. Government Printing Office.
Netter, F. M. 1965. *Reproductive systems.* CIBA Collection of Medical Illustrations, vol. 2. CIBA.
New York State Department of Motor Vehicles. 1969. *Motorcycle accidents* (res. rep. no. 1969–12).
Nowlis, H. H. 1969. *Drugs on the college campus.* Anchor Books.
Nydick, M., Bustos, J., Dale, J. H., Jr., and Rawson, R. W. 1961. Gynecomastia in adolescent boys. *J. Am. Med. Assoc.* 178:449–454.

O'Connor, J., Shelley, E. M., and Stern, L. O. 1974. Behavioral rhythms related to the menstrual cycle. In *Biorhythms and human reproduction,* ed. M. Ferin, F. Halberg, R. M. Richart, and R. L. Vande Wiele. Wiley.

Odell, W. D., and Moyer, D. L. 1971. *Physiology of reproduction.* Mosby.

Offer, D. 1969. *The psychological world of the teenager.* Basic Books.

Office of Civil Defense and Public Health Service. 1965. *Family guide emergency care.*

O'Malley, B. W., and Schrader, W. T. 1976. The receptors of steroid hormones. *Sci. Am.* 234(2):32–43.

Orley, J., Flórian, E., Jurányi, R., and Nyomárkay, I. 1969. Vaginal discharge in puberty: A survey of 1000 adolescents. *Gynaecologia (Basel)* 168: 191–202.

Pascal, R. 1953. *The German Sturm und Drang.* Manchester University Press.

Patton, R. G., and Gardner, L. I. 1969. Short stature associated with maternal deprivation syndrome. In *Endocrine and genetic diseases of childhood,* ed. L. I. Gardner. Saunders.

Paulsen, C. A. 1974. The testes. In *Textbook of endocrinology,* ed. R. H. Williams. Saunders.

Paulsen, E. P. 1972. Obesity in children and adolescents. In *Pediatrics,* 15th ed., ed. H. L. Barnett and A. H. Einhorn. Appleton-Century-Crofts.

Pennington, G. W., and Dewhurst, C. J. 1969. Hormone excretion in premenarcheal girls. *Arch. Dis. Child.* 44:629–636.

Penny, R., Guyda, H. J., Baghdassarian, A., Johanson, A. J., and Blizzard, R. M. 1970. Correlation of serum follicle stimulating hormone (FSH) and luteinizing hormone (LH) as measured by radioimmunoassay in disorders of sexual development. *J. Clin. Invest.* 49:1847–1852.

Pospisilova-Zuzakova, V., Stukovsky, R., and Valsik, J. A. 1965. The menarche in Whites, Negresses, and Mulatto women of Havana. *Z. Aerztl. Fortbild.* (Jena) 59:500–516.

Porter, J. C., Kamberi, I. A., and Grazia, Y. R. 1971. Pituitary blood flow and portal vessels. In *Frontiers in neuroendocrinology, 1971,* ed. L. Martini and W. F. Ganong. London: Oxford University Press.

Powell, G. F., Brasel, J. A., and Blizzard, R. M. 1967. Emotional deprivation and growth retardation simulating idiopathic hypopituitarism. 1. Clinical evaluation of the syndrome. *N. Engl. J. Med.* 276:1271–1278.

Prabhakar, A. K., Sundaram, K. R., Ramanujacharyulu, T. K. T. S., and Taskar, A. D. 1972. Influence of socio-economic factors on the age of the appearance of different puberty signs. *Indian J. Med. Res.* 60:789–792.

Prader, A. 1974. Growth and development. In *Clinical endocrinology,* ed. by A. Lobhart. Springer-Verlag.

Prader, A., Tanner, J. M., and von Harnack, G. A. 1963. Catch-up growth following illness or starvation. *J. Pediatr.* 62:646.

Puberty and cancer. 1970. *Br. Med. J.* 3:722–723.

Rafaelsen, O. J., Bech, P., Christiansen, J., Christrup, H., Nyboe, J., and Rafaelsen, L. 1973. Cannabis and alcohol effects on simulated car driving. *Science* 179:920–923.

Rakoff, A. E. 1968. Endocrine mechanisms in psychogenic amenorrhea. In *Endocrinology and human behavior,* ed. R. P. Michael. London: Oxford University Press.

Reichlin, S. 1974. Neuroendocrinology. In *Textbook of endocrinology,* 5th ed., ed. R. H. Williams. Saunders.

Reiter, E. O., and Kulin, H. E. 1972. Sexual maturation in the female: Normal development and precocious puberty. *Pediatr. Clin. N. Am.* 19:581–603.

Reynolds, E. L., and Wines, J. V. 1951. Physical changes associated with adolescence in boys. *Am. J. Dis. Child.* 82:529–547.

Rifkind, A. B., Kulin, H. E., Rayford, P. L., Cargille, C. M., and Ross, G. T. 1970. Twenty-four hour urinary luteinizing hormone (LH) and follicle stimulating hormone (FSH) excretion in normal children. *J. Clin. Endocrinol. Metab.* 31:517–525.

Rifkind, A. B., Kulin, H. E., and Ross, G. T. 1967. Follicle stimulating hormone (FSH) and luteinizing hormone (LH) in the urine of pre-pubertal children. *J. Clin. Invest.* 12:1123–1128.

Ritchie, J. M. 1975. The aliphatic alcohols. In *The pharmacological basis of therapeutics,* 5th ed. Macmillan.

Rivlin, R. S. 1969. Thyroid hormone and the adolescent growth spurt: Clinical and fundamental considerations. In *Adolescent nutrition and growth,* ed. F. Heald. Appleton-Century-Crofts.

Roche, A. F., French, N. Y., and Da Vila, D. H. 1971. Areolar size during pubescence. *Hum. Biol.* 43:210–223.

Root, A. W. 1972. *Human pituitary growth hormone.* Charles C Thomas.

Root, A. W. 1973*a.* Endocrinology of puberty. 1. Normal sexual maturation. *J. Pediatr.* 83:1–19.

Root, A. W. 1973*b.* Endocrinology of puberty. 2. Aberrations of sexual maturation. *J. Pediatr.* 83:187–200.

Rose, R. M., Holaday, J. W., and Bernstein, I. S. 1971. Plasma testosterone, dominance rank, and aggressive behavior in male rhesus monkeys. *Nature* 231:366–368.

Ross, G. T., and Vande Wiele, R. L. 1974. The ovaries. In *Textbook of endocrinology,* ed. R. H. Williams. Saunders.

Saez, J. M., Morera, A. M., and Bertrand, J. 1972. *Plasma concentrations of estrone (E_1) and estradiol (E_2) before puberty in humans.* International Congress of Endocrinology, Washington, D. C., June 18–24. Abstr. 306.

Salmon, U. J., and Geist, S. H. 1943. Effect of androgens upon libido in women. *J. Clin. Endocrinol. Metab.* 3:235–238.

Scammon, R. E. 1930. The measurement of the body in childhood. In *The measurement of man,* ed. J. A. Harris, C. M. Jackson, D. G. Paterson, and R. E. Scammon. University of Minnesota Press.

Schachter, S., and Singer, J. E. 1962. Cognitive, social and physiological determinants of emotional state. *Psychol. Rev.* 69:379–399.

Schon, M., and Sutherland, A. M. 1960. The role of hormones in human behavior. 3. Changes in female sexuality after hypophysectomy. *J. Clin. Endocrinol. Metab.* 20:833–841.

Schrocter, A. L. 1972. Rectal gonorrhea. In *Epidemic venereal disease. Proceedings of the second international symposium on venereal disease.* American Social Health Association and Pfizer Laboratories Division.

Scott, E. M., Illsley, R., and Thomson, A. M. 1956. A psychological investigation of primigravidae. 2. Maternal social class, age, physique and intelligence. *J. Obstet. Gynaecol. Br. Emp.* 63:338–343.

Seat belts: Helpful or harmful? 1962. *J. Trauma* 2:303–304.

Shehadeh, N. H., and Kligman, A. M. 1963. The bacteriology of acne. *Arch. Dermatol.* 88:829–831.

Shock, N. W. 1944. Basal blood pressure and pulse rate in adolescents. *Am. J. Dis. Child.* 68:16–22.

Shock, N. W., and Soley, M. H. 1939. Average values for basal respiratory functions in adolescents and adults. *J. Nutr.* 18:143–153.

Shuster, L., ed. 1962. *Readings in pharmacology.* Little, Brown.

Sims, E. A., Goldman, R. F., Gluck, C. M., Horton, E. S., Kelleher, P. C., and Rowe, D. W. 1968. Experimental obesity in man. *Trans. Assoc. Am. Physicians* 81:153–170.

Sinclair, D. 1973. *Human growth after birth.* London: Oxford University Press.

Sizonenko, P. C., Burr, I. M., Kaplan, S. L., and Grumbach, M. M. 1970. Hormonal changes in puberty. 2. Correlation of serum luteinizing hormones and follicle stimulating hormone with stages of puberty and bone age in normal girls. *Pediatr. Res.* 4:36–45.

Smith, D. C., and Rice, G. R. 1972. Community aspects of pediatric practice. In *Pediatrics,* 15th ed., ed. H. L. Barnett and A. H. Einhorn. Appleton-Century-Crofts.

Solomon, D., ed. 1966. *LSD: The consciousness-expanding drug.* Putnam Medallion Books.

Staff, J. 1955. *Collected papers on aviation medicine.* London: Butterworth.

Stedman's Medical Dictionary, 22d ed. Williams and Wilkins.

Stewart, W. D., Danto, J. L., and Stuart, M. 1974. *Dermatology,* 3d ed. Mosby.

Stolz, R. S., and Stolz, L. M. 1951. *Somatic development of adolescent boys: A study of the growth of boys during the second decade of life.* Macmillan.

Stunkard, A. J. 1975. Obesity. In *Comprehensive textbook of psychiatry,* vol. 2, 2d ed., ed. A. M. Freedman, H. I. Kaplan, and B. J. Sadock. Williams and Wilkins.

Tanner, J. M. 1962. *Growth at adolescence,* 2d ed. Oxford: Blackwell.

Tanner, J. M. 1966*a*. Growth and physique in different populations of mankind. In *The biology of human adaptability,* ed. P. T. Baker and J. S. Weiner. Oxford: Clarendon Press.

Tanner, J. M. 1966*b*. The secular trend towards earlier physical maturation. *Trans. Soc. Geneeskd.* 44:524–538.

Tanner, J. M. 1970. Physical growth. In *Carmichael's manual of child psychology,* vol. 1, 3d ed., ed. P. H. Mussen. Wiley.

Tanner, J. M. 1973. Growing up. *Sci. Am.* 229(3):34–43.

Tanner, J. M., and Gupta, D. 1968. A longitudinal study of individual steroid excretion in children aged 8 to 12. *J. Endocrinol.* 41:139–159.

Tanner, J. M., and Israelsohn, W. J. 1963. Parent-child correlations for body measurements of children between the ages of one month and seven years. *Ann. Hum. Genet.* 26:245–259.

Tanner, J. M., Taylor, G. R., and the editors of Time-Life Books. 1969. *Growth.* Time-Life Books.

Tart, C. T. 1970. Marihuana intoxication: Common experiences. *Nature* 226:701.

Taylor, R. L., Maurer, J. I., and Tinklenberg, J. R. 1970. Management of "bad trips" in an evolving drug scene. *J. Am. Med. Assoc.* 213:422–425.

Tepperman, J. 1973. *Metabolic and endocrine physiology,* 3d ed. Year Book Medical Publishers.

Thomson, A. M. 1959. Maternal stature and reproductive efficiency. *Eugen. Rev.* 51:157–162.

Thompson, D'Arcy W. 1942. *Growth and form,* 2d ed. London: Cambridge University Press.

Tillman, W. A., and Hobbs, G. E. 1949. The accident prone automobile driver. *Am. J. Psychiatry* 105:321.

Tinklenberg, J., ed. 1975. *Marijuana and health hazards.* Academic Press.

Udry, J. R., and Morris, N. M. 1968. Distribution of coitus in the menstrual cycle. *Nature* 220:593–596.

U.S. Bureau of the Census. 1975. Projections of the population of the United States: 1975 to 2050. *Curr. Population Rep.,* ser. P-25, no. 601. U.S. Government Printing Office.

U.S. Department of Health, Education, and Welfare. 1964. *Accident handbook: A new approach to family safety.* Boston: The Children's Hospital Medical Center.

U.S. National Center for Health Statistics. 1970. Selected symptoms of psychological distress, United States. *Vital Health Stat.* ser. 11, no. 37.

U.S. National Center for Health Statistics. 1974. Mortality trends for leading causes of death, United States: 1950–1969. *Vital Health Stat.* ser. 20, no. 16.

U.S. National Center for Health Statistics. 1975a. Examination and health history findings among children and youths, 6–17 years, United States. *Vital Health Stat.* ser. 11, no. 129.

U.S. National Center for Health Statistics. 1975b. Self-reported health behavior and attitudes of youths, 12–17 years, United States. *Vital Health Stat.* ser. 11, no. 147.

U.S. President's Advisory Committee on Youth. 1974. *Youth.* University of Chicago Press.

U.S. Public Health Service. 1964. *Smoking and health: Report of the Advisory Committee to the Surgeon General of the Public Health Service,* pub. no. 1103.

U.S. Public Health Service. 1967. *The health consequences of smoking: A Public Health Service review: 1967,* pub. no. 1696.

U.S. Public Health Service. 1968. *The health consequences of smoking: 1968 supplement to the 1967 PHS review,* pub. no. 1696-1.

U.S. Public Health Service. 1969. *The health consequences of smoking: 1969 supplement to the 1967 PHS review,* pub. no. 1696-2.

U.S. Public Health Service. 1970. *The facts about smoking and health,* pub. no. 1712.

U.S. Public Health Service, National Center for Health Statistics. 1974. *Vital statistics of the United States: 1970.*

Usdin, E., and Efron, D. H. 1972. *Psychotropic drugs and related compounds,* 2d ed. U.S. Department of Health, Education, and Welfare pub. no. (HSM) 72–9074.

Ushakov, G. K. 1971. Anorexia nervosa. In *Modern perspectives in adolescent psychiatry,* ed. J. G. Howells. Edinburgh: Oliver and Boyd.

Van Wyk, J. J. 1972. The thyroid. In *Pediatrics,* 15th ed., ed. H. L. Barnett and A. H. Einhorn. Appleton-Century-Crofts.

Vaughan, V. C., and McKay, R. J., eds. 1975. *Nelson textbook of pediatrics,* 10th ed. Saunders.

Volle, R. L., and Koelle, G. B. 1975. Ganghom's stimulating and blocking agents. In *The pharmacological basis of therapeutics,* 5th ed., ed. L. S. Goodman and A. Gilman. Macmillan.

Wallach, E. E., Root, A. W., and Garcia, C. R. 1970. Serum gonadotropin responses to estrogen and progestogen in recently castrated human females. *J. Clin. Endocrinol. Metab.* 31:376–381.

Washburn, S. L., and Lancaster, C. S. 1968. The evolution of hunting. In *Perspectives on human evolution,* vol. 1, ed. S. L. Washburn and P. C. Jay. Holt, Rinehart and Winston.

Weil, W. B., Jr., and Kohrman, A. F. 1968. Diabetes mellitus in children. In *Pediatrics,* 15th ed., ed. H. L. Barnett and A. H. Einhorn. Appleton-Century-Crofts.

Weiland, R. G., Yen, S. S. C., and Pohlman, C. 1970. Serum testosterone levels and testosterone binding affinity in prepubertal and adolescent males: Correlation with gonadotropins. *Am. J. Med. Sci.* 259:358–360.

Weiner, I. B. 1970. *Psychological disturbance in adolescence.* Wiley.

Weir, J., Dunn, J., and Jones, E. G. 1971. Race and age at menarche. *Am. J. Obstet. Gynecol.* 111:594–596.

Welldon, J. E. C., 1866. *Rhetoric of Aristotle.*

Wells, H. G. 1934. *Experiment in autobiography.* Macmillan.

Wettenhall, H. N. B., and Roche, A. F. 1965. Tall girls: Assessment and management. *Aust. Pediatr. J.* 1:210–216.

Wetzel, R., Reich, T., and McClure, J. 1971. Phase of the menstrual cycle and self-referrals to a suicide prevention service. *Br. J. Psychiatry* 119: 523–524.

Widdowson, E. M. 1951. Mental contentment and physical growth. *Lancet* 1:1316–1318.

Widholm, O., and Kantero, R. 1971. A statistical analysis of the menstrual patterns of 8,000 Finnish girls and their mothers. *Acta Obstet. Gynecol. Scand. Suppl.* 14:1–36.

Wieland, R. G., Chen, J. C., Zorn, E. M., and Hallberg, M. C. 1971. Correlations of growth, pubertal staging, growth hormone, gonadotropins, and testosterone levels during the pubertal growth spurt in males. *J. Pediatr.* 79: 999–1002.

Wilkins, L. 1965. *The diagnosis and treatment of endocrine disorders in childhood and adolescence,* 3d ed. Charles C Thomas.

Williams, R. H., ed. 1974. *Textbook of endocrinology,* 5th ed. Saunders.

Wilson, E. O., Eisner, T., Briggs, W. R., Dickerson, R. E., Metzenberg, R. L., O'Brien, R. D., Sussman, M., and Boggs, W. E. 1973. *Life on Earth.* Sinauer.

Winter, J. S. D., and Faiman, C. 1972. Pituitary-gonadal relations in male children and adolescents. *Pediatr. Res.* 6:126–135.

Wintrobe, M. M., Tharu, G. W., Adams, R., Braunwald, E., Isselbacher, K. J., and Petersdorf, R. G., eds. 1974. *Harrison's principles of internal medicine,* 7th ed. McGraw-Hill.

Wolstenhome, G. E. W., and O'Connor, M., eds. 1967. *Endocrinology of the testis.* Little, Brown.

Woodring, P. 1970. Retrospect and prospect. *Saturday Review* (September 19):66.

World Almanac and Book of Facts. 1976. Newspaper Enterprise Assoc., Inc., p. 364.

World Health Organization. 1965. Health problems of adolescence. *W. H. O. Tech. Rep. Ser.,* no. 308.

World Health Organization. 1968. Sport. *World Health* (September).

World Health Organization. 1975*a*. Road accidents. *World Health* (October).

World Health Organization. 1975*b*. Sexually transmitted diseases. *World Health* (May).

World Health Organization Expert Committee. 1975. Smoking and its effects on health. *W. H. O. Tech. Rep. Ser.,* no. 568.

World Health Organization Expert Committee on Drug Dependence. 1974. Twentieth report. *W. H. O. Tech. Rep. Ser.,* no. 551.

Yen, S. S. C., and Vicic, W. J. 1970. Serum follicle stimulating hormone levels in puberty. *Am. J. Obstet. Gynecol.* 106:134–137.

Young, W. C., and Yerkes, R. M. 1943. Factors influencing the reproductive cycle in the chimpanzee: The period of adolescent sterility and related problems. *Endocrinology* 33:121–154.

Zacharias, L., Rand, W. M., and Wurtman, R. J. 1976. A prospective study of sexual development and growth in American girls: The statistics of menarche. *Obstet. Gynecol. Surv.* (suppl.) 31:325–337.

Zacharias, L., and Wurtman, R. J. 1964. Blindness: Its relation to age of menarche. *Science* 144:1154–1155.

Zacharias, L., Wurtman, R. J., and Schatzoff, M. 1970. Sexual maturation in contemporary American girls. *Am. J. Obstet. Gynecol.* 108:833–846.

Index